MY BROTHER'S KEEPER

A THIRTY-YEAR QUEST TO BRING TWO KILLERS TO JUSTICE

CHRIS RUSSO BLACKWOOD
FOREWORD BY TED KERGAN

WILDBLUE
PRESS

WildBluePress.com

MY BROTHER'S KEEPER published by:
WILDBLUE PRESS
P.O. Box 102440
Denver, Colorado 80250

WILDBLUE PRESS is registered at the U.S. Patent and Trademark Offices.

ISBN 978-1-947290-01-3   Trade Paperback
ISBN 978-1-947290-00-6   eBook

Interior Formatting/Book Cover Design by Elijah Toten
www.totencreative.com

Then the Lord said to Cain, "Where is Abel, your brother?"

And He said, "I do not know. Am I my brother's keeper?"

- Genesis 4:9

TABLE OF CONTENTS

Foreword   7

Prologue   11

Chapter 1: Where's Gary?   13

Chapter 2: Ted and Gary   22

Chapter 3: Hello Gary   25

Chapter 4: Las Vegas   32

Chapter 5: Blood in the trunk   40

Chapter 6: Leila Mulla   51

Chapter 7: Ted and Gary   60

Chapter 8: Ronald Dunnagan   62

Chapter 9: Dear Diary   69

Chapter 10: No Body   75

Chapter 11: Finding the Landmark   84

Chapter 12: After Life   92

Chapter 13: Cold Case Hot   97

Chapter 14: Ted and Gary   106

Chapter 15: A Confession 110

Chapter 16: The Real Leila 125

Chapter 17: Pretermit 136

Chapter 18: Ron's New Friend 145

Chapter 19: What's the Deal? 153

Chapter 20: Back in town 162

Chapter 21: At last 172

Chapter 22: Ted and Gary 182

Chapter 23: Wade 185

Chapter 24: The Magees 195

Chapter 25: All Eyes on Leila 208

Chapter 26: Verdict 224

Chapter 27: Entirely New Level 238

Victim Impact Statement 243

Epilogue 246

Acknowledgements 252

Photos 254

FOREWORD

I picked up the phone in my Lafayette office one afternoon in September 2012 and said hello to a pleasant voice from the past. I hadn't spoken to Memry Tucker, the daughter of a long-time business associate, in years.

Memry calmly dropped a bomb. She had news about the unsolved murder of my older brother, Gary Kergan. I was speechless. How was Memry, of all people, involved in a case that had been closed for nearly 30 years?

By the time Memry and I hung up, my head was swimming in even more questions. What unfolded over the next three years was amazing. I had doubts about this book, because I wasn't sure the story could be told in a way others would believe – uncanny coincidences and weird twists of fate.

These pages demonstrate author Chris Blackwood's dedication and marvelous gift of storytelling. She captures the best example of Gary's legacy – all the people who fought so long and hard for justice for him. These were mostly people he never knew. That's the impact my brother had on people.

I'm tempted to say I was fortunate to cross paths with them. But was it fortune? As I would come to learn, Gary had been looking down the entire time, guiding and protecting me as he always had.

Ted Kergan
August 2017

MY
BROTHER'S
KEEPER

PROLOGUE

Ted Kergan was only six years old in 1959 when he nearly killed himself on his hand-me-down bike. Sheer exhilaration had seduced him with the thrill of racing down the cracked sidewalks of Detroit's Ellwood Avenue, but his concentration failed and the bike flipped without warning. Little Ted felt himself go airborne, limbs twisting out of control. Time seemed to snap into slow motion. The moment hung in the air.

He landed on a fire hydrant.

His torso bore the point of impact with the hydrant's top nut.

His mother was there in a flash, and even though the hydrant didn't pierce his skin, she realized he must have sustained internal injuries. She rushed him to nearby Beaumont Hospital, and X-rays confirmed the damage; Ted's liver was practically torn in half. The emergency operation went on for hours, and doctors said the tedious surgery to rejoin the torn organ was akin to "sewing together a wet paper tissue." When the surgeon's work was done, no one really knew if Ted would survive, or whether hepatitis of the traumatized liver would set in.

He awoke to the sounds of soft beeps and swishing noises, and found himself lying flat in a hospital bed. His mother was crying next to him, but when he tried to reach for her, his hands wouldn't move. They were held in place by leather straps. Mama leaned close to comfort him and explained that he was restrained to prevent him from accidentally tangling or rearranging the web of tubes attached to his body. But there was nothing she could do to spare him the coming weeks in that sterile hospital bed. It would be months before Ted returned to his first grade class at Shrine of the Little Flower Catholic School.

His mama spent as much time as she could at Ted's side, but her home sewing business was the family's livelihood, and she didn't dare neglect it. Many times, she sent Ted's brother, Gary, to be with him at the hospital. At ten years old, Gary was the "man" of their family, having assumed that fate the day after Ted was born, when their Dad suffered a fatal heart attack. Gary embraced the role almost like a badge of honor, and developed an outgoing, confident manner, with a touch of swagger.

Tube by tube, Ted was weaned away from that hospital bed, and slowly rewove himself back into life as a Catholic school student and altar boy, under the guidance of a priest who gifted him and his siblings a free parochial school education after their father died. But things were never the same. Lingering fragility was a concern. Teachers kept Ted isolated from rambunctious students and their proclivity for accidents. His mama kept a much closer eye on him. Gary became Ted's protector. Whenever Ted looked over his shoulder, Gary was right behind him.

Flash forward to the annual frosh day in high school, where upperclassmen like Gary made slaves, or at least fools, of the freshman class. While Ted's ninth grade classmates succumbed to every silly or outrageous command, he sauntered about the small parochial institution unencumbered. There would be no hazing for Ted. This was the result of a plan for Ted's life that his brother Gary set in motion the day Ted fell from his bike. It was one Gary defended for the rest of his young life: No one touched Ted. As long as Gary was with him, no one would dare.

But what would happen if the tables turned and Gary became the victim?

CHAPTER 1

WHERE'S GARY?

What happened to Gary?

The question banged around in Ted Kergan's dream like a pinball. *Ding! What happened to Gary? Ding! What happened to Gary? Ding! What happened to Gary?* Louder and faster, Ted's dream world merged with consciousness until he snapped awake. Eyes open, he still felt disoriented. His six-foot-four frame had folded itself onto his couch, sometime after midnight. Now he untangled his stiff limbs while he tried to untangle his thoughts.

Where the hell is Gary? Great, I have him to thank for a crappy half night's sleep on the sofa.

He glanced at the security chain on the front door. It was still unlatched in anticipation of Gary's arrival with important financing news about expanding their South Louisiana chain of Sonic Drive-Ins. Gary had called around eleven the night before, letting Ted know he would arrive at Ted's condominium around twelve-thirty. Gary's home was close by. So where the hell was he?

Ted found himself no less helpless now than he'd been in his dream. Sitting alone in his condo with his head buried in his hands, he pondered what was at stake; the expected news was life altering. The Kergan Brothers were set to sign one of Sonic's first development agreements, consequently adding significantly to their chain of fourteen Sonic restaurants.

Ted's brain began clicking through the timeline. Gary had met with bankers in McComb, Mississippi, to seal the deal the day before. Also, in order to be closer to their new territory, he had lately spent a lot of time at a Baton Rouge apartment he and another business associate shared. Ted wondered, was Gary there when he called?

They talked at least half a dozen times daily, either in person or on the phone. During their last conversation, Ted had thought Gary sounded awful, hoarse, and wheezing. Gary had confirmed he wasn't feeling well, possibly with the flu.

A list of possibilities ran through Ted's mind. Maybe Gary stayed overnight at the Baton Rouge apartment, and simply fell asleep before he could call back to tell Ted he was spending the night there. Or maybe he skipped visiting Ted and decided to make the seventy-eight mile trip straight back home.

But an uneasy feeling in the pit of his stomach was just reaching his throat when the wall phone in the kitchen rang, commencing a day Ted would never forget. It was just after 7:00 a.m. on Thursday, November 29, 1984. Gary's wife, Susie, was on the line with a panicked voice. She outlined in stark tones what Ted was already thinking; Gary had never spent the night away from home without calling.

Ted quickly showered and dressed, as he plotted his next move and strove to fight off worst-case scenarios. It was a short drive to the Acadia Parish Sheriff's Office in the small town of Crowley, Louisiana. Its historic downtown district on Court Circle, literally a circle around the circa 1888 courthouse, was home to everything official in Crowley, including the sheriff's office. Ted's good friend, newly elected Sheriff Ken Goss, greeted him warmly and empathized with his situation but cautioned him that not much could be done immediately, since, at that time, a missing person's report could not be filed for twenty-four hours. Additionally, the report had to be filed in the jurisdiction where the person went missing. When Ted last heard from his brother, Gary was definitely in Louisiana's capital city, located in the heart of East Baton Rouge Parish. Even though Baton Rouge was barely an hour's drive, it was light years away from the small-town law enforcement Ted experienced in Crowley. The capital city's force was bigger and much busier. As an outsider to police operations there, Ted wondered if he would find Baton Rouge police were a lot less friendly too. Over a cup of coffee, Sheriff Goss and Ted came up with an interim plan. Ted would continue on to Baton Rouge and begin searching for his brother, door to door if necessary, starting at the Fairway View apartment that Gary rented as an auxiliary office. Sheriff Goss put out an all-points bulletin on Gary Kergan's 1984 Cadillac Eldorado, a champagne beige two-door sedan.

Ted tried to control his anxiety, but Ken sensed it and kindly cut their meeting short so Ted could head to Baton Rouge. Back in his vehicle, he opened the glove box, pulled out his special-issue Acadia Parish Deputy Sheriff badge, and stuffed it into his pants pocket. Ted flashed back to Gary calling him mere months before, commanding Ted to come down immediately to the sheriff's office. As Ted had done so many times, he stopped what he was doing to comply with Gary's request. Even though he was thirty years old, Ted often deferred to his brother, who was only three years older, yet still cast that fatherly aura. Gary had arranged for himself and Ted to be commissioned as Acadia Parish sheriff's deputies. The impromptu swearing-in ceremony was just another one of Gary's got-to-make-it-happen moves. Ted never thought to ask why or how Gary finagled those official badges.

Minutes later, with the sun to his back, Ted merged onto eastbound I-10. After he passed the city of Lafayette, the heart of Louisiana's Acadiana region, Ted began the eighteen-mile trek over the raised interstate crossing the expansive Atchafalaya Basin with a sense of foreboding that was as dark and murky as the massive cypress tupelo swamp. He tried not to think about how many men had died in that swamp, whether in accidents or at the hands of murderers who were certain alligators would pick any evidence clean. Even in late November, the trees glistened green throughout the muddy basin waters.

What a contrast this terrain presented to the Kergan brothers' home turf in suburban Detroit. The brothers had matriculated through a Vatican II-guided parochial school in the 1960s, and then discovered a passion for entrepreneurial endeavors. As teenagers, Gary and Ted became enamored with a controversial multi-level marketing company called Dare to Be Great, created by business evangelist Glenn Turner. The brothers shared more with Turner than a desire to excel. Turner was raised by a poor, single mother, and found success at the hands of good business mentors. Gary and Ted had the utmost respect for their own mother, with the formidable name of Grace Harriet Patricia Frances McGraw Kergan, who bravely stepped up to become head of household after their father's sudden death.

Turner's cosmetic company, Koscot, had become a $100 million business in three years, bigger than Amway at its height. Turner crafted Dare To Be Great because Koscot had a need for training materials and sales courses. Many, including Gary and Ted Kergan, flocked to Dare to Be Great seminars and came away impressed by Turner's evangelistic approach, hoping to join more than eight hundred others who became millionaires through Koscot and Dare to Be Great.

Glenn Turner was eventually charged with aiding and abetting a pyramid scheme related to a subsequent company, and spent five years in an Arizona prison. Nevertheless, disciples of Dare to Be Great moved forward with tenants of the sales and motivation program, following Turner's challenge: "Some people are waiting for something to turn up. Why not try starting with your sleeves and go to work?" Besides providing a business foundation for the brothers, the Dare to Be Great program and one of its Detroit distributors, Jim Freeman, showed them how to network and form lasting business relationships.

Gary met his wife, Susie, at Wayne State University, a city college in Detroit, where he was enrolled in a pre-med curriculum. Sparks flew when they found themselves in the same speed-reading course. Gary found what he was looking for in a partner with Susie, who was intellectually his equal.

The speed-reader's version is Gary's family was Catholic; Susie's was Episcopalian. So the couple agreed to marry in a Presbyterian Church.

Married life was fine, but it wasn't long before the lure of making money and an entrepreneurial spirit enveloped Gary. His savvy skills as a sales representative had made him a natural at pharmaceutical sales. Still, he wasn't his own boss.

It was Jim Freeman who lured Gary Kergan to Louisiana, away from his pharmaceutical sales job in Utah. It was 1975, when Gary, upon hearing the story of Don Gravlee, Freeman's brother-in-law and one of the very first Sonic Drive-In restaurant franchisees, packed up his wife and young son, Wade, and headed south, deep into the Bayou State. It was there that Gravlee and Freeman put Gary to work earning credit toward a franchise with sweat equity as a Sonic manager. Although Sonic Drive-Ins would afford him the opportunity to be his own boss, the road to that goal was a long slog.

Gravlee's sons provided far less sweat equity, which would have meant actually showing up and working, and instead brought more of an entitled mentality to the idea of working with Gary Kergan in the enterprise. He put in long hours and continually chronicled daily goings-on to brother Ted, still back home in Detroit. On one occasion, at a particularly low moment, Gary had to break up a fist fight between a couple of rednecks at his very rural restaurant and got hurt in the process. When Ted heard Gary relate the blow-by-blow details during their next evening phone call, he made the decision to move to Louisiana that year, 1977, and join the business with Gary to help with the struggles at the stores. He would also be there to help Gary deal with the spoiled, unruly Gravlee boys.

Don Gravlee Sr. knew Troy Smith before he conceived Sonic Drive-Ins, back in the 1950s when Smith ran a Top Hat root beer stand in Shawnee, Oklahoma. When Troy Smith branched out to franchise his trademark Sonic restaurants in the 1960s, fellow Oklahoman Don Gravlee was one of his first partners, eventually growing his Sonic business in several states, including Louisiana. By the mid-1970s, three of his four sons had relocated to South Louisiana to soak up the resulting largesse. Donnie, Mark, and Mitch Gravlee, the roughest of the three brothers, were constant irritations to Ted and Gary Kergan, both during and outside of work hours. With tension mounting between the two camps, Don Gravlee Sr. and Gary Kergan agreed to split up their Sonic restaurants on a Friday the 13th in April of 1979.

A troubling animosity lingered, however, and Ted Kergan found himself remembering several ugly incidents between his brother and Mitch Gravlee, as he sped toward Baton Rouge on I-10. One such incident started with a car chase between the two, ending with Gary running away on foot and hiding from a furious Mitch Gravlee in a Lafayette furniture store. Ted had also heard his brother tell a story about Mitch Gravlee calling late at night, directing him to bring cash to the back room of a Lafayette bar. Gary entered the room in the midst of a card game to find one player pointing a gun at Mitch Gravlee, waiting for his winnings to be delivered. Mitch had a fondness for nightlife, and a lot of Sonic co-workers joined him on after-hours jaunts. Ted had accompanied Mitch Gravlee on a few such nights, and he knew Gary had as well.

Could Gary's disappearance somehow involve Mitch Gravlee?

It was midday when Ted reached The Fairway View apartments, just a couple hundred yards off I-10 at the College Drive exit. The drive to the back of the vanilla-looking complex paralleled a municipal golf course, reminding Ted of Gary's home on Bayou Bend golf course. Mitch Gravlee owned a home on the other side of that same golf course. But then, Bayou Bend was the most upscale neighborhood in the small town of Crowley.

Ted thought about how many times in the last few months Gary had driven the same route he had just taken from Crowley to Baton Rouge. While Ted was used to staying in their Acadiana territory, taking care of the nitty-gritty detail work for their fourteen restaurants, Gary was constantly on the move, recently tying up loose ends on their new Sonic development agreement, one Ted thought was overly ambitious. As Ted entered the ground floor Fairway View apartment unit No. 136 in Baton Rouge, he didn't know what to expect. Gary's Cadillac was not parked outside. He looked around in the bedrooms and bathroom, halfway expecting Gary to emerge from one of the rooms surprised to see Ted there. There was no sign of Gary, yet nothing in the apartment seemed amiss. The living room was set up as a boardroom, complete with large conference table and comfortable chairs. Ted picked up a square push-button phone near the table and punched out the number for Larry Tucker, Gary's office roommate at Fairway View and their business partner in the upcoming Sonic development agreement venture. Larry owned Sonic franchises of his own and was living with his family in Amory, a north Mississippi town of seven thousand, an hour's flight, or a five-and-a-half-hour drive from Baton Rouge.

When Larry answered the phone, Ted skipped the formalities. "Have you talked to Gary? He didn't come home last night."

Larry was an intense man with a fair complexion and reddish hair, and he had become close to Gary Kergan through their numerous Sonic-related business deals. They worked together for twelve-hour days, and would meet at Ruth's Chris Steak House most evenings for a nightcap and business wrap up. After the steakhouse closed at eleven-thirty, Larry and Gary often returned to their nearby office/apartment and swapped stories. Larry was married with two daughters.

In Larry's eyes, Gary was the leader, the dreamer, the big picture guy. Gary could do anything; he had tremendous confidence. He wasn't cocky, just confident. Nothing scared him. Ted was the nuts and bolts guy. He was in the background, always taking care of the minutia. Larry Tucker thought brothers Ted and Gary were inseparable. Ted and Larry were not close yet. That would change over the next thirty years.

Larry Tucker had spoken to Gary Kergan the night he went missing. He recalled Gary as feeling sick; they had joked about trying a Schnapps remedy. The two of them had an easy relationship, and it flowed seamlessly from serious business into playtime. Now Larry racked his brain, trying to recall anything Gary said or did that might be a clue.

Days before, there had been a slip of paper on the table at the apartment with the name Erika and a phone number scrawled on it in Gary's handwriting. Larry had tossed it into the bathroom wastebasket. Later that same night, Gary unexpectedly stopped by the apartment. After talking over a little business, the two went out for drinks.

At the time, Larry had no problem confronting Gary about finding and tossing Erika's name and number. Gary thanked him, saying, "You know, you probably saved me from going out on my wife." Once they were back in the apartment, Larry settled in for bed and heard Gary shuffling around in the bathroom.

The next morning, Larry discovered Gary's bed made, and knew he had not slept at their Fairway View apartment the night before. He found the bathroom's trash from the day before in the kitchen garbage but couldn't find the note with Erika's name and phone number on it. Did Gary go through the trash and retrieve that slip of paper? Where was Gary?

Who was Erika anyway? Larry had a lot of questions about that evening.

It was the last time Larry Tucker saw Gary Kergan. "I was naive about it all, but I knew something was really wrong," he recalled. "Ted told me he was going to fill out a missing person's report. I hung up the phone and turned to Connie and said, 'Gary's dead.' That's how well I thought I knew Gary. But I didn't really know him at all."

Within forty-eight hours, Larry Tucker was on a plane from Tupelo to Baton Rouge to help with the search.

CHAPTER 2

TED AND GARY

Thirteen-year-old Gary Kergan was having one of his frequent bursts of inexplicable confidence. This self-assurance was what his ten-year-old brother Ted most admired about him, and what he most tried to emulate. That didn't prevent little Ted from being caught off guard when Gary spoke up out of the blue. "You know Ted, since Mom can't afford to move us out of this house, the only way we're ever going to get any space for ourselves is if we go upstairs and turn the attic into a bedroom for us. Finish it out. Really do it right! We could make it a real project...," Gary drifted off, already visualizing the task.

Ted was excited by his big brother's idea, but his ten years in the world hadn't given him any knowledge of home construction. "But where do you even start with a job like that? We can't exactly use our own house for practice."

"We won't have to practice! I've asked around. There are books you can buy, or even check out at the library, and they tell you how to do everything, step-by-step!"

"What, we just follow them, and then actually do it?"

"Why not? Listen, you don't have to be a genius, you just have to be serious about getting it done."

Although Gary was only three years older, he was the father figure for Ted and he embraced the role. It fell to him when their dad died shortly after Ted was born, and a crooked lawyer wound up with their father's insurance money. Their mother earned a living out of their home as a seamstress.

She drove an old car, and both boys appreciated how hard she worked to keep them all together inside their tiny house.

To Ted's surprise, their mom gave Gary and Ted permission to work unsupervised on their attic project. The idea didn't fade out and the urge didn't go away. For Ted, it was scary but made him feel giddy at the same time. They actually were going to go through with this.

Gary went ahead and obtained all the written instructions on how to finish out an attic space and make it livable. Ted went along with the difficult work sessions required, and didn't complain much in spite of his age. In truth, he rode on the magic carpet of Gary's confidence and optimism.

One of the neighbor men noticed them working and asked what they were up to. He guffawed at the idea of two boys their ages building out an attic and turning it into a big bedroom with nothing but a few hand tools. From that day on, whenever he saw them he made it a point to challenge them on their knowledge of whichever task they were doing.

But Gary had already read up on each step before they started on it, and the neighbor never stumped him, not even once. Ted's biggest thrill on the job was being part of a team of boys who were rearranging a grown man's understanding of what two motivated boys could do.

His pride helped offset the fact that even though Gary was Ted's protector in many ways, they were still brothers, and thus when it came time to do the electrical wiring, it was Ted's job to touch the ends of the wires to see if they were live or not. He got shocked a couple of times, but Gary only extended brotherly sympathy of the so-what-you'll-live variety. He even managed to get Ted to laugh it off as a lesson in "what the electric chair feels like!"

No matter, because once they were into the job, they both felt a heavy obligation to avoid disappointing their mother. The idea of making her sorry she gave them a chance at this was powerful enough to keep them showing up for work every day after school.

Which they did, and, after the weeks rolled by, the brothers finished their new upstairs bedroom. They lost no time in moving in. Naturally, Ted and Gary felt stronger and more confident because of their accomplishment. They had taken on a big project for the first time, working as a team. Now they basked in the resulting sense of feeling capable.

The attic project turned out to be more than a new bedroom for two industrious boys. It was a real world demonstration of where this new sense of capability could take them. It was hard proof of their ability to find success at something good, in spite of the family's poverty.

Coded into their muscles now was the knowledge that they could imagine, they could plan, and they could build. Years later, Ted would realize that while they had confirmed their mother's faith in them, this was also when they began building a lasting foundation of it for themselves.

CHAPTER 3

HELLO GARY

Ted Kergan combed Baton Rouge looking for his brother, feeling more frantic by the hour. He had brought along Gary's Rolodex and flipped the tabbed pages one at a time, phoning each and every contact. He tried to walk in his brother's footsteps, following a route to surrounding grocery and convenience stores, gas stations, even dry cleaners. Then he widened the circumference of his search, visiting their Sonic franchises, talking to managers and employees. He called every hospital between Baton Rouge and Crowley. He checked in with Baton Rouge police.

No one had seen Gary, yet it was completely out of character for him to go missing and not tell anyone his whereabouts.

Ted made stops at Ruth's Chris Steak House, and next door at a discotheque called Del Lago, both around the corner from the Fairway View apartment office. On his drive back to Crowley Thursday evening, taking the same I-10 westward route Gary should have taken home the night before, Ted drove extra slowly, peering countless times over the sides of the raised expressway. He stopped more than once to check if Gary had somehow driven his car off the road and into the gnarly swamp.

But Ted found no clues and no solace along the way. Once back in his own condominium, he reluctantly related his lack of progress to Gary's wife, Susie, and their young son, Wade, who had suffered the wait at home. It was a long, sleepless night for all of them.

The next day, Friday, November 30, was slated to be an important day for Gary. He had a real estate closing at 3:00 p.m. for a new residence in Hammond, thirty miles east of Baton Rouge. It was part of the new Sonic empire being constructed by the Kergan Brothers Company. Gary was so serious about it, his family planned to move to Hammond and oversee restaurants in that region.

Now younger brother Ted was at wit's end, trying to imagine what kind of trauma could be keeping Gary out of touch. He drove to the attorney's Hammond office with the desperate hope that Gary would somehow show up for the closing appointment. At this point, Ted had not talked to Gary in twenty-four hours. The brothers usually spoke multiple times daily, communicating in their own special language. Decades before text messaging was available, Ted and Gary Kergan carried on conversations using just the first letter of each word. Both brothers were wicked smart and talked about everything, changing subjects, conversing back and forth, seemingly confusing to onlookers, but making perfect sense to the brothers.

Though it was Gary who had enrolled in a pre-med curriculum at Wayne State University before his entrepreneurial side took over, younger brother Ted was his intellectual equal. Ted picked up the first volume in their home set of encyclopedias as an eight-year-old, and read the whole book. He proceeded to devour every volume in the entire set. The brothers were used to matching wits, albeit in Kergan speak.

Ted wished he could have one more straightforward talk with his brother right now. In the last few weeks, he sensed Gary was holding back something during their multi-tiered sessions, and he felt it was a huge burden to Gary. After all, the brothers normally conversed about anything and everything. Ted wondered if that silent subject had anything to do with Gary's disappearance. What had been troubling him?

Both Kergan brothers were nervous about this new Sonic agreement and opening *forty-five* new Sonic restaurants in New Orleans, an area where Sonic had no brand awareness and where the process of building was daunting. Ted thought the brothers were overcommitting with this agreement. Gary felt that way too.

Weeks before, the brothers traveled to Sonic's corporate office in Oklahoma, where Gary instructed Ted to burst into the CEO's office and get them out of the burgeoning business arrangement. They both knew it was going to be incredibly expensive to build the New Orleans' Sonic Drive-Ins.

No, Ted reasoned, if Gary was worried about business, he would have no problem relaying that. Ted pondered more deeply about his brother's tendencies. He had always been somewhat envious of how easily Gary met and connected with people. Ted saw himself as an introvert. Gary and Susie were such a good match, two strong-willed people who had become involved in the Crowley community. Instead of choosing either of their childhood faiths, since Gary was Catholic and Susie was Episcopalian, the couple decided to join the Church of Jesus Christ of Latter Day Saints and became part of the close-knit Mormon congregation. Gary coached son Wade's ball teams and took him on hunting and fishing trips just like a native Louisianan. On the other hand, Gary sometimes connected with the wrong people. Damn, he was a terrible judge of character, thought Ted. Because of that naïveté, coupled with his generous "give you the shirt off his back" tendencies, Ted believed Gary Kergan could be easily led astray.

Ted traveled through the darkest parts of his brother's character traits, searching for answers, but he felt defeated and alone. Gary had always stood beside Ted during tough times, but where was he now?

Reeling in his heart of hearts, Ted knew that if Gary failed to show up at that office for the real estate closing, something was terribly wrong. He tried to conjure up any reason that would keep Gary away from him, away from his family, away from this real estate closing that was so important to both his professional and personal life. Ted knew that the brothers had made up their minds to proceed with the Sonic development agreement, and that meant wild horses would not keep Gary from closing on his new home in Hammond. Whatever was keeping him away was clearly very serious. Ted felt certain the circumstances were devastating, possibly even lethal. As time ticked away, an overwhelming sense of grief worked on him bit by bit until it completely enveloped him. At 3:30 p.m., with no sign of Gary at the prescribed site of the closing, Ted became physically ill, overwhelmed by the feeling he would never see his brother again.

After a brief period of sorrow, Ted pulled himself together and drove back to Baton Rouge to continue the search. At least he had help; with an official missing report now filed by the Baton Rouge Police Department, along with the all-points bulletin on Gary's Cadillac Eldorado, detectives were actively involved in the case. This didn't slow Ted down. He continued routes around Baton Rouge that Friday evening, stopping any place he thought Gary might have been and questioning anyone who might have seen him. He went back to Ruth's Chris Steak House, to other restaurants, clubs, even convenience stores in the area surrounding the Fairway View apartments. But he learned nothing.

How could Gary just disappear? It was getting late, past closing time for many establishments, and Ted had exhausted every idea or hunch about where Gary might have stopped. Ted was mentally and physically exhausted as well. It had been almost 48 hours since that last, brief phone conversation with his brother. Beyond desperate, he postponed his long drive back home and pulled himself together to consider any last-ditch, final stops in the search. At this time of night, only bars and clubs were open. Since Ted had already been to all the restaurants and clubs in the area of the Fairway View apartment, he wondered if there was another place, maybe further afield.

He remembered a strip club in North Baton Rouge that Mitch Gravlee had taken him to a couple of years before. The Night Spot was almost ten miles from the apartment in the opposite direction from Gary's route home. Although Ted and Gary had never been there together, Ted knew Gary was aware of the place, set amid a row of strip clubs in North Baton Rouge. They had talked about Mitch Gravlee and his appetite for dancing women and drink, and they knew it had led him to a variety of clubs, including The Night Spot.

The Hollywood Street interstate exit was the opposite of what its name indicated. Instead of swaying palm trees, hills, and mansions, Ted saw a million lights of Exxon's refinery city on the river to the west, and a street lined with cramped, dingy frame houses on his way to Plank Road. As he made the left turn into another way of life, Ted had no problem finding a parking spot near The Night Spot's only door. He sat there for just a minute, reconsidering. Did he really want to go into this dive? This was a real long shot, but Ted was out of options, and that alone drove him to cut the ignition and enter a strange portal that would soon become his new reality.

The Night Spot lounge had been recently acquired by Gary and Dorothy Magee. Plank Road, where The North Baton Rouge club was located, was a defining artery in that declining neighborhood. It operated under a steady and profitable system of the time. Although it has long been closed, The Night Spot was described by a former patron as an old bump and grind joint with only white female dancers clad in pasties and G-strings who danced on a raised stage, which wrapped around the center bar for a crowd made up solely of white males. There were no lap dances and no back rooms. People didn't clap for dancers in those days. The atmosphere was quieter. Customers came from all over the community to wind down from their jobs. Some were white-collar professionals employed in downtown Baton Rouge, while others worked at the nearby plants. They drank beer and whisky, talked about current events, politics, and sports while watching practically naked women dance. If they got out of line, they were cut off and told to leave and sometimes the police were called for those who didn't comply.

At six feet four, Ted Kergan was four inches taller than Gary. Ted was also twenty pounds heavier. Nevertheless, the family resemblance was undeniable. As Ted Kergan pushed open the door of The Night Spot, a place he had only been once before in his life, two days of a blurry existence came into focus for him. One of the dancers immediately approached him with a knowing smile, greeting Ted with "Hello Gary!" Her proclamation of mistaken identity was confirmation that his brother was fairly well known there.

"No, I'm Gary's brother, Ted. Could you take me to your manager?"

Gary Magee, a quiet type, had long, jet black hair that fell down to his waist. His wife, Dorothy, worked very hard behind the bar, but also danced and supervised the girls. Their bar was one of the few in the area not affiliated with the Sons of Silence biker gang, but the Magees tolerated the bikers because they needed their women employed as dancers. Among the crowd every night were bikers acting as spotters to make sure their women were working and handling things properly. Disputes were not always settled peacefully. Bloodstains on the sidewalk outside The Night Spot remained from the stabbing death of a Sons of Silence chief. Despite this, The Night Spot was not considered by most to be a dangerous place.

Ten or twelve women danced a couple of sets on stage, after which they came down to sell drinks, visit with customers, and collect tips in the interim. Men sat around the bar (maintaining a mandatory and legally enforced three-foot distance from the dancers atop) or they sat at one of the eighteen four-man tables around the establishment's single, large room. The Magees kept a tally of the drinks sold by individual dancers by putting straws for each dancer in marked cups behind the bar. Dancers were paid $2 on $5 drinks plus tips from the customers. Ted watched the Friday night scene unfold while he followed the dancer to the bar, where she pointed to Dorothy Magee.

"Could I buy you a drink?" Ted asked Dorothy. She nodded, signaling to the bartender. That was Ted's queue to continue.

"Do you know my brother, Gary Kergan?" Ted asked. Dorothy Magee nodded again. "Was he here Wednesday night?" For the third time, Dorothy Magee nodded. Ted asked more questions, but The Night Spot co-owner remained tight-lipped, knowing better than to answer too many questions from a stranger. A stupid move like that could get her bar shut down.

Ted took a $100 bill from his wallet and tore it in half.

"If you find out anything else about Gary, call me and I'll give you the other half," Ted told her as he handed her one-half of the bill, stuffing the other half back into his wallet. Again, Dorothy Magee nodded.

Ted made his way back to the door. He lingered outside, hoping Dorothy Magee would follow him and give up some other clues. He marveled about how just how miraculous it was to locate Gary's whereabouts from the night he went missing. It was akin to finding a needle in a haystack.

He was excited and frightened all at once.

CHAPTER 4

LAS VEGAS

Gary Kergan's missing person case was assigned to Baton Rouge police detectives Bob Howle and R.E. Thompson. Howle and Thompson made an interesting team. Although both were veteran police officers and excellent detectives, they approached this puzzle from different angles. Hard-charging, New York native Howle didn't bother to use the social skills common to Southern-bred folks, but you could almost see the wheels turning under his slick, combed-back hair. Bob Howle was always processing things mentally, positioning himself where he thought an investigation was heading. He couldn't care less if anyone actually liked him on a personal level. And he enjoyed a drink or two, or more. On the other hand, R.E. Thompson followed in the footsteps of his father, a captain with the Baton Rouge Police Department. His dress included a few cowboy accents, particularly the enormous belt buckles in vogue during those years following the "Urban Cowboy" movie movement. He honed his social skills and used them to navigate to where he wanted to go.

They worked around the clock investigating the disappearance of Gary Kergan that first weekend of December. Such a missing person case was a big deal, even more so if it turned out to be a homicide. As 1984 was winding to a close, Baton Rouge detectives had only investigated a couple of dozen murders, most of those the result of domestic disputes. A young, reputable businessman missing as the possible result of foul play became front page news.

Ted called early Saturday morning to tell the two detectives about his enlightening encounter with the dancer who mistook him for Gary at The Night Spot the previous evening. Ted also told them about meeting other dancers and the club's owners, Gary and Dorothy Magee. Finally, Ted related the story about giving Dorothy Magee half of a $100 bill.

Howle and Thompson were impressed with Ted's detective work and met him at the Fairway View office/apartment on Saturday afternoon to search for evidence. Finding nothing unusual there, the two detectives said goodbye to Ted and proceeded to The Night Spot lounge on Plank Road. Saturday was Carla Carmichael's first day working at The Night Spot, but she had frequented the lounge as a patron during the prior week and told detectives she was indeed there in the early hours of Thursday, November 29. She remembered seeing Gary Kergan sitting at a table with a dancer she knew only as Erika. Howle and Thompson then showed Gary's photo to Brooksie Ardoin, another dancer, who also said she recognized Gary and knew that he owned several Sonic restaurants. She confirmed that Gary was there to see Erika that night, and added she saw Gary Kergan leave the club with Erika after the 2:00 a.m. closing time. Contacted by telephone, Night Spot proprietor Gary Magee revealed that Erika was her stage name. The dancer's real name was Leila Mulla. Magee obtained this information from Leila Mulla's "go-go dancer license," which described her as a white female, born 6/17/65, 5'2", 130 pounds, brown hair and listed a Louisiana identification card number. Howle and Thompson ran a computer analysis of that identification card, issued to Leila Mulla on November 1. The card revealed an address of 1021 Decatur Street in New Orleans. Apartment owner Joe Valenti verified a man named Ron Dunnagan had once resided at a nearby address, 1019 Decatur Street, where he lived with a woman named Chris Mulla, but that he was no longer there.

On Sunday morning, December 2, Detectives Robert Sedesky and Jerry Callahan, colleagues of Howle and Thompson, struck gold while they continued perusing the databases for information on Leila. They found other aliases: Chris Mulla, Chris Jacobs, Chrissy Jacobs, Chris Moniker, and Chrissy Moniker. They also found she had a second license on file, this one giving her address as 2956 Byron Street, Apt. B in Baton Rouge, just blocks from The Night Spot. Howle and Thompson reported to the address that same day and were again joined by Ted Kergan.

The detectives had a newfound respect for Ted because he made the connection to The Night Spot. It didn't hurt that Ted was deputized by Acadia Parish Sheriff's office. While waiting for duplex owner John Guedry to arrive at the scene, detectives questioned neighbors while an anxious Ted Kergan frantically kicked at an air conditioning unit in an attempt to gain entry into the back of the duplex. He had no intention of waiting on keys from the duplex owner. If his brother was still inside and alive, he might need help right away.

As hard as he tried, Ted couldn't get the window unit to budge. Still, he kept kicking.

Evelyn McAllister lived next door, with the front door of the duplex facing the side of her residence. She had observed a man and a woman moving out of the apartment a couple of days before. Ms. McAllister, a good candidate for nosy Neighborhood Watch block captain, said the couple who lived there tried to sell her furniture, and that two men arrived later and loaded bedroom furniture, tables, and a chest of drawers into their red pickup truck.

Ms. McAllister watched from her window while this couple packed the rest of their belongings into their Plymouth Valiant and pulled away. Behind the duplex, another neighbor, 18-year-old Marie Meadows, was also approached by the same man and woman on the day of their quick exit. Although Ms. Meadows was not acquainted with them, they offered to give her a broom, mop, lamp, two yellow cups, a small mirror, and two plastic feeding bottles for hamsters. Ms. Meadows followed them to their duplex to pick up the items. The detectives had Ms. Meadows turn over her "gifts" as evidence, and she substantiated that the couple did indeed leave in a Plymouth Valiant.

John Guedry finally arrived at the scene and opened up the duplex. Howle and Thompson perused the dwelling first. When they came out, the detectives told Ted Kergan that "there was blood all over the place" but no sign of Gary Kergan. Landlord John Guedry produced a copy of the lease agreement signed by "Mike Karakas." Guedry acknowledged he received a telephone call from the man he knew as Mike Karakas, saying they were moving out. Karakas did not request that his $75 deposit money be returned, but instead asked Guedry if he wanted to buy furniture. Guedry responded by asking for a phone number to follow up on the furniture purchase at a later time. When police checked the number, it was bogus. Guedry remembered he proceeded to the duplex the day he received the phone call and found damage to the bedroom, holes in the walls and doors he said was not there before he rented the apartment to Mike Karakas on November 2. Howle and Thompson accompanied Guedry back into the duplex to witness and log the damage. Ted Kergan was close behind, checking out damage in the duplex's only bedroom, where there was evidence of a fight. Guidry pointed out damage to the bedroom's door, a hole penetrating all the way through it; a hole in the bedroom closet's sliding door; and another hole in the west wall of the bedroom. He also showed detectives several marks on the closet facing, which he said were not there before the house was inhabited by Karakas. All of the marks appeared to have been made with two different types of objects. Detectives also noticed what appeared to be bloodstains on the door, ceiling, closet doors, and on the door casing. There was also a small amount of something that looked like blood on the living room wall. As detectives tallied the mounting evidence, Guedry explained that on October 21, before Mike Karakas resided there, a shooting occurred in the same duplex. The victim was shot in the leg by his roommate. Detectives Howle and Thompson contacted the investigating officer in that shooting case, who proceeded to the Byron Street duplex to clarify details about that event. The officer said no human blood splattering was present during his investigation of the October shooting at the duplex. Furthermore, Howle and Thompson pursued the victim of the October shooting, who admitted being shot but added he did not bleed in the apartment. Following the incident, the victim had surgery at a nearby hospital, where a technologist there confirmed his blood type was A positive. Blood found at the Byron Street duplex was type O positive. Back at the scene of the crime, Howle and Thompson were joined by Dwayne Fontenot, a police officer with the Crime Scene Search Division, who photographed the residence, including all of the damage and what appeared to be blood in various places. Afterward, the two detectives locked up and sent the keys to the district attorney's chief investigator, Hillar Moore. Those keys were waiting for Moore when he arrived for work the next morning, Monday, December 3.

Thirty-year-old Moore loved his job. He had tapped into his bloody passion while studying forensics and crime scene analysis as part of the requirements for his LSU degree in criminal justice. While still in school, the New Orleans native interned for District Attorney Ossie Brown and was introduced to nether regions of Baton Rouge that he had never known existed. His colleagues, hardened investigators who touted experience over books, amused themselves by assigning the college boy late-night crime scenes in seedier areas of town. Much to their chagrin, Moore relished each and every investigation, quickly catching the DA's attention and, upon graduation, full-time employment. A decade's worth of deciphering clues, to satisfy the "beyond a reasonable doubt" burden for the office's cases, had turned the outwardly easygoing Moore into a savvy workhorse who had become the chief investigator. Beyond still photos and individual pieces of evidence from crime scenes, Moore could link his experience with the necessary language to provide trial-worthy descriptions for the DA's prosecuting attorneys to win cases that were scheduled to be heard a year or even two years after the crimes had been committed.

Early that same Monday morning, Gary and Dorothy Magee drove from their suburban home to downtown Baton Rouge for questioning, as requested by Howle and Thompson. While the detectives recorded the bar owners' statements on cassette tapes, Gary Magee said he was personally acquainted with Gary Kergan and that he dropped a lot of money in the lounge, further clarifying that he bought plenty of drinks for the dancers. He estimated Gary Kergan had been a patron of the bar for about a year. Over a period of the last month, Gary Magee had seen Gary Kergan in the bar sitting with Leila Mulla on several/multiple (?) occasions. Magee said on the record that Gary arrived around midnight on November 28 and that he saw him leave with Leila Mulla around two a.m. on November 29. Finally, Magee said he knew Leila Mulla lived with someone named Ron and that he occasionally came into the lounge.

Dorothy Magee's statement mirrored her husband's, with one addition. She noted that two weeks before November 28, Gary Kergan approached her at the lounge around 11:00 p.m. and asked if Leila could leave early. Dorothy responded by saying she could leave early, but if she did she wouldn't be paid. Gary and Leila left together at closing that night as well. Dorothy Magee said all she knew about Ron was that he was either Leila's husband or boyfriend.

Officer Jerry Callahan, assisting in the investigation, continued collecting oral statements from dancers and patrons at The Night Spot. A couple of fellow dancers noted that Leila was a quiet loner who kept to herself. Sandra Germany said she didn't know "Erika's old man" but that Leila often met him after work across the street in the Krispy Kreme parking lot for a ride home. Callahan also questioned Dale Spears, a Night Spot patron, who had been out on a date with Leila on November 23. Spears told him they had dinner at The Mirror Steak House on Airline Highway and afterward went to a friend's mobile home for sex, adding that he did not pay for the sex. During their date, Leila told Spears she used to work on Bourbon Street in New Orleans, that she was currently living on Byron Street, and that she came to Baton Rouge on a Greyhound bus. Spears had noticed her exiting a Plymouth Valiant at The Night Spot the week before. She also told Spears she did not have any problem with her "male roommate" if she went out.

Durel Glenn, manager of The Key Club, which was located next door to The Night Spot, recognized Leila's male roommate in the photo Officer Callahan showed him of Ron Dunnagan. He added that man had been at The Key Club for one drink on either November 27 or 28, but he couldn't be sure of which date.

Officer Callahan's last subject was John Langlinais, now owner of Playboys Penthouse, located on Airline Highway, who also recognized in the photo a man he knew as Ron Dunnagan. Langlinais told the officer Ron came by Playboys Penthouse in early November to try to obtain a job for Leila. Ron continued to return every few days, checking for Leila's dancing license, which had been mailed to the Playboys Penthouse. John Langlinais and Ron Dunnagan had history. Ron Dunnagan worked for Langlinais as a bartender at The Night Spot in previous years when Langlinais was its owner. Langlinais told Officer Callahan he suspected Ron stole $300 from the bar one night by not ringing up all the sales through the cash register. In short, Langlinais simply did not trust Ron Dunnagan.

Evidence seemed to mount while statements were taken,

but as it did, questions increased. If Leila Mulla, aka Erika, and Ron Dunnagan were indeed a couple, who was Mike Karakas? Who left Baton Rouge in a hurry in that Plymouth Valiant? The weekend of investigation bore fruit but Leila's and Ron's trail had gone cold. Before DA Chief Investigator Moore had the chance to travel to the North Baton Rouge crime scene Monday, December 3, he received an extremely informative call. Gary Kergan's car, a 1984 champagne beige Cadillac Eldorado, had just been located in a parking lot on Severn Avenue in Metairie, a suburb of New Orleans.

CHAPTER 5

BLOOD IN THE TRUNK

When Anthony Freddi drove into his office parking lot at 2612 Severn Avenue in Metairie that Monday morning, he noticed the new champagne beige Cadillac Eldorado sedan was still there. He had first seen the car parked there when he arrived at work around 8:30 a.m. the previous Thursday morning, November 29, 1984. Knowing it didn't belong to anyone who worked there, it seemed to Freddi that something was fishy. Four days had passed and Freddi thought it was time to call the police.

When a police officer arrived, he peered through the windows and noticed a man's sports coat and checkbook on the back seat of the locked car. There was no obvious damage to the car. Following procedure, the policeman ran the license plate through the National Crime Information Center database and discovered the abandoned Cadillac was registered to a gentleman by the name of Gary Kergan, who had been reported missing in Baton Rouge days before.

Dealer's Wrecker Service was dispatched to transport the Caddy to Jefferson Parish Sheriff Department's Auto Theft Division's impound lot, also located in Metairie. Detectives Bob Howle and R.E. Thompson were contacted and they quickly made their way to Metairie to inspect the car, which was connected to their case. Once the Cadillac was parked inside the secured police lot, Howle and Thompson asked employees of Dealer's Wrecker to force open the trunk's lock. Peering into the crevice, detectives stepped back. A large pool of dried blood was on the passenger side of the trunk. Howle flashed a knowing glance to Thompson. To these two partners, it spoke volumes.

After pondering the blood, they inspected the rest of the crime puzzle pieces in the trunk: brown briefcase, five coin changers still unopened and encased in their cardboard boxes, a set of keys, a knife in a black sheath, and assorted papers. Once they completed their visual examination, they shut the trunk and secured the car for transport to the Louisiana State Police Crime Laboratory in Baton Rouge.

Acadia Parish Sheriff Ken Goss had originally put out the all-points bulletin on Gary's Cadillac, so he was also notified when the missing car was discovered. He immediately called Ted to let him know the Cadillac was on its way to Baton Rouge. Naturally, Ted wanted to see that car himself; there was no way Ted would accept a second-hand description about the state of that vehicle. Goss had Larry Tucker meet Ted at the State Police Crime Lab, located in Baton Rouge's mid-city area. Inside the lab, a state trooper pulled Larry Tucker off to the side, out of Ted's earshot, letting Larry know about the large pool of blood in the car's trunk. The trooper suggested Larry keep Ted from looking into the trunk. Larry knew there was no way that was going to happen. Instead, Larry prepared Ted for what he was going to see, then backed off to give him room to approach the back of the car alone.

Ted glanced briefly into the trunk and quickly retreated. "Your blood runs cold," He explained, remembering. "You steel yourself beforehand. You sort of see the blood, but you sort of don't. There's stuff thrown everywhere in the trunk. So I'm thinking, 'Is that a lot of blood? What does that mean?' Then your defense mechanisms put you in denial. It was just another level of horror."

Ted asked a trooper what the amount of blood meant. At first, the officer didn't answer, but Ted persisted.

"That's a substantial amount of blood," the trooper

finally told him. The remark later proved to be a gentle understatement. The odd-shaped pool of coagulated blood was a foot wide in some areas. Patches of dried blood stained a number of items in the trunk, including coin changer boxes and bank deposit slips.

Meanwhile, Larry Tucker took a long gander into the trunk, then questioned crime lab technician James Churchman, who was fully engaged in collecting all the evidence the car held – both inside and outside. He summed it up: the victim was already dead when placed in the trunk or he had died there. There was too much blood for any other alternative end but death. Even with mounting bad news from the days before, both men had held out a glimmer of hope that they would find Gary alive. But seeing the car and that large body of blood in the trunk sucked all hope out of Ted Kergan. As his inner voice of reason finally overcame the one in denial, he accepted the fact that by the time the early hours of Thursday, November 29 had rolled around, his brother lay dead in the trunk of his own car.

As the sun set on Monday, December 3, Ted called his business office in Crowley and asked his colleague, Doris Reiners, to summon a Catholic priest to Gary's home. Susie, Wade, his mother, and his sister were all gathered there, awaiting news. Even though Susie was a practicing Mormon, Ted's mother was a staunch Catholic and he knew the presence of a priest would help comfort her. As Ted and Larry began the long journey west to Crowley on the elevated expressway through the swamp, Ted conjured up a painful memory. This wasn't the first time he had told a group close to him the worst possible news. A young male employee who began working at Sonic in central Louisiana, before he was promoted to manage a Sonic in Hammond, Louisiana, was killed in a robbery at that drive-in. Ted traveled to Alexandria along with law enforcement officials to deliver the horrible news to the deceased's love ones. Ted remembered their loss of control over facial expressions, over their bodies in general. The memory was unbelievably painful. Now he was about to ratchet up that pain, as the task fell upon him to deliver the most personal and dreadful news of all to his own family.

Since the drive took more than an hour, it gave Ted and Larry time to consider how to handle this brutal burden and approach breaking the news. They decided a child who just lost his father shouldn't have to see his mother's and grandmother's rawest emotions. This day's memory would leave enough indelible marks.

Since Larry had a good relationship with Wade, he would take Wade into his bedroom and, in words a ten-year-old child could comprehend, tell him that his dad was never coming home. Ted would break the news to everyone else. When they entered his late brother's home, Ted found it full of Susie's fellow congregants from the Church of Jesus Christ of Latter Day Saints. The Catholic priest was also in their midst. Their chatter ceased as all eyes focused on Ted. He took a deep breath and then told them the authorities located Gary's car and there was evidence that Gary was not coming back.

He hoped that would be enough of an explanation. After all, those few words were hard enough to muster without choking up. But the three women couldn't accept such a simple ending to their beloved Gary's young life, so they pressed Ted for details. Looking into their devastated faces, he reluctantly described the pool of blood found in the trunk. Susie Kergan's own defense mechanisms kicked in as she implored Ted to find out more information. Surely, there had to be more facts, something to prove Gary could still be alive. Ted assured her that was all he knew.

Back in his bedroom, Wade accepted the news quietly, but there was no way for Larry to know how the child internalized such a blow. Yes, Wade seemed to understand that his father would not be at home that night, but what about all those tomorrows, all those milestone moments when a son needs his father? Larry couldn't read the boy's emotions, but he felt like he, himself, had been punched in the gut.

***

Ted's whole world had changed. That day marked a turning point in his life. Gary was dead and things would never be the same. Since Ted lost his own father the day after he was born, Gary had been the man of the house, the person everyone looked to for answers. Now that heavy mantle had passed to him. More than that, Ted missed his brother, who had been his childhood mentor and was now his best friend. If Ted had a problem, he always knew Gary would have the solution. There was such an uncanny closeness between the brothers. He spent his life playing with Gary, going to school with Gary, now running a business with Gary. They had shared everything. It was the worst day of Ted Kergan's life.

Two days later, on the fifth of December in Baton Rouge, the blood in the trunk of the car also triggered an arrest warrant for Leila Mulla as a material witness to the whereabouts of Gary Kergan. She was the last person seen with Gary, who, along with being missing, was now presumed dead. Louisiana District Judge Joseph F. Keogh authorized the arrest warrant. Pertinent information on Leila, including her many aliases and her new status as "wanted" by authorities in East Baton Rouge Parish, was entered into the national criminal database. Acting upon change of address forms procured from federal authorities with the U.S. Postal Service, detectives believed Leila and Ron might be on their way to San Diego, and notified authorities there. Imagine their surprise when the call came from Las Vegas instead.

As soon as Leila had applied for a dancer's license, a routine background check produced the warrant for her arrest as a material witness in the murder of Gary Kergan. Authorities in Clark County, Nevada took her into custody Friday, December 7, at around 3:00 p.m. Meanwhile, Ron Dunnagan remained waiting in the decade-old Plymouth Valiant outside in the parking lot, wondering why it was taking Leila so long to procure a simple dancer's license in a place known as a Mecca for dancing girls. Finally, curiosity got the best of him and when he entered the government facility, Ron Dunnagan was also detained, although officially "captured at last" for an outstanding contempt of city court warrant for failure to appear back in Louisiana.

Howle and Thompson knew they had to get to Las Vegas quickly before Ron was released. Authorities could only hold him for twenty-four hours on the contempt of court warrant. "We've got them," Detectives Howle and Thompson told Ted, who continued his daily routine of showing up at Baton Rouge police headquarters with his Acadia Parish Sheriff's badge in his pocket. They asked Ted if he had any connections to get them to Las Vegas in a hurry. Howle and Thompson assumed he would call his travel agent or his preferred airline. But Ted Kergan was on another plane entirely. He now knew Gary was dead and he blamed Leila Mulla and Ron Dunnagan. He fixated, wondering what had happened that night. How in the world had his brother been lured away from that bar by a woman he barely knew?

Yet Ted knew Gary would willingly help anyone. He also knew his brother had a daring, edgy side. That combination of personality traits led to Gary's undoing. Now Ted had to turn the page from looking for his missing brother to bringing justice to the two people he considered responsible for Gary's death. Still reeling from news of Gary's murder and his odd relationship with an exotic dancer, Ted grabbed a Baton Rouge telephone book and flipped to the yellow pages, finding an ad for 24/7 Jets. He dialed the New Orleans number, telling the company representative he needed a jet right way. He added that he would like to charge fees for the jet to his American Express card.

Time was at a premium. Howle and Thompson went home to pack their bags. Ted only had enough time to get to a convenience store to buy toiletries. Within two hours, a Lear jet, rented using Ted's American Express card, was at the Baton Rouge airport ready to transport him and the two Baton Rouge detectives to Las Vegas to interview the two suspects.

By 9:00 p.m. local time on that same day, December 7, Bob Howle was interrogating Leila in the break room at the detention center. In mandated police style, the conversation began with Howle advising Leila of her Miranda rights. Then Leila launched the first of several different versions about how Gary Kergan was murdered.

"Did you know Gary Kergan?" Howle questioned.

"Yes," replied Leila. "The man who owns Sonic Drive-Ins."

"Have you ever left The Night Spot lounge with him?"

Leila went on to describe Gary as "a trick" and yes, she had brought him home with her to the Byron Street duplex a couple of times during the month of November. With Ron Dunnagan present at the duplex both times, she said she and Gary retreated to the bedroom for sex. In the early morning hours of November 29, she initially said Gary left after he paid for her services.

"Did Gary Kergan deserve to die?" asked the detective.

"No," replied Leila.

"Did Ronald Dunnagan intentionally kill Gary Kergan?"

"Yes," said Mulla. "Ron killed Gary, but it was not intentional."

She wove a tale of a drunken Gary Kergan who wanted rough sex prompting Ron, who was hiding in a closet, to enter the bedroom. At that time, Leila said, she retreated to the couch in the living room. From that vantage point, she saw nothing but heard a struggle and noises emanating from the bedroom. Leila said Ron exited the bedroom, panicked, and later placed Gary's body in the trunk of his own car. Ron got behind the wheel of the Cadillac and pulled away from the duplex while she remained there.

"You should talk to Ron for the rest of the story," she advised Howle, adding that she wanted an attorney before answering any more questions.

It was now early Saturday morning, December 8, 1984. A Las Vegas homicide detective, Bernie Alvin, verified Ron's and Leila's new Las Vegas address on Palos Verdes Street, which is closer to the University of Nevada Las Vegas than to the famous strip. Alvin accompanied Baton Rouge detectives and Ted Kergan to the apartment to make sure it was secure while they waited on the search warrant to be approved. Later that same day, detectives obtained an arrest warrant for Ron Dunnagan, using Leila Mulla's statement as probable cause. The charge was second-degree murder.

On the next day, Sunday, December 9, detectives in Las Vegas secured search warrants for Ron and Leila's new apartment at 4050 Palos Verdes Street. It had been leased by Dunnagan in his own name, and in that of his "wife" Ericka Sylvan, another of Leila's aliases. Apartment 16 on the ground floor was an average one-room studio with a floor-to-ceiling built-in dividing the living and bedroom areas. Sergeant Bobby Hitt of the Las Vegas Robbery Division acted as the affiant, joined by investigator Bob Corse, the two Baton Rouge detectives, and Ted Kergan. Among the items secured as evidence were three revolvers, a semi-automatic pistol, two boxes of ammunition, brass knuckles, a folding knife, and a container of plastic cable ties. In the apartment, detectives later found a pair of handcuffs made in Spain with the marking E.I.C. There was also a variety of identification materials, including birth certificates for William Earl Dove and Philomena Ann Lillis and a social security card in the name of Peggy Sue Spurlock. In the apartment's only closet, located among hanging clothing, a toolbox, and red duffle bag, was a four-foot metal locker-style chest. Inside was a clown costume and items used in magic tricks.

Ted Kergan located the real treasure trove of evidence. In a bureau drawer, he found Leila's Hallmark diary along with her "personal monthly plan book," her red spiral notebook with handwritten entries, and her Mead writing tablet diary. In the mid-1980s, before the advent of personal computers and cell phones, monthly planners contained much more than appointments. They often contained names, addresses, and all kinds of other personal information. Looking through Leila Mulla's planners and diaries was like looking through that brief period of her life with binoculars. It was an up close and personal picture of the life of a very troubled teenager, obsessed with her looks, her weight, and her measurements.

Within the diaries were plenty of silly rants, but also lots of damning entries. Ted flipped through the pages, skipping the trivia and focusing on what was going on in Leila Mulla's life during the month of November, 1984. Many of the passages didn't make any sense to him, until, astounded, he saw his brother's name mentioned. Who else could be "Sonic Gary" to this young woman, the same woman who left The Night Spot with his brother? As he continued reading, Ted gleaned that Leila Mulla had revealed in her own handwriting a plan to "get" Gary Kergan and to "hit Gary next time." Ted also found a mysterious hand-drawn map, one depicting the levee, with a winding road and rough-shingled building drawn on one side and the close-up version of the levee with trees, trash, and an "X" marking on the other. For Ted, the diaries and this map were all the evidence he needed to know that Leila Mulla and her companion, Ron Dunnagan, planned and killed his brother.

On Monday morning, detectives proceeded to the Las Vegas North Commerce Street lot, where Ron Dunnagan's Valiant was impounded, to search the vehicle. Bob Corse was again on hand to photograph evidence. Amid the trash and disgusting grime accrued in the car during their cross-country journey, there was no real evidence. That same day, December 10, Ron and Leila waived extradition back to Louisiana. It didn't take detectives long to find out Ron Dunnagan had street smarts. He managed to have a short, yet meaningful conversation with Leila before they were taken back to Baton Rouge. Due to a lapse in judgment by Howle, the two were transported to the airport in one car instead of two. This gave them time together in the back seat. If they became separated, Ron told Leila to contact him at his mother's home in Bossier City, where they had made a pit stop on their journey west.

After 9:00 p.m. on December 12, the entire Las Vegas entourage, including Leila, Ron, Bob Howle, R.E. Thompson, and Ted Kergan arrived at the Baton Rouge airport on a commercial flight. Leila and Ron, in the custody of the two detectives, had no idea Gary Kergan's brother was on the same flight or that he had been in Las Vegas helping to collect evidence against them. Upon arrival, Leila's charges were upgraded to first-degree murder. Again, presented with her Miranda rights, she signed the form but asked for an attorney before answering any questions. She then spent the first of many nights in the East Baton Rouge Parish Sheriff Office's downtown jail. Ron, on the other hand, was originally charged with second-degree murder and acknowledged his Miranda rights as administered by Howle and Thompson, but he refused to sign the form. He agreed to answer questions and related his story about the night of the murder.

He said yes, he knew Gary Kergan, the Sonic Man, but he did not kill him. Ron said Gary left the Byron Street Duplex around 3:15 the morning of November 29. During questioning, Ron became slightly more animated, challenging, "How do you know he just didn't leave town and run off? You don't have a body, do you?"

Two days later, on December 14, which was fifteen days after Gary Kergan disappeared, charges against Ronald Dalton Dunnagan were upgraded to first-degree murder.

Who was this odd couple? At first glance, Leila Mulla was a nineteen-year-old beauty and Ron Dunnagan was a thirty-six-year-old simpleton with street smarts, a very odd couple to say the least. There had to be much more beneath the surface.

CHAPTER 6

LEILA MULLA

At nineteen, Leila Mulla bore a striking resemblance to a young Madonna, but Leila was a different kind of performer. She learned early that acting out got her what she wanted. From the small stage of her posh Kent, Ohio, home as the youngest of six children, to raunchy nightclub platforms in New Orleans' famed French Quarter, Leila danced for a stable of men and used a variety of names. Most recently, she was known as Erika. Big hair and gobs of dark makeup complemented her half-Syrian ancestry. Beneath it all shined the flame of youth, so blinding, so attractive that it blocked almost everything else about her.

Leila was the youngest of six children born to a stay-at-home mother and immigrant physician father. Both parents were unusually tough on all of the siblings, demanding excellence and obedience. Theirs was a "spare the rod, spoil the child" volatile household, even where Leila was concerned. Her siblings pursued careers in medicine, teaching, and diplomacy under the unwavering eyes of their taskmaster parents. As a prominent obstetrician-gynecologist on staff at three area hospitals, Dr. Nejdat Mulla upheld the strict family regime, yet found a soft spot for his youngest daughter, who had learned to please and manipulate at an early age. Her Catholic mother, formerly a nurse, prayed for her strong-willed daughter.

Leila took violin lessons, performed in the Theodore Roosevelt High symphony orchestra and joined her high school cross-country track teammates at the state meet. By that time, her family had moved into a huge home on a lake in exclusive Sugar Bush Knolls, slightly north of Kent, Ohio. At the age of sixteen, Leila was a violin prodigy, track star, and honor student. Her two older brothers, Omar and Nejdat, were away at college, choosing not to matriculate at nearby Kent State University. Family life began to unravel for those remaining in the house, including Leila, older brothers Sean and Kahil, and sister, Wadia.

Facing lofty expectations for college graduation followed by advanced degrees, Leila's focus became hazy. She got involved with a peer group of burnouts who introduced her to tobacco and alcohol. Too many rebellious teen-age incidents had combined to propel Leila to a crossroads pointing toward a destructive destiny, such that, by the time she reached her senior year, she had succeeded in pushing her parents to their limits.

The popular confrontational way to handle teenage drinkers and druggies in the 1980s was with an intervention, so Nejdat and Betty Mulla carted Leila off to Edwin Shaw, a rather creepy Akron, Ohio, drug rehabilitation hospital, in 1983, midway through her senior year at Kent's Theodore Roosevelt High School, where wayward Leila's psyche was prodded. This former hospital for tuberculosis patients sat on a hundred acres of property, which had included Sunshine Village, a one-time home for orphans and abused children, and a cemetery for 246 who died during their confinement there. The hospital was reputed to be haunted with ghosts of tuberculosis patients and suicidal children who roamed the buildings and grounds. With such glimpses between hallucinations and reality, it had to be hard to concentrate on detoxification and sober living.

Leila met and befriended Rick Jaskiewicz, a fellow recoveree at Edwin Shaw, who was later accused of driving under the influence resulting in an accident in March, 1983, in which an off-duty policeman and his wife were killed.

A few months later, in June, Jaskiewicz was sentenced to prison for those two counts of vehicular homicide.

Leila was supposedly rehabilitated when she returned home to Kent from Edwin Shaw that same summer, after spending six weeks there, but that reformed period didn't last long. More erratic behavior prompted Leila's parents to send her away again for treatment in July, this time to Cleveland's Hitchcock House, a women's halfway house still in its infancy, located in a bequeathed older home in the downtown area.

Rick Jaskiewicz wrote Leila from prison. In August, his letter addressed to her parents' home in Kent was forwarded to her at Hitchcock House. "I have this weird feeling you're not at home no more. Is that true or what?" Rick Jaskiewicz wrote in a letter dated August 4. "Are you going to the halfway house? Or, are you already there?"

By late summer of 1983, Leila decided to escape the throes of drug rehab, her newfound group of teens struggling with recovery, and her parents' dominance once and for all. She ran away from Hitchcock House and made her way south. Leila later said she feared for her safety at Hitchcock House and longed to go to Los Angeles. She claimed she hitchhiked alone and somehow mixed up the "LAs," ending up not in Los Angeles but in New Orleans as the city rushed to make final preparations for the 1984 Louisiana World Exposition.

This expo ended up being a big disappointment for New Orleans. The Crescent City, so named for its position in a large bend of the Mississippi River, had to scale back many of its original grandiose plans due to lack of funds. Still, with the theme "World of Rivers," the event was an ambitiously grand display on 81-plus riverfront acres in the city's warehouse district. While many visited the expo multiple times, it didn't attract anywhere near the desired number of out-of-town visitors. The ones who came wanted to experience all of New Orleans, not only the exposition, but also the adjacent, historic French Quarter. The juxtaposition of a shiny new World's Exposition and jazz music-powered strip joints on Bourbon Street attracted Leila Mulla and an array of money-grubbing opportunists.

She wasn't in New Orleans long before she was arrested for shoplifting. Leila claimed all her possessions were stolen when she arrived, so she had to steal clothing in order to obtain a job as a restaurant server. As quickly as she lost her possessions, Leila lost that job, turning to dancing and prostitution for money.

"I'm thinking about throwing my roomy out! I really don't want to but I think I need to," she wrote in a letter to Rick Jaskiewicz, who was serving prison time back in Ohio. "Also, I met some rich folks and I need to see what I can get from them. I need a joint right now but I don't got one to smoke. My friend went out to sell some and didn't leave me any... I should go out and hustle."

She moved in with a Canadian musician but that didn't last long. With no place to live, Leila attracted the attention of another Decatur Street complex resident, Ronald Dunnagan, a 36-year-old simpleton who made his living by entertaining as a costumed clown in front of St. Louis Cathedral in Jackson Square and later, by working in a shop that sold pornography. This match made in the French Quarter reeked of co-dependency. She was just eighteen, pursuing a treacherous, high-risk lifestyle in a dangerous place. He was much older and could play the role of protector with his stable of weapons, including a small arsenal of guns, knives, and brass knuckles. On the other hand, Ron had a child-like connection to clowning and really enjoyed performing his self-taught magic tricks and fashioning balloon animals for children. Even though he loved his avocation, Ron eventually stopped working as a clown because Leila thought his work was demeaning and clowns were downright creepy. Leila found that Ron Dunnagan, just like other men in her life, was easily manipulated.

"Tonight Ron massaged my crotch," Leila wrote in one of her diaries. "I get embarrassed cause I shake when I come so I kept stopping him."

"We then partied," another diary entry related. "I really love Ron & never want us to split apart. Amen."

Leila returned home for several weeks during the Christmas holidays in 1983 and was back in Kent for her brother Omar's wedding in June, 1984, just days after her nineteenth birthday on June 17. As she moved around freely, Leila kept a 1984 calendar of her cash payments for dancing and prostitution. However, when the couple suddenly moved sixty miles westward on I-10 to Baton Rouge on November 2, 1984, the calendar's cash notations became less frequent and Leila identified one benefactor as "Sonic Gary."

Leila chronicled her every move. She believed she would someday be famous, perhaps a model or an actress, maybe even a writer. Leila definitely enjoyed being on stage. As a teenager, she took a modeling course and, despite her religious Irish Catholic mother being in the audience, Leila had no problem strutting her stuff in lingerie for the course's finale, which was staged at a restaurant/bar. In 1984, Leila also kept a Hallmark diary, its cover adorned with a hooded lady sitting on a mountaintop watching the sunset, William Arthur Ward's quote flowed across in free-form script: "If you can imagine it, you can achieve it. If you can dream it, you can become it." In her first entry on July 4, 1984, she called the Hallmark diary "a goals and improvement book." Each day's entry contained the usual laundry list of goal items like diet and exercise plans, prayer, and reading tasks. Leila was fastidious about dieting to maintain her figure, jotting her measurements down in a Mead tablet on July 27, 1984 ... "Waist 28 1/2... 1 thigh 23 1/4 ... Hips 36 1/2. Weight 131."

There were daily entries which read "Be nice to Ron" and notations of appointments with johns throughout. In a different journal, a spiral-bound notebook, Leila also made a checklist of daily goals. These included: *Give Ron a blowjob, wake up happy, don't be bossy, eat only fruits and vegetables,* and *call home.* On October 29, 1984, Leila noted in the spiral-bound notebook that she was in Baton Rouge all day, in preparation for moving with Ron to apartment B at 2956 Byron Street.

Oct, 31, 1984 (Halloween Night)
Today we took a long walk & no Baton Rouge. That's tomorrow. My client was ok today. Thank God we are moving & it's my last day at the club. I made up a story about a modeling job in a magazine.
It was dead for Halloween in the club. I've come a long way 'cause I remember last Halloween.
I gotta go, G-nite

Leila poured out her heart and soul in the fourth and most interesting of her journals, a three-ring, spiral bound notebook.

"November 4, 1984 (Sunday)
I'm in New Orleans right now. There's tension here rite [sic] now. I ate like a pig again & I hate it. I hate eating lots. Ron asked me my fantasies today - I couldn't say... I dream I'm skinny & wealthy. Every man & woman wants me. I meet a man who is adorabley [sic] handsome & has money. We make love to slow music - dancing & moving & feeling everything. I do love Ron - lots, but I need something fresh sometimes. I do want to make money w/tricks."

***

Leila moved from New Orleans with Ron, to a dilapidated duplex on Byron Street, just blocks from The Night Spot. She was making a living, but not living her fantasy. That fantasy was so private, so intimate that she couldn't share it with Ron, not even when he had asked her directly just days after they moved to Baton Rouge.

Gary Kergan's name first appeared in this spiral notebook on Friday, November 9, 1984.

"It's late - 5 a.m. - Gary didn't find me. (Trick)". Gary Kergan's name appeared a total of five times in the notebook. On Monday, November 12, Leila wrote:

"Tonite was odd. Ron wants to play again & he should give it a rest. Gary wants some sugar. I won't take a $10 or $20 trick like I almost had tonite. We ate at Pancho's - not bad. I got loaded - I hate that! Tomorrow I fast. I need to calm down about everything. I have tomorrow off work. Amen."

A short entry just three days later noted: *"I had $240 from Sonic Gary & plan to get him next time. Ron hid in the closet - That good man."* Plan to get him? The phrasing got even darker on November 16, as Leila wrote: *"I do love Ron. I had $100 trick & fried shrimp dinner. I wasn't really hungry ok. I drank a lot accidentally. Jimmy's not home. I couldn't drive - wet roads. No license. The movie was good. Practice w/Ron tomorrow. Hit Gary Next Time!"* The last entry naming Gary appeared routine. On November 21, she writes: *"Gary on Sat. Or Fri."* The next day, Thursday, November 22, was Thanksgiving. Thus, Friday and Saturday wrapped up the holiday weekend and Gary Kergan spent the time with his family. Leila and Ron spent their Thanksgiving picnicking and hiking in the woods. On Saturday, November 24, Leila noted in her diary, *"Neither trick came today. Serves me right for worrying, bitching & complaining."* Her final diary entry came on Tuesday, November 27. *"I had off today & have been waiting for _____ all nite & I guess it's not time."*

Had Leila called Gary and made a plea to see him,

enticing him to come to The Night Spot? When he said he was sick, did Leila lean on him harder? After all, she documented how she and Ron had concocted a very detailed plan. It was almost the end of the month and, as they learned later, Ron Dunnagan was adamant he wouldn't pay another month's rent in Baton Rouge.

On her cash-payment calendar, Leila filled November 1984 squares with amounts of her tips and prostitution money, usually anywhere from $52 to $94 a day, much less than her "tips" from dancing nights in New Orleans. However, on a trio of days in Baton Rouge, Leila would make more than $100 each day in tips. On her best day for tips, she received $240, perhaps from Gary Kergan.

In the early morning hours of November 29, 1984, Leila stepped down from the stage for the last time, picked up the familiar Jack Daniels libation, stirring it with her marked straw as she made her way across the floor to Gary Kergan's table. Gary had been a regular for the last few months at The Night Spot, where his empathetic and outgoing nature touched owners Gary and Dorothy Magee. On several occasions, after The Night Spot's 2:00 a.m. closing time, he followed the Magees home, where Dorothy Magee prepared breakfast for the three of them.

On this night, he donned a long-sleeve, white dress shirt, open at the neck to reveal chest hair. He had left the jacket of his gray and green plaid pattern suit, along with other paraphernalia from his workday, in the trunk of his Eldorado. As was the style in the mid-1980s, Gary's jewelry was 14-karat gold and flashy. He wore gold diamond rings on the ring fingers of each hand and a gold diamond watch. Regular patrons knew him as Sonic Gary, personable and very charismatic. Everybody there knew he had money and the tale circulated that he might carry cash from his Sonic restaurants' daily sales with him on his late nightclub jaunts. He befriended dancers and patrons alike, tipped well and never got out of line.

In the early hours of November 29, while his brother, Ted, waited at his Crowley apartment for an update on their impending business expansion, Gary had inexplicably changed his plan to head home and was sitting at his regular table watching and waiting, while one of the youngest dancing gyrators, a dark-haired beauty, finished her shift. Even though he wasn't feeling well, Gary remained at The Night Spot until closing at 2:00 a.m., eyes focused on Leila while she exited the stage and made her way into the shabby anteroom to transform from practically naked tease into an overly made up but still needy nineteen-year-old. While the last call drinks were being finished, Gary chatted with Leila, whom he knew by one of her aliases, Erika. Men made their way to the door, exiting their evening's escape. Some dancers reunited with their waiting biker boyfriends. Gary Magee and his wife watched the closing scene at their bar unfold, as it had night after night. The Magees and a cadre of Leila's dancing companions saw her and Gary Kergan leave The Night Spot together.

None of this made any sense to Ted. He talked to his brother just a couple of hours before this dive closed. Gary told him he was sick and on his way home. Why would Gary suddenly change his plans without calling him? Why on earth would he head to The Night Spot? And who was this Leila Mulla?

CHAPTER 7

TED AND GARY

The Kergan brothers attended the same Catholic school, and both boys also joined the Boy Scouts. Their Scouting program included weeklong camping trips out into the wilds of scouting camp-dom, where you might, as songwriter Allan Sherman so adroitly put it back in 1963, get eaten by a bear.

The tradition of these trips was for the dads to all come along and get in some serious bonding time with their sons. They also shared chaperone duties with the other men. The scoutmasters were determined that these young bucks were not only going to return home sober, but free from the duties of shared parenthood with any of the local girls.

In the case of Gary and Ted, the pair was known to the local scout leaders well enough that Gary was allowed to be Ted's "chaperone" without any adult assigned to them. The men who made the decision knew Gary and had witnessed his protective attitude toward Ted, which seemed to erase any doubts they may have harbored. Either way, when the stalwart scouts split up into teams for white water rafting on a dangerous stretch of Michigan's Rifle River, it was Gary on "dad duty" while the two brothers screamed like elated maniacs at the thrill of shooting the tumbling rapids and surviving to tell the tale.

When Ted became a freshman in high school, the tradition of hazing by the juniors and seniors was already deeply ingrained. Ted saw the levels of petty humiliation or dangerous risk being heaped upon his classmates and knew down in his bones that having Gary in the senior class was saving him a world of hurt. With the level of trauma and the amount of hospitalization Ted had already endured, he had no taste at all for physical confrontation, but the way the hazing sometimes played out made it tough to predict who would come out of it okay and who wouldn't. All it took was one stern warning from Gary and word spread among the others. If you mess with Ted, you are messing with Gary. Gary was already big enough to discourage anyone from wanting to mess with him, too.

The bubble of protection around Ted felt so familiar, he could trace it back to being two or three years old. His mother wanted to add a couple of small rooms to the back of their house, which required deep concrete footers poured into deep holes to form pillars of support for the new slab. Ted was an active toddler and, unsupervised one day for long enough to make his escape from adult authority, he somehow managed to locate one of the deep pillar holes before it was filled with anything, and fell in. As an adult, he not only remembered his panic and despair as that little boy, he could still feel it in his body. Currents of a primal fear of being buried alive ran through him, unable to escape from the narrow pit. Something Ted recalled just as clearly as an adult was his overjoyed relief when Gary showed up, seemingly out of nowhere, and pulled him out of the terrifying trap.

CHAPTER 8

RONALD DUNNAGAN

Ronald Dalton Dunnagan had been on both sides of a beating, plenty of times during his life. Growing up in Sacramento, California, Ron was horrifically tortured by his stepfather, Mike Karakas. There were countless, conventional beatings at the end of Karakas' worn leather belt, often resulting in blood blisters. But his stepfather's brand of discipline went further. Ron's sister, Patty Sigler, recalled times when they were commanded to strip and lie naked under their respective beds. Ron's "punishment" had extra punitive measures: Ron had to lie face down under the bed with head on one brick and shins on another and struggle to keep his torso from touching the floor. Mike Karakas' ideas of "discipline" took many different forms.

"He would make us for days at a time stand on our knees up against the wall. One time my step-dad caught my brother looking around," said Patty Sigler, the childhood memory seared into her brain. "Yeah, caught him looking, turning around like this, and my stepdad came over and bashed his head up against the wall and blood ran down the wall ... kinda broke his nose. Yeah, it was on a concrete floor, standing on our knees all day."

Another time, when Ron was around ten years old, Mike Karakas tried to teach his stepson a lesson when he forgot to take out the trash.

"He was just a little boy, you know, and there was a jar in the trash," said Patty Sigler, relating the story. "This was outside the house, and, well, you know, I heard my parents talking, I didn't see it happen. But anyway, he slung the trash into my brother's face on the outside of the house. It was dark and he slung it into his face and put a big knot like this on his head. His forehead, uh-huh. And he had a concussion but they didn't take him to a hospital."

Their mother, Blanche, also a victim of Karakas' abuse, felt powerless and outwitted in trying to stop her children's torture. Mike Karakas' son and namesake, Mike, lived in the same household but was spared beatings and instead spoiled by his biological father. Ron later used the name "Mike Karakas" as an alias to rent the Byron Street apartment. Both biological siblings would later be diagnosed with schizophrenia; Ron as a paranoid schizophrenic. Patty wondered whether the condition was a birthright or if it was a result of their childhood trauma. Either way, paranoid schizophrenia hampered Ron Dunnagan from any semblance of a normal life. His world was often dark, isolated, and fragmented.

Shortly after Blanche divorced Mike Karakas, she remarried and moved her children to Louisiana. Blanche and family ran a country grocery store in Shreveport, where an old door in the back separated business from the family's living quarters. Thirteen-year-old Vickie Ann Staggs lived with her parents, Ann and Ray Hickman, and sister, Carolyn, just across the street. Although he was twenty-one, Ron spent his time engaging in silly teen activities with Vickie and her friends. Then he started visiting Vickie during her high school recesses. Since Vickie was really eager to get away from her strict, older adoptive parents, she saw Ron as her ticket out of her parents' house and as a way to quit school. The mismatched couple met with Vickie's parents, the Hickmans, and revealed their plan to marry. Ray Hickman was okay with the wedding, but he made Vickie and Ron promise that Vickie would remain in school.

So at thirteen, Vickie married Ron Dunnagan but she

didn't move far. The newlyweds began their life together in a trailer behind the Hickmans' house. Marital bliss, if any, was short lived. Within months, Vickie became pregnant and quit school against her father's wishes. Two daughters, Angelique and Tammy, arrived within two years, and the Dunnagans moved to a trailer park behind a towing service off Market Street. Ron soon ignited a fire at their mobile home, and then he slapped Vickie across the face, commanding her to shed tears for the insurance adjuster in an attempt to collect on the fire. Not long afterward, Vickie said, Ron brought home an older man for Vickie to "date." It wasn't long before sixteen-year-old Vickie bolted from living with Ron at his sister's house to taking her two daughters and moving in with this older man.

"So, anyway, then he (Ron) came over there one day and he told me to open the door and I said, 'I'm not opening the door.' He was mad, you know, and I just acted like I wasn't there and then I told him, 'Well, I'm not opening the door.' He said, 'If you don't open this door I'm gonna bust it down,' so I opened the door and he kicked the man's TV and busted it and then grabbed a knife and he says, 'I'm gonna kill all of you," but then I told him I was calling the police. Then he left. And so then I left and went to Arkansas with this other guy, because my real (biological) dad lived up there."

After Ron filed suit for desertion against Vickie, her mom went to Arkansas and coaxed her into moving to Shreveport once again, back in the house with Ron, his sister Patty, and her husband once again.

"So I did, and then just one night out of the clear blue he says, 'I'm going to the store,' and I said okay," Vickie remembered. "He says, 'I'm gonna take Angelique with me,' I said, 'Okay, she'd like that.' She was just a baby, you know, a toddler. Tammy was an infant in the baby bed and I remember Tammy slept in Patty's room with them. When he came back, I said, 'Well, where's Angelique?' He says, 'We're moving to Michigan or you'll never see her again.'

I said, 'Well, where is she?' you know, and by then I had a little temper too and I told him, 'You better go get her and you better go get her now.' He says, 'Well, she's at the hospital. They're watching her till I pick her up.' And, I didn't believe him. I said, 'You better get her,' you know, and I told Patty she better open that room door and let me get Tammy. And, I tried to kick the door down, couldn't, but anyway, she was at his mother's house. He had taken her to his mother's house. And, then he said we was moving to Michigan or else I wouldn't get the kids back. His dad lived in Michigan and that's when we went there."

In Almont, Michigan, Ron Dunnagan returned to their mobile home one day after work to find Vickie and some friends playing cards. Unprovoked, Ron honed in on one teenager and violently beat him.

"We were arguing about it later and I went in the bathroom with Angelique and he come in there with a knife and he grabbed her and put the knife to her throat and told me that if I left, you know, he'd come and kill her. And so I just started screaming and he told me shut up.

"He said, 'I'll put the knife up if you shut up.' So, I shut up and he went and put the knife up. And, when he did, I grabbed her and Tammy, went out the back door, went down four trailers, knocked on these people's door, which was two women, and told them I needed a place to hide. When I told them what happened, they called the police, and I stayed there, you know, a couple of hours till the police come, and then they took him to jail. And then I was still there two days later and the third day I called them to see what the status was. They had him in for a mental evaluation and they were fixing to release him. They said if you gotta go, you better go now and so I told my next-door neighbor. She was pregnant. I said, 'Look, I'm grabbing the kids' clothes and I'm going. If there's anything in the house you want, baby bed, anything, go in an' get it now before he gets here and you can have it, and I drove from Michigan back to Arkansas and that's where I got a divorce."

Vickie Staggs said she never looked back upon that portion of her life after she packed up her two baby girls and left that mobile home. She made sure Ron Dunnagan couldn't locate her. Vickie didn't want him anywhere around her daughters.

"He would just go off for no reason. I was scared of him."

Their 1974 divorce was final within thirty days and Vickie did not hear from Ron Dunnagan until 1989. Ron became a self-taught clown, moving from North Louisiana to Las Vegas in the mid-1970s. He alternated performing magic tricks as a costumed clown and working as a casino barker, hauling around a four-foot green locker-style treasure chest filled with the magical trappings of a clown and a growing stash of weapons. He learned how to win a little gambling money playing cards and also continued his fondness for smoking marijuana. Maybe smoking weed drowned out constant suicidal thoughts, lessening the hold schizophrenia had on him. Or maybe it deepened the divide between the happy, engaging clown and the isolated, suspicious loaner who failed at a number of suicide attempts.

Finally, in the late 1970s, Ron and his locker-style chest made their way back to Louisiana. Its costume and magic tricks remained inside when Ron turned to more serious employment for several years in the late 1970s with Exxon as a Seaman Mate 1 in Baton Rouge. During this time, Ron met John Langlinais, who, at that time, owned The Night Spot lounge on Plank Road. Ron went to work at night as a bartender there. He would seek out Langlinais a few years later when Leila was looking for a place to dance in Baton Rouge.

True to his life pattern as a drifter, Ron didn't stay anywhere long. He lived for a brief stint in a Baton Rouge suburb named Denham Springs, then moved on to New Orleans. Along the way, a string of arrests for traffic tickets and other minor infractions resulted in a few fugitive warrants, probably because Ron never bothered showing up for the court dates.

As he did regularly at different times in his life, Ron sought refuge at a homeless shelter. In New Orleans, he lived off and on at Ozanam Inn on Camp Street, operated by the Brothers of the Good Shepherd as a "hospice for homeless men." Ron Dunnagan found employment at a French Quarter shop selling pornography while nursing a broken arm that prohibited him from clowning. When he met Leila Mulla at his apartment building, Ron was working at that store on Decatur Street, where he had been arrested a couple of times on various obscenity and permit violations.

In Ron's mind, working at the porn shop was always temporary. He longed to make his living as a clown. Shortly thereafter, much to Leila's chagrin, Ron re-opened his magic trunk and broke out his clown costume for jobs in the French Quarter. She thought his face-painted pandering was embarrassing and demeaning. Ron thought of it as an acquired art and, along with selling and smoking marijuana, dressing as a clown allowed him to escape from his schizophrenia plague.

Partnered with young and beautiful Leila Mulla, he sold drugs while she danced and prostituted. Ron was totally smitten by her, but it seemed Leila needed a daily reminder to return his affection. During their last few months in New Orleans, Leila made daily journal notations of "be nice to Ron." In the final week of October, the couple made plans to move to Baton Rouge, and on November 2, 1984, they were in Baton Rouge setting up house in the Byron Street duplex.

Once in their new environs, Ron paid a visit to his former boss, John Langlinais, seeking a place for Leila to dance and make some real money on the side. He found Langlinais no longer owned The Night Spot but new owners Gary and Wanda Magee were happy to have the nineteen-year-old dark-headed looker in their stable of moneymaking ladies. Ron rented a duplex near the club on Byron Street from a man named John Guedry, paying the deposit and signing the lease with the name of his father and stepbrother, Mike Karakas. He also used Karakas' name to hook up gas and electric utilities at the Byron Street address. Leila had a variety of aliases. She danced using the name Erika. Their South Central Bell landline account was in the name of Chris Jacobs, another alias. On November 11, Leila noted in her diary that they "shot guns which hurt my ears," went to two movies, snuck in one and played all day.

It seemed they didn't plan to stay long in Baton Rouge. Ron continued to sell drugs, but Leila was the real moneymaker during that month, November 1984. It appeared Leila was the breadwinner while Ron played househusband. She danced at The Night Spot and brought johns home to Byron Street for sex. At least some of the time, Ron Dunnagan hid in an apartment closet and watched. According to Leila, he was in the duplex when she brought Gary Kergan to the Byron Street duplex in the early hours of November 29.

"(Ron) told me what they were accusing him of; that they saw him carry a trunk out of his apartment," said Patty Sigler, Ron's sister, who recalled many years later Ron's version of those late November days. "But he was moving, is what he said, and he carried his magic stuff, you know, in the trunk, all his stuff. He carried that trunk around everywhere he went ... Yeah, he would open it and pull out his stuff, you know. Well, he mentioned that he was accused of killing a man. He was accused of killing a man and someone said they saw him carry a trunk out of the house but he said he wasn't carrying nobody out in a trunk; it was his work stuff. This is what he told me: that trunk that they saw him put in the car was his magic stuff."

CHAPTER 9

DEAR DIARY

Baton Rouge was always a temporary stop for Leila and Ron. She wanted to accumulate money for a move to California to begin modeling and morph into a more glamorous lifestyle. Ron was happy to follow along. They never intended to pay landlord John Guedry a second month's rent for the Byron Street duplex.

It's unclear why Leila and Ron moved from New Orleans to Baton Rouge. What is clear is that Leila took an immediate dislike to Baton Rouge. One day after their move, she wrote in her diary: *"Baton Rouge is hicks & niggers. It's either money or lust & I must take #1 so I'll be ok & protected."* As she settled into prostitution just hours later, Leila noted: *"Work was good $ ... Terrible people. I can't understand them and have a hard time talking to them. They're very country and can be mean."* By the very next day, November 9, Leila had already met Gary Kergan at The Night Spot and became laser focused. That day, Gary first appeared in her diary: *"It's late - 5 a.m. - Gary didn't find me (trick)."*

Their leased North Baton Rouge neighborhood sprang up in the shadow of the Standard Oil, later Exxon, refiner. Domiciles for its blue-collar workers lined the narrow streets. During the decades since the Great Depression, the old wood siding on those shotgun-style houses had been painted over and over. Some families eventually moved to the suburbs, leaving pockets of blue-collar workers and renters. "Separate but equal" segregation policies in Baton

Rouge during the 1970s gave way to a "separate but equal" reality. Those who could afford it, black or white, moved on. In the early 1980s, Byron Street was home to a mixture of long-time residents, hard-working families, and a few transients. It was a microcosm of Baton Rouge in those days before crack cocaine led to skyrocketing murder statistics.

While New Orleans' French Quarter was more of a melting pot of cultures and means, north Baton Rouge was dominated by blue-collar, working class neighborhoods. Caucasian-owned businesses dotted the landscape. Between The Night Spot dive and Byron Street duplex, there were landmarks like Krispy Kreme Doughnuts, where Ron Dunnagan often occupied a booth waiting for Leila's shift at The Night Spot across the street to end, and Tony's Seafood, where long lines of seafood buyers often formed outside the small fruit-stand-turned-market. The steeple of St. Gerald Majella Catholic Church marked the highest architectural point in the vicinity, and the church, with its white Ionic columns and pediment found so often in Southern plantations and state houses, was easily one of the more regal looking buildings in the zip code. This was like a foreign country to an upper-class daughter of privilege from suburban Kent, Ohio, even though she had strayed so far from those roots.

Gary Kergan had a foot in both worlds. He was raised by a single mother without a lot of means, so he learned to bootstrap his way through the world with a dogged entrepreneurial work ethic. Though he was rising on the ladder of fortune and aspired to a country club lifestyle, he could not forget his roots. Gary connected with people on many levels and found it as easy to converse in a boardroom as in a barroom. As a result, it wasn't odd that Gary became friends with Night Spot owners Gary and Wanda Magee, or that he was attracted to Leila, a beautiful damsel in distress, who dangled her vulnerability like bait.

In the month prior to November 29, Leila's Hallmark diary detailed eerie preparations and practices. On November

15, she wrote that she made $240 from Sonic Gary and planned to *"get him next time. Ron hid in the closet - that good man."* The very next day's entry said in part: *Practice w//Ron tomorrow. Hit Gary next time!* On November 17, this mismatched couple purchased feed mice and a black male guinea pig. Two days later, they added a female Guinea pig to their menagerie. That diary entry proclaimed the mice had rabies and were *"hopping around weird."* Leila noted that *"The time is short so I must make use."* Then, on November 20, she said: *The Guinea pig I believe does not have Rabbies [sic]. It's weird here in Baton Rouge. Satan's trying to keep us here, but it won't work. Ron & I are 1 [one] & will stay that way."*

Gary Kergan had no idea he was being duped when they left The Night Spot at closing time and entered her seedy Byron Street rental in the early morning hours of November 29, 1984. She led him through the cheap wood-paneled, sparsely furnished living room past the tiny galley kitchen and bathroom, where they turned right to go into the duplex's only bedroom. Gary had been there before and thought he knew what to expect. They would drink and have sex. He would pay her and then be off to Crowley, where his brother, his wife, his child, and that weighty Sonic business development agreement all waited for him.

This night was not like the others. Ron Dunnagan was also in the duplex. Whether his presence was apparent or he waited in a closet ready to pounce, Gary unknowingly walked into a complete setup. Having left all business and personal effects behind in his 1984 Cadillac Eldorado, Gary entered the last hour of his life stripped of any armor. One thing became clear: Gary Kergan put up an extraordinary fight for his life in that dingy, paneled bedroom. He was removed from the Byron Street duplex dead or clinging to life, and was placed in the trunk of his own vehicle. This at the hands of a woman he had known for about four weeks.

Somewhere between the Byron Street duplex and an

office parking lot across from the iconic circular Landmark Hotel in the New Orleans' suburb of Metairie, Gary Kergan's lifeless body was removed from the Eldorado's trunk by Ron Dunnagan and/or Leila Mulla. But where? There was a very tight timeline immediately following the murder. First, the frantic ride in Gary's Cadillac to the Landmark Hotel took at least one hour. Sixty very nervous minutes, certainly many more if they stopped to dump evidence and remains along the route, in the early hours of November 29, on a dark, eastbound expressway flanked by miles and miles of nothing but tree-lined swamp.

What goes through a nineteen-year-old mind after a scene like that? What is her partner in crime thinking less than an hour after brutally beating a benefactor? Were they in one car or were there two cars? With all of the variables, the biggest unanswered question remained: Where did they stash the body?

Ted Kergan had found that curious hand-drawn map in their apartment days later in Las Vegas. Scrawled across a piece of lined notebook paper turned on its side, landscape style, was a page-dividing line marked "levee." Above the levee line were squiggles marked "trash" and above that, hand-drawn trees sticking out between the word "water," which is repeated three times. A bullseye, drawn and retraced over and over again so its lines are much heavier than anything else in the drawing, is set amid the trash pile, just above the levee line. The other side of the map is more detailed, labeled with the same script. The levee line is at the top of the page. Crossing over the levee on a double-line road, there is a bridge and "Swerve" sign, then a two-way railroad track crossing. Moving further down the road, a square building is drawn on one side, its front door facing the road. On the map is this description: *Building looks like it has reddish black soot looking on top. Top made out of cypress or cedar wood.* The last line on the bottom of the lined sheet is chilling: *Drove Coupe De Ville lite [sic] gray color.*

Levees line lakes and rivers across South Louisiana, but those keeping the winding Mississippi River in its banks are the most pronounced. Double the hundred plus miles of the riverbank's levees between Baton Rouge and New Orleans, since there are levees on each side of the river. That meant more than two hundred miles of potential area that the map portrayed. The only clues to which portion of the levee is depicted on the map are the building, the railroad tracks, and a "Gulf Station." Of course, there was no way to tell the scale of the map and whether or not the images and distances between them were drawn to scale. Finally, although it seems to be the case, was the map actually drawn to identify the dumping ground?

Once they reached New Orleans, Leila and Ron tied up loose ends, changing their New Orleans post office box address to a box in San Diego. They ditched the victim's car and Leila maintained they took a taxicab for the sixty plus mile journey back to Baton Rouge. Whatever their method of transportation, the couple were back at the Byron Street duplex before dawn broke on November 29, 1984, cleaning residue from the struggle and packing for their move.

Their timeline was super tight. If they left their apartment in Gary's Cadillac at 3:30 a.m. with Gary's remains in the trunk, they could have arrived in suburban Metairie no earlier than 4:30 a.m. If they stopped to discard the remains, they would have arrived in Metairie even later. They were spotted back at the Byron Street duplex by 7:00 a.m. Then they cleaned up the duplex and doled out their belongings. Later that morning, Leila and Ron hit the road in Ron's two-toned 1975 black-over-blue Plymouth Valiant containing everything they owned. But where was the cash and jewelry they stole from Gary Kergan? They were no doubt disappointed in the amount of cash, a lot less than the windfall they expected. Gary's jewelry, including two rings and a watch, fashioned in 14-karat gold and embellished with diamonds, helped sweetened the pot. The pair made a pit stop at Ron's mother's home in Bossier City, a north Louisiana hamlet on the eastern bank of the Red River facing its sister city, Shreveport, on the other bank.

Matriarch Blanche née Bonnette, watched with interest as her son ushered Leila Mulla into her home amid the regular family assemblage of grandchildren. Ron Dunnagan's only marriage had lasted just a couple of years and relatives weren't used to seeing him with a beautiful young woman. Leila headed straight to the bathroom and showered. Relatives later commented that they both looked dirty and road weary, but there was little time for observation and interaction. Ron and Leila left a mere hour later, headed west toward a new life, confident they had gotten away with murder.

CHAPTER 10

NO BODY

Baton Rouge Mayor President Pat Screen had a serious substance abuse problem. Symptoms of his illness rocked through Baton Rouge city parish government in waves. Screen was re-elected to his second term in the fall of 1984, and continued to rely on close allies to keep his administration upright and moving forward. Unlike Screen, District Attorney Ossie Brown failed to garner support from the majority of people in East Baton Rouge Parish and was defeated in his bid for a third term in office on November 7, 1984. This was three weeks before Gary Kergan was fatally targeted. Mere months before that, Brown escaped federal conviction on extortion, mail fraud, and perjury charges stemming from a failure to prosecute two prominent Baton Rouge citizens on possession of cocaine charges. The epic story played out in front page newspaper stories all summer long.

No doubt, the scandal helped put an end to Brown's thirty-year political career. He was succeeded as Baton Rouge's chief prosecutor by fifty-eight-year-old Republican attorney Bryan Bush, who, in the words of Brown's campaign coordinator, "profited from being the right man at the right place at the right time." But until the last day of 1984, Ossie Brown was still district attorney for East Baton Rouge Parish and in charge of prosecuting the murder of Gary Kergan.

Ted Kergan found himself in the midst of this political changing of the guard while he pushed for action and answers regarding Gary's murder case. It was Ossie Brown's final month as the head of the office charged with prosecuting Leila Mulla and Ronald Dunnagan, who were relegated to the parish jail, both charged with the first-degree murder of Gary Kergan. For Ted, the wheels of justice were grinding much too slowly. With the help of Larry Tucker, Ted mounted his own searches for his brother's remains, which he reasoned had to be somewhere between the Byron Street duplex and the suburban New Orleans parking lot where Gary's car was located.

So Ted drove the desolate sixty-something mile route between Baton Rouge and New Orleans on I-10 numerous times, stopping at each of the many overpasses and bridges while Larry got out of the car and peered into murky bayous and canals, even surveying vast Lake Pontchartrain along the way. They took exits off into the swamp onto roads forming islands between more bodies of water, rumored to be body dumping grounds for New Orleans' organized crime. Finally, tired and frustrated, they had exhausted places to look. While taking a break one evening at Ruth's Chris Steak House, Larry Tucker's favorite hangout, he commiserated with owner/restaurateur T.J. Moran, a friend of the brothers.

Moran suggested a meeting with the man at the top, Mayor Pat Screen, as a means to help intensify the official investigation. The meeting was quickly arranged and political greenhorn Larry Tucker negotiated his way to the mayor's third floor office in the city's downtown beehive-busy municipal building on St. Louis Street. Screen greeted him warmly, seemingly interested and empathetic. As a former star quarterback for Baton Rouge's LSU Tigers football team, Screen had earned local celebrity status long before he graduated from law school and began a political career. In spite of his ongoing battle with substance abuse, he was personable and popular in the community.

Screen appeared attentive and assured Tucker, with a warmth that was hard to distinguish from patronizing political nice-speak, that he would see what he could do. Just one request, he quickly added. Would Larry like to buy tickets to a barbecue benefitting his mayoral campaign? Of course was the only fathomable answer, even after the mayor disclosed the tickets' price tag was $10,000. Once the money was produced, Screen produced the printed tickets from his desk drawer. Each seemed to have gotten what he wanted. When Larry related the story about the meeting to Ted, Ted told Larry to keep the tickets and attend the barbecue. Larry began to laugh as he pulled the tickets out of his pocket and pointed to the date of the campaign's fund-raising barbecue. It had taken place several weeks earlier! This political bamboozlement opened doors, nevertheless, and Ted was given his own desk at the police station and a more open ear from Baton Rouge law enforcement. He vowed from the beginning to do whatever it took to find out what happened to Gary. Buying tickets to a barbecue that had already taken place was just part of whatever it took. As long as he wasn't interfering with the official murder investigation, Ted relied on his own moxie to find answers himself.

Louisiana State Police loaned their helicopter so that city and state police could fly along both sides of the interstate highway between Baton Rouge and New Orleans, searching from the air for any spot that looked like it might hold Gary Kergan's remains. The same agencies combed the areas by car, but nothing was discovered. Ted met with Louisiana Department of Wildlife and Fisheries' Chief Burt Angelle and asked him to release an official statement saying he had his enforcement agents taking their boats for a closer look into South Louisiana's waterways, which are as plentiful and meandering as spider veins.

"You don't remember me, do you?" Angelle asked Ted. Angelle owned a car dealer adjacent to a Kergan Brothers' Sonic Drive-In in Breaux Bridge, La., just outside of Lafayette. Ted's employees provided the workers plenty of Sonic treats. It was a kindness Angelle had not forgotten.

Angelle readily pledged his agency's support, although both understood there would be only a statement issued, not any actual boat searches. Ted's ruse was two-fold: to put pressure on Leila and Ron to confess what they had done with Gary Kergan's body, and to encourage local fishermen to conduct their own private searches for the remains.

On Friday, December 14, two days after Leila Mulla and Ronald Dunnagan were extradited from Las Vegas back to Baton Rouge, Ted appeared with Ossie Brown in front of television cameras at a somber press conference. He said his family had given up any hope of finding Gary alive. Also on the dais was Acadia Parish Sheriff Ken Goss, who had accompanied his friend from Crowley to Baton Rouge for the news event. Ted Kergan announced his family was sponsoring a $100,000 reward and opening a Gary S. Kergan Factfinders Hotline for information leading to the recovery of Gary's body.

Ossie Brown, looking every bit the part of an old school man of the cloth with his best Baptist preacher style delivery, waxed on about diligently prosecuting the case, asserting "We know more than we are telling you." Someone had leaked to the press that Leila's diaries and notebooks had been entered into evidence. Amid her goals and daily dribs and drabs, Leila continually mentioned spirits, one spirit in particular named "Squeekee." Occasionally, there were notes about magic and even a library list of books on witchcraft. But were these references to something sinister, or just the silly curiosity of a nineteen-year-old woman? Without prompting or questioning, Brown suggested to those assembled for the press conference that the killing might have been cult related but declined to discuss that angle further. What a can of worms to uncork at a press conference. The mass suicide of cult leader Jim Jones' Peoples Temple followers at Jonestown, Guyana, had occurred only a few years before.

Brown was no stranger to the world of cults and massacres. As a private criminal defense attorney in 1970, he was responsible for the acquittal of one of the twenty-six men prosecuted in the My Lai Massacre, the mass killing of several hundred unarmed civilians by U.S. soldiers in South Vietnam. The event was deemed the most shocking episode of the Vietnam War, and it was one of the most celebrated cases of his career.

Brown promised to convene a grand jury to indict Leila and Ron the very next week, which was the week before the Christmas holidays, and two weeks before Ossie Brown's deadline to move his personal effects out of the district attorney's office prior to Bryan Bush's inauguration on January 1, 1985. That grand jury was never convened.

Days later, in an effort to salvage some semblance of the holidays, Ted drove his sister-in-law, Susie, and nephew, Wade, to the New Orleans airport so they could travel to visit family in Michigan for Christmas and at least enjoy a change of scenery. "They were just going crazy sitting around the house and looking at each other," Ted Kergan told a reporter for the Morning Advocate, Baton Rouge's daily newspaper, in an article that appeared on Christmas Eve. "Kergan said he virtually lived at the police station as he followed each step of the investigation." After all, he was a single man on a singular mission. There was no Christmas celebration for Ted Kergan that year.

"We will find Gary. It's the last thing I can do for him," Ted said in the article. "He's got to be out there. I don't know what the hell I am going to do."

He related a heartbreaking story to the reporter about Wade, who asked who was going to take him to buy his mother's Christmas present since his Dad was not home. So of course, Ted took his nephew Christmas shopping at a nearby mall, where several people stopped to offer condolences. "Gee, Dad knew a lot of people," Wade told him.

When the reporter broached a question about the continuing health of their Sonic restaurant business, Ted

Kergan was quick to say the business was in good shape but, with the special rapport between him and his brother gone, things would be a lot different for him going forward. The brothers were so close; they had even recently purchased matching cars, Datsun 280ZXs, and matching motorcycles. Ted's days were so different now. He missed the half dozen daily calls with Gary. No one else spoke their mysterious language. He would never have the ease of that type of abbreviated conversation with another person.

"It's like somebody grabbed the puzzle and shook it up and threw it on the ground," Ted told the reporter. "You still have the puzzle but how do you put it back together? You don't have somebody looking over your shoulder. How do you piece it together?"

As 1985 dawned, the case was barely percolating, partially due to staff shakeup in the new district attorney's office. Some of Ossie Brown's longtime staff members even filed suit against new District Attorney Bryan Bush when he dismissed and replaced them with his own staff choices. It was more political wrangling that took time away from the caseload. Susie Kergan came forward in late January, telling the same daily newspaper reporter who interviewed Ted that she wanted to meet with Leila Mulla, the woman who was charged with murdering her husband.

"Maybe something I would say to her would touch her heart in a way that she would feel like she could talk to me or talk to somebody and get it done and get it out and say where he is. All I'm interested in is finding my husband so that we can lay him properly to rest."

Susie, a petite, determined woman with dark eyes and short, curly hair, said the Crowley community had rallied around her and she was particularly comforted by members of her church, the Church of Jesus Christ of Latter-day Saints. She described her husband of twelve years as very generous, giving, and almost naive in his trust of people. It was very difficult at home without him. Susie related that son Wade often punched his pillow at night while sleeping.

"I can only imagine what he was dreaming," she said in the article.

"We would like to see the grand jury held," Susie said in response to a question about the status of the murder case. "We're wondering when that's going to happen.... If it wasn't for Ted, they (detectives) would not have gone as far as they have."

In February, Ronald Dunnagan appeared before Louisiana District Judge Frank Saia and requested a new public defender. It seemed he wasn't happy with the progress of David Price, his court-appointed attorney. Within a week, Michele Fournet joined Price, both from the Public Defender's Office, to defend Ron Dunnagan. As strategies on both sides of the case were being formed, reporter Steve Wheeler pondered the real question for readers of The Morning Advocate on February 22: "Is it possible for the state to convict someone without producing the murder victim?"

A judge and an LSU law professor both weighed in for Wheeler's editorial, saying it was possible but certainly not an easy task. The burden on the state was three-fold. First, prosecutors must prove beyond a reasonable doubt that a death had occurred resulting from criminal action. Second, the state must prove the persons charged with the crime actually committed the offense. Finally, the prosecutor had the additional burden of proving the act that caused the death of the victim occurred within the jurisdiction of the court hearing the case. Thus, this case had to be proven almost entirely with circumstantial evidence. Meanwhile, District Court Judge Frank Saia ordered Leila and Ron to provide blood and hair samples for the state to compare to evidence from the crime scene and the Cadillac Eldorado.

A couple of weeks later, the winds of March found District Attorney Bryan Bush back pedaling. "I'm having real problems not having a body," Bush told a local newspaper reporter. He said his staff was investigating crimes other than murder that might have occurred in conjunction with Gary Kergan's disappearance. When blood and hair samples taken from Leila and Ron did not match samples taken from Gary Kergan's Cadillac Eldorado, Ron's attorney Michele Fournet filed a writ of habeas corpus, a formal request that Ron be brought before the court to determine if he was being illegally held. There was no proof Gary Kergan was dead, or, if he was, that Ron Dunnagan killed him. On March 18, Judge Saia ruled on the motion and ordered Ron released from jail.

"When the law is clear, you just have to follow it," he said. "I didn't have any discretion. It's just very difficult to prove a murder case when you can't prove someone is dead. I sympathize with the victim's family. The district attorney didn't have any choice either. I feel a jury would have probably had to acquit him." Saia added the state could still prosecute Ron if Gary Kergan's body was found or if new evidence was uncovered. However, if Ron was tried and acquitted, the state would not have the opportunity to charge him again.

On Monday, March 18, 1985, Ronald Dunnagan, carrying a large brown paper bag bearing his personal effects, walked out of the downtown Baton Rouge jail, relieved of all charges. His dark hair was parted on the side and combed behind his ears, flowing to his shoulder, and his mustache and beard were neatly trimmed. The cuffs on his two-tone cowboy-style shirt were unsnapped as he stared stone-faced into the faces of the assembled media.

"I'm not guilty," he told reporters waiting outside.

"We were shocked to learn this morning that District Attorney Bryan Bush made it possible for Mr. Dunnagan to leave the parish prison a free man," began a prepared statement from Ted Kergan. "Our family believes that our system of justice provides for justice to be done without jeopardizing the rights of the accused. It also provides for submission of charges such as these to a grand jury when there is shown evidence of guilt. District Attorney Bush has not done this. He has chosen, unilaterally, to avoid the normal process of submitting the matter to independent grand jurors."

Ted Kergan was beyond upset. It seemed to him that the district attorney was letting the case slip away. He emphasized how outraged his family was with Ron's release and said they were in the process of arranging a meeting with the State Attorney General's office to request the matter be presented to a grand jury. Louisiana state law provided for the attorney general's office to step in to prosecute any criminal cases in any of the 64 parishes within the state, the widest berth possible. The attorney general's office could also present matters to grand juries for consideration. Judge Frank Saia telephoned Walter Smith with the attorney general's office to determine how that office responded and whether it would take over the case.

"I wouldn't touch the case," replied Smith. "I agree completely with what Bush did."

Two days later, on March 20, Judge Saia ruled on the motion from Leila Mulla's defense attorney, C. Frank Holthaus, and released Leila from custody to her parents, Nejdat and Betty Mulla. They had traveled from Ohio to Baton Rouge, and were present in the courtroom. Leila walked demurely from the downtown jail under heavy sheriff deputies' guard shortly after 11:00 a.m., dressed all in white: a soft suit with skirt modestly hemmed at mid-calf, white cuffed socks, white tennis shoes and her hair pulled neatly back away from her face. She went directly to her attorney's office, where her parents waited to take her home to Kent.

Assistant District Attorney Prem Burns, who handled the case, revealed that former District Attorney Ossie Brown offered Leila a plea bargain before January 1. Under the proposal, all charges against Leila would be dropped if she agreed to testify against Ron Dunnagan at trial. Leila declined the offer. No body meant no murder trial... for now.

CHAPTER 11

FINDING THE LANDMARK

Ted Kergan remembered every detail of the day he found out Ron Dunnagan was released from East Baton Rouge Parish Prison. He was working at his Sonic Drive-In in Amite, about forty miles from Baton Rouge, when he received a series of confusing and conflicting phone calls.

That day, March 18, 1985, had started off well. Early that morning, Ted received a telephone call from a private investigator he hired for the case. The investigator reported that everything looked good. Standing on the courthouse steps, Assistant District Attorney Prem Burns told reporters her office was ready to prosecute. Ted's hopes soared with the news about the case, but that feeling was short-lived. An hour later, he received a second call from the investigator, who told him things had quickly reversed.

"They're going to let them go," he said. "The district attorney said he is not going to prosecute, because there is no body."

Events rapidly progressed. Ron Dunnagan was unceremoniously released from the East Baton Rouge Parish jail the same day, before Ted had time to drive the short distance to Baton Rouge. For Ted Kergan, forty miles might as well have been four hundred. He instructed the private investigator to follow Ron, but the crafty clown-man gave him the slip.

When Leila was released from jail two days later, he learned her parents were there waiting to take her home. Ted wondered what life was like back at her home in Kent, Ohio. For months, the Kent Record Courier, her town's daily paper, chronicled the murder and its aftermath for Leila's neighbors and friends to discuss and digest. No doubt it was a major topic of conversation in the university town. Leila's father was a prominent obstetrician/gynecologist and her mother was well known for volunteer work at St Patrick Catholic Church.

Surely Leila was catching the sounds of whispers behind her back. Ted hoped she was very uncomfortable. What was she doing back home in Kent? Was it something reputable or was she already back to her old habits and the oldest profession?

Ted could not believe the murder investigation was really over. He tried to get back into some type of rhythm, but his life was so different now. As the weeks passed since Leila Mulla and Ron Dunnagan were released from custody, Ted's emotions were still as raw as the day he found out they had been freed. It was like being struck by a knockout punch. After all, Leila herself had said that Gary was murdered and that there was blood all over their apartment and in the trunk of Gary's car. Lots of people at The Night Spot saw Gary and Leila leave the bar together. Why did the district attorney's office suddenly get cold feet and decide not to prosecute? While they had not yet found Gary's body, there was plenty of other evidence, certainly enough to win convictions. Ted played the details of the case out in his mind over and over again; it just didn't make sense to him that they had refused prosecution. There were no other suspects, no information pointing to any other scenario.

It was tough trying to regroup his Sonic restaurant business, and Ted knew he now needed to pay attention to both the details and the overall strategic picture that Gary had always painted so effortlessly as part of his charismatic persona. He remained convinced that Leila Mulla and Ron Dunnagan killed his brother, and the idea that they were permitted to weave themselves back into their former lives was too much to tolerate. Eventually no one around them would even know or remember that Ron and Leila had once been arrested and charged with the first-degree murder of Gary Kergan.

Ted made a promise to himself and his deceased brother to use every resource he could muster to bring them to justice. Those murderers were released simply because Gary's body had not yet been located. Ted knew the more time passed, the harder that task became.

Several months passed in a hurry, and one day in June, 1985, Ted received a telephone call from Susie Kergan, Gary's wife, that sent a shock through every nerve in his body. He had trouble understanding her; she was breathless and fearful while she recounted a call from a man who said he knew where to find Gary Kergan's body. The caller said he became acquainted with Leila following her release from jail.

When Ted returned his call, the man claimed Leila said she and her partner murdered Gary Kergan and, more importantly, that Leila provided the location of Gary Kergan's body. That man, or "Confidential Informant," as he became known, demanded Ted pay for the information. The confidential informant feared he would be forced to move from his current hometown in the Atlanta area if his identity were ever revealed.

But the $100,000 reward, which the Kergan family initially offered for information leading to the recovery of Gary's body, had been withdrawn months before. The reward money was offered initially in an attempt to find someone who might sellout Leila and Ron, someone who knew what they did with Gary Kergan's remains. Secondly, with reward money on the table, there would be lots of people out looking for Gary's body. Whether or not they located anything, the sheer knowledge that the reward was in place might cause Leila and Ron to cut a deal. From a practical standpoint, Ted literally had to put $100,000 in a bank account for the offer of the reward to be valid. When none of the numerous leads was actionable, the tip hotline was disconnected and the offer of the reward was withdrawn.

Now Ted listened intently to everything the caller had to say before telling him he would think it over and get back to him. Ted immediately called Ken Goss at the Acadia Parish Sheriff's Office and gave him the informant's name. Soon Ted discovered he was not just any anonymous caller. The informant's credentials checked out, and so did his job, which placed him in direct daily contact with Leila Mulla.

Ted and the sheriff came up with a plan. At Ted's expense, the confidential informant would fly to New Orleans and travel around the corner to the Holiday Inn on Williams Boulevard. At the hotel, deputies would set up surveillance equipment in one room and monitoring equipment in an adjoining room, where Ted Kergan would meet with the confidential informant and try to obtain enough evidence to re-open the case. Whatever this man had to say, Ken Goss wanted to make sure he said it on the record and that the full weight of the law was behind the questioning.

Goss gave Ted instructions about what questions to ask and what answers had to be obtained in order for the witness to be put on the record in the case. After the right questions were answered between the two men alone in the hotel room, Ted would take the confidential informant to deputies in the adjoining room and ask him to repeat the answers for the deputies. The thinking was that if indeed the confidential informant had information that would lead to the prosecution of Leila Mulla, he should have gone to the authorities in the first place, not to Ted Kergan seeking money in exchange for this information. Thus, the trap was set for the confidential informant, forcing him to go on the record.

On June 20, 1985, two months after Leila and Ron were released from the East Baton Rouge Parish jail, Officer Steven Monachello with the Criminal Investigation Bureau of Louisiana State Police traveled from Baton Rouge and joined Ted Kergan and Acadia Parish Sheriff Deputies Charles LaFosse, Ralph Lacombe, and Keith Latiolais in a room filled with surveillance equipment on the twelfth floor of the Holiday Inn in Kenner.

Just after 10:30 in the morning, the confidential informant knocked on the door of Ted Kergan's room, next door to the deputies' surveillance post. For two hours, Ted Kergan and the confidential informant conversed as Ted deftly asked questions he rehearsed earlier, while the deputies listened and audio recorded their discussion. From his answers, it was obvious the informant had daily contact with Leila Mulla in a setting where she could have easily revealed information about Gary Kergan's murder. Ted and the CI agreed to meet again in the same room at 3:30 p.m. to exchange money and more information.

At that second meeting, with authorities still listening and the tape rolling again, the confidential informant began circling around the salient points. Ted Kergan took charge of the conversation, asking the informant if he knew what happened to Gary and if he would tell Ted only if he was given the reward money. "Yes" was his answer to both questions.

The informant told Ted his brother was indeed killed by Leila and Ron, but that locating the body would be difficult. Gary's body was dismembered by Ron Dunnagan, the CI explained. He continued, saying the murder took place at Leila's duplex on Byron Street in Baton Rouge and that Leila was involved in a satanic worshipping group and received her direction from Ron Dunnagan. According to the informant, Leila said she was directed by Ron to kill someone with money. Since she was a prostitute and already acquainted with Gary Kergan, whom she knew as Sonic Gary, she lured Gary back to her apartment in the early hours of November 29, where they had sex and drank champagne. There were two bottles of champagne. The first bottle was consumed by

Gary and Leila. However, the second bottle was laced with cyanide poisoning and Leila knowingly served Gary Kergan a glass from the tainted bottle. Gary became unconscious and Ron came into the bedroom and moved Gary's body to the bathtub, where he dismembered it. During this time, the Informant said, Leila left the room to watch television in the adjoining living room. She said Ron placed body parts in six separate garbage bags and put them into the trunk of Gary Kergan's Cadillac. Leila joined Ron in the front seat of the Cadillac and they proceeded to drive to suburban New Orleans, where the body was placed in six different dumpsters, each containing one garbage bag.

The story set Ted's head reeling. Poison? Dismemberment? Neither of these elements came through in Leila's statement. Before he could wrap his head around this startling disclosure, Ted motioned for the informant to follow him to the door adjoining the room where the law enforcement officials were conducting surveillance.

"Come on in," Ted invited, motioning for the informant to look through the door. It took a few seconds for him to realize it was a set up.

He fell to his knees and began dry heaving.

Once he regained his composure, the informant took a lie detector test, which he passed. He had never been to New Orleans or its suburban areas of Metairie and Kenner near the airport, yet he directed Ted and the officers from the Holiday Inn across busy Veterans Boulevard to a nearby area several blocks square, known collectively as Fat City. This nightlife hotbed of discotheques, massage parlors, and restaurants was deemed "the French Quarter of Jefferson Parish."

The informant attempted to point out the dumpsters Leila had mapped out to him. In the case of one unusual building, he recognized it only through Leila's description; he had never seen the iconic round tower of the Landmark Hotel in Metairie. As Ted Kergan looked from the hotel's dumpsters in the back of the parking lot to the top of the tall cylindrical hotel building, he remembered attending meetings and conferences in the hotel's 16th floor circular penthouse ballroom, which offered a panoramic view of Jefferson Parish and of the New Orleans skyline. He tried to imagine what role the hotel and its adjacent dumpsters played in the murder narrative. He had not yet processed that his brother's body could have actually been dismembered. At first mention, the word seemed so cold and clinical, yet the desecration it entailed made Ted's blood boil. Then, he quickly regrouped. No way Gary was dismembered, Ted thought, discounting that possibility. Dismemberment didn't fit the killer's tight timeline the night of the murder. Ted remembered being at the Byron Street duplex crime scene. There was not enough blood evidence there and the bathroom was spotless. This was several days after the murder and they would have been able to smell human decomposition in the drains and elsewhere. Besides, that place was so tiny; there was simply not enough room anywhere to accomplish dismemberment without leaving a substantial mess and evidence behind.

The informant was whisked away to the New Orleans airport the same day, headed back home. The officers continued to survey dumpsters in the Fat City area and determined all were owned by one of six companies, whose names and phone numbers were prominently displayed on the dumpsters themselves. The next day, officers contacted those dumpster companies and learned that garbage from those suburban New Orleans trash sites could be in one of two landfills. However, each landfill received between one hundred and five hundred loads of garbage per day. The officers realized that sheer volume of garbage made it virtually impossible to retrieve Gary's body from either landfill. A reluctant Ted Kergan admitted it as well. What he still couldn't admit, couldn't abide, was this new possibility that his brother's body had been dismembered. Another chilling discovery that day was that the office parking lot, located at 2612 Severn Avenue in Metairie, which was also the one where Gary Kergan's car was found just days after the murder, was located directly across the street from the Landmark Hotel.

Weeks later, Ted Kergan received a package containing information that proved the confidential informant had been in daily contact with Leila Mulla for eight months just after Gary Kergan was murdered. He never saw or heard from the CI again.

CHAPTER 12

AFTER LIFE

Leila Mulla spent most of 1985 in an Atlanta mental hospital, suffering a nervous breakdown and experiencing suicidal tendencies, following her release from East Baton Rouge Parish Prison. Although those records are sealed, one thing is certain: deep in that institutional cocoon, Leila was protected from her demons, real and imagined. When her psychiatrist brought a Catholic priest into one of their sessions in an attempt to gain her confession so her therapy could move forward with honesty, she thwarted the priest's efforts and managed to get reassigned to a different psychiatrist.

Initially, Leila was determined to leave the facility. She struggled to cope with the institutional regime and to maintain her equilibrium with prescription medicine. Finally, Thorazine kept her on a somewhat even keel and she continued her stay at the Atlanta hospital. By the end of 1985, Leila was released from the facility, but she remained under her newer psychiatrist's care. She and her mother, Elizabeth, moved into an Atlanta apartment in an attempt to transition Leila back into a normal existence. Leila got a retail job at a shopping mall and kept up with her therapy sessions. After a few weeks, Elizabeth was feeling confident with Leila's new and more stable routine. Buoyed by overconfidence or desperate for hope, she returned home to Kent, leaving her daughter alone in the Atlanta apartment.

It didn't take long for Leila to hook up with an unsavory band of druggies. Shortly afterward, when mom returned to

Atlanta unannounced, she found the apartment filled with drugs and Leila's new stoned friends. She immediately carted Leila back to the same Atlanta hospital, this time for admission into their drug rehabilitation program.

By mid-1986, Leila finished with rehab. She moved into her parent's Kent, Ohio home, supposedly for the greater stability it provided, but she was soon back to her old tricks. In December, she hooked up with former boyfriend, Rick Jaskiewicz, after he was released from prison on the two vehicular homicide charges. She alternated staying part-time at home with living part-time with Rick, and again took to making her living through a revolving mix of exotic dancing and prostitution. This time she worked her trade at clubs in the Cleveland area, right under the noses of her unknowing parents. In the red Mercury Lynx they bought for her, Leila kept a bag with her tools of the trade: fancy dancing shoes, makeup galore, and assorted hair accoutrements. This go-round, her clients provided a high-dollar return for her services and she needed to look the part.

Leila never told Rick about her arrest in Baton Rouge on a murder charge, but he knew all about it, anyway. A friend had visited him in prison in 1985 and brought newspaper stories about the murder.

Despite the hard street edge to their lives, the lovers engaged in a sort of magical thinking. They mused about how they could shuck his criminal background, along with their mutual substance abuse issues, and somehow live straight lives. They seemed to believe the dream was within reach.

It was never to be. Rick Jaskiewicz returned to prison for parole violations in July of 1987, while Leila was left to her own devices back in Kent.

In early 1989, Leila packed up her Mercury Lynx and drove from her parents' home three hours south to Nelsonville, Ohio. Rick Jaskiewicz had been released from serving his third parole violation prison stint in February, and was pursuing courses in logging there at Hocking College.

He was surprised that she showed up at all, since he had been incarcerated for the better part of a year. Yet there she was, and furthermore, Leila declared she was ready to move in with him.

Jaskiewicz was ready for sex, but he quickly realized something was peculiar with his partner. Rick could tell Leila was hiding her body, even though the two were already intimately acquainted. He probed until she revealed the reason: she was barely showing, but Leila was definitely pregnant.

This was too much for Rick. Not only did he already have a girlfriend, but Leila's pregnancy suddenly made that other relationship loom up in importance to him. He ordered Leila to leave. They never spoke again.

Leila's staunch Catholic parents were dismayed by their unmarried daughter's pregnancy. For them, abortion was out of the question. They urged her to give the baby up for adoption. Leila cajoled them into thinking she planned to do exactly that, but nevertheless the atmosphere in the household was now akin to an armed camp.

Leila's brother, Kahil, offered a means for a truce; he suggested Leila come to live with his wife Cathy's kinfolks near them in Dayton, Kentucky. An agreement was reached and she spent the remainder of her pregnancy in Dayton, where she gave birth to a son in December 1990.

Despite her parents' pleas for the adoption option, Leila chose to raise Adam herself. Mom and baby son took up residence in a tiny, neatly kept apartment in nearby Covington, Kentucky. She worked as a secretary during the day, and went out most evenings instead of going home. Soon she was frequently leaving her young child with a babysitter.

Leila was at a Cincinnati area bar on New Year's Eve of 1991, when she met another Rick, this one named Rick Stockmeier. A midnight kiss on the cheek was all it took to spark a relationship between Rick and this twenty-six-year-old single mother of a toddler. He was stable enough, with a job at Cincinnati Gear. Rick fell in love with Leila as well as her blonde, curly-haired child, and he was serious enough about them both to help them get into a better apartment. Then he upped the ante by moving Leila and Adam in with him. They married in 1994 and remained in the Cincinnati area, far away from the Mullas' home base in Kent.

It wasn't a "happily ever after" situation. The marriage was rocky. Leila admitted she and Rick both had problems.

Rick and a partner purchased several franchises for rotisserie chicken restaurants called Kenny Rogers Roasters, which was singer/songwriter Kenny Rogers' venture into the fast food business. Things didn't go well for Rick on a small scale, just as they didn't go well for the entire company. Kenny Rogers Roasters company entered Chapter 11 bankruptcy in March 1998, and was bought out. The Stockmeiers ended up in debt.

Rick turned to selling cars and became depressed, so Leila thought a change in geography might help. They moved to Philadelphia and lived in the same apartment complex as Leila's sister, Wadia Mulla. Here, Rick and Leila welcomed a daughter in 1996. The marriage continued to have its ups and downs. Leila worked at Bloomingdales in Philadelphia and Rick dabbled at a few different jobs. He yearned to have his own business, prompting another move, this time to Cape May, New Jersey, where Leila's mother owned an oceanfront condominium. Rick opened a cookie business, but quickly realized he couldn't sustain it in a place where business was mostly seasonal. Soon, they were back in the Cincinnati area. Leila decided it was time to make her own money. With two brothers and a sister who were doctors, she turned toward the medical profession and entered nursing school in Cincinnati. To the surprise of those in the family who doubted her, Leila graduated from Good Samaritan School of Nursing on December 13, 2000.

As she neared the age of forty in 2005, Leila underwent a midlife crisis of sorts. She began an affair with a doctor colleague. Then Leila moved out of the family home, living and partying with single nurse friends in the Cincinnati area. In his anger and hurt, Rick lashed out. Leila filed for a restraining order. Ultimately, she decided to divorce Rick Stockmeier and leave her two children behind, moving to New York City. She obtained a nursing license there on August 8, 2006. In Astoria, Queens, among the nondescript businesses and apartment buildings, Leila found what she was looking for: a place where she could quietly work as a nurse, a place where she could blend in and get lost. The children, as it so often happens, became collateral damage to her change of priorities.

Meanwhile, back in Cincinnati, Rick Stockmeier's attorney was conducting research in preparation for the couple's divorce, and uncovered Leila's old arrest record for the murder of Gary Kergan. Rick Stockmeier was stunned by the news. Leila had never disclosed anything to him about the murder charge at any time during their long relationship. All he knew about that part of her past was that she had once lived in Louisiana and never wanted to return.

For a very long time, Leila had managed to bury her past in Baton Rouge. Even as she slogged through psychiatric treatment and returned to drugs and prostitution, or became a mother, married and divorced, or pursued a career in nursing, there was one thing she did not do. For twenty-eight years, she had absolutely no contact with Ronald Dunnagan.

It would have been easy enough to find him. Ron lived quietly, either working as a clown/casino barker in Las Vegas or surviving on disability payments in the Bossier City area. It was clear she had no desire to talk to him ever again.

CHAPTER 13

COLD CASE HOT

Memry Tucker wasn't sure what propelled her into a career in law enforcement, whether it was extreme fascination with childhood Nancy Drew books, or the murder of her dad's best friend in 1984, when Memry was nine years old.

She had vivid memories of being intrigued by both. Her bookcase full of Nancy Drew books, with their gold and navy bindings, was situated in her upstairs bedroom in the Tucker home in Amory, Mississippi. Memry would sit and read on the staircase outside the bedroom door, looking down the steps into a view of the kitchen and the old-fashioned rotary dial telephone mounted on one wall.

During the days and weeks after Gary Kergan was reported missing, Memry's father, Larry Tucker, spent plenty of time pacing and talking with one ear pressed to the receiver. The fear and desperation he expressed during those calls were branded into her memories of that time. She recalled the chaos her father experienced during that time. She also remembered Gary Kergan, who had always been friendly and ever smiling during the summer trip both families had taken to the Gulf of Mexico. Gary's son, Wade, was close to Memry's age, and the two had gotten along well together.

"I grew up wanting to solve murders," she revealed three decades later. "I wanted to be a cop my entire life, probably because of Gary." At the age of nineteen, Memry began a career in law enforcement and the dream became reality. Her first job was as a deputy for the East Baton Rouge Parish Sheriff's Office, assigned to a remote substation.

After marrying and adopting two young boys from Russia, then the USSR, Memry chose to become a full-time homemaker, at least until her boys were old enough to be in school. By the time she was ready to do so, years later, she was anxious to re-join the work force. Memry submitted her résumé and received a call from East Baton Rouge's new district attorney, Hillar Moore III, who hired her for a new position, victim assistance coordinator.

In that role, Memry learned everything about the trial process so she could provide support for victims' family members. She helped her charges negotiate the court gauntlet, running them through the maze of hearings, statuses, and motions. She familiarized them with the unique language integral to the legal system. Memry also gained knowledge about both sides of the trial process. This experience catapulted her into an investigator role with Prem Burns, who was the assistant district attorney assigned to many high-profile cases.

In the small world of the Baton Rouge Police Department, Memry easily befriended detectives in the homicide division. This included Ross Williams, who called her one day in February 2011, asking about something she had not thought about in a very long time.

"Do you recognize the name Larry Tucker? And what about this address in Mississippi? Do you know a guy named Gary Kergan?"

Memry Tucker's head was reeling. "Larry Tucker is my dad and that address in Mississippi matched the home where I was reared," she told Williams. "Gary Kergan," she added, "yes, I knew Gary Kergan."

Ross Williams explained to her the newly created Cold Case Division was looking through several hundred case files, and one file, the 1984 murder case of a man called "Sonic Gary," stood out as a good choice to be re-opened.

In the case file, another man, Larry Tucker, from Amory, Mississippi, gave a statement to police back in 1984, saying he had shared an office with Gary Kergan in a Baton Rouge apartment and both were Sonic Drive-In franchisees. Because the Tucker family lived in Mississippi at that time and because Memry was only a child then, she had no idea Gary Kergan's murder took place in Baton Rouge. After all, the Kergans lived in Crowley at that time. She had assumed all these years that Gary Kergan was murdered in or near Crowley.

Memry Tucker couldn't wait to get her hands on that case file. She called her father and related the news about the possibility that Gary Kergan's murder case would be re-opened. It was the first real adult conversation the father and daughter had about the case and their mutual disappointment over the release of the "alleged" perpetrators in 1985.

Gary Kergan's death had altered Memry's life in so many ways. It not only ignited her desire to have a career in law enforcement, it prompted her family's permanent move to Baton Rouge in 1985. Gary's death introduced Ted Kergan into Memry's life, someone she would grow up knowing as a member of her extended family. Memry quickly decided not to tell Ted about Baton Rouge Police's Cold Case Division and its interest in the murder of "Sonic Gary," at least not yet. She couldn't stand to see Ted heartbroken once more. Instead, she decided it would be best to work behind the scenes because of her close connections to it all, and moved quietly into the investigation.

Memry Tucker found herself at ground zero for this cold case investigation, in the midst of a series of weird connections to the original Kergan murder case. Her big boss, District Attorney Hillar Moore III, had been the original crime scene investigator at the tiny duplex at 2956 Byron Street. Another boss, Assistant District Attorney Prem Burns, was the original prosecutor for the case. Every old school detective in the office remembered the details, including her partner, Leo

Innerarity, who worked for the ABC Board back in 1984. He pulled Leila Mulla's identification card. That card connected her real name to the woman known only as "Erika" to those at The Night Spot. Leo Innerarity remembered the case well, and his former partner before Memry just happened to be R.E. Thompson, one of the original detectives assigned to the Kergan murder case.

Memry helped Cold Case Division Department Head John "Buck" Dauthier track down former Night Spot dancers, police officers, and other pertinent details. The two joined Detective Joe Rawls to question Bob Howle, R.E. Thompson's former partner and fellow investigator in the case. Howle was currently serving life in prison at Louisiana State Penitentiary at Angola for an unrelated murder. Several years after the Kergan murder, Bob Howle had gotten into a heated dispute with a man about Howle's girlfriend in the front yard of Howle's home. Howle shot and killed the man in what he claimed was self-defense. He refused a plea deal, went to trial, and was subsequently convicted.

In the spring of 2012, Joe Rawls, John "Buck" Dauthier, and Memry Tucker made the trek to question Howle about the case at Louisiana State Penitentiary, a little more than an hour's drive north of Baton Rouge. The last twenty miles down Highway 966 became more remote while it bisected the Tunica Hills and ended up at the prison's gates close to the Mississippi River. Howle was incarcerated in the prison's hospital ward, suffering from terminal cancer. It was hard for him to speak. He needed additional oxygen just to breathe. He insisted the three detectives sit around his hospital bed. Joe Rawls and Buck Dauthier sat on a tiny couch, leaving Memry to position herself inside an adjacent antique wheelchair. The detectives brought case reports, but Howle didn't need any reminders. Like everyone else who was involved in the case, he remembered every detail of the investigation. Howle offered to help, but admitted he was not in good enough physical condition to be a witness.

There was no need. It had taken almost two years but Buck Dauthier and his fellow detectives had finally gathered enough information and potential witnesses to convince prosecutors to re-open the case of "Sonic Gary."

So far, Memry had resisted the urge to call Ted Kergan, not wanting to get his hopes up in case her department decided not to pursue the case. There had always been blood evidence from the trunk of Gary Kergan's Eldorado Cadillac, but the Baton Rouge Police Department had made a lot of progress. At last this evidence sample's DNA could be compared to Wade Kergan's DNA for a possible match. Memry Tucker went ahead and placed a call to break this news to a surprised Ted Kergan.

His first reaction was guarded. Was there really a genuine commitment by the District Attorney's Office after all these years? Absolutely, Memry confirmed. Instantly, the emotional wall went down and Ted Kergan became ecstatic. Once he came into contact with Buck Dauthier of the Cold Case Division, Ted felt like they had not missed a step in the process of finding his brother's killers.

Ted hadn't missed a step, either. He had followed Leila Mulla and Ron Dunnagan all these years. He knew where they lived, where she worked, and so much more about both of them. As technology advanced, Ted was able to use his own equipment and early forms of social media to locate them. He obtained plenty of additional information by hiring private investigators. Maybe, he thought to himself in the depths of his being, he had even been expecting the case to be officially re-opened.

After getting Ted's approval, Buck Dauthier contacted Wade, who was instructed to go to a nearby Detroit Police Station. There a detective extracted Wade's DNA for testing and forwarded it to Baton Rouge. The samples not only matched, they also revealed that Wade's DNA proved he was an offspring of the man whose blood was in the trunk. The match put the "Sonic Gary" cold case on the front burner. It was the first case opened by Baton Rouge Police's new Cold Case Division, funded by a federal grant, enough money to cover detectives' payroll in the complex investigation.

On one hand, Ted Kergan felt confident about convicting his brother's murderers. He had been tracking their whereabouts ever since they were released from East Baton Rouge Parish jail in March of 1985. On the other hand, Ted's life was so different now. Sonic Corporate had released Ted from the ambitious development agreement after Gary's death. And while it took time to regroup, Kergan Brothers' Sonic Drive-Ins were now flourishing with fifty-eight locations.

Personally, Ted stepped into the role of family patriarch after Gary died. He took care of his now-deceased mother, who openly mourned Gary's tragic death until the day she herself passed on. He kept up a close relationship with his sister-in-law, Susie, and his nephew, Wade, even after they moved to Michigan three years after Gary's death. When Ted visited Susie months before her death from cancer in 2007, she showed him a video she had prepared to be played at her funeral. Ted wept when he saw it contained so many memories of Gary. Although she was happily remarried, Susie revealed to Ted that Gary remained the love of her life.

After Susie's death, Ted continued his close relationship with nephew Wade, who finally returned to Louisiana when Ted got married in January, 1992. Ted had met Ann in New Orleans during the summer of 1991. Their eyes first met when Ann came through the doors of Maximo's restaurant. It was, as they say, love at first sight. Their whirlwind courtship took everyone by surprise, particularly those closest to them.

Ted told Ann about Gary's death not long after they met, which by then was more than six years after the murder. Ann's heart broke for Ted and she could not imagine the pain Gary's loss caused. Although he remained vigilant in stalking Gary's killers for twenty more years, Ted chose not to involve Ann in any of his clandestine efforts. Their home was his safe place, a place whose atmosphere wasn't dampened by a constant death knell. Ted let something slip that made Ann realize he was following Leila's and Ron's tracks. At first she was hurt by the news, but it didn't take her long to understand why Ted had to keep it up and also why he couldn't let his quest infiltrate their home environment. She was grateful for his thoughtfulness in keeping their home a sanctuary, especially for son Jean Luc's sake, and reacted with cautious optimism. More than anything, she didn't want Ted to be crushed again.

Ted and Larry Tucker were also in a cautiously celebratory mood. This time, they were older and wiser, knowing Ron Dunnagan and Leila Mulla had slipped through authorities' hands once before. Ted vowed it wouldn't happen again. He was ready to pledge whatever time and resources that effort took. Friends rallied to help. Ann Edelman, a Baton Rouge public relations professional and old friend of Larry Tucker, became totally intrigued by the re-opening of this case, which she had heard so much about through the years. She had also worked with Ted and his Sonic business through the years, and gained a feel for the close bond between the brothers. Along with Ted and Larry, Ann Edelman also had a keen eye for detail. They formed a triumvirate of sorts and began their own re-investigation of the murder of a charismatic man who continued to motivate them from the grave.

In an attempt to find Gary Kergan's remains, Buck Dauthier got in touch with authorities in every Louisiana Parish holding unidentified bodies. None of them matched the DNA now positively identified as that of Gary Kergan.

Next, he meticulously assembled a plan to again arrest the only two suspects in the case, Ronald and Leila. Dauthier's reconnaissance uncovered the fact that Ron was still in the Bossier City area, staying mostly at the home of his forty-one-year-old daughter, Tammy Williams, along with her husband and some of her brood of children. Police detectives knew little about Dunnagan, except that he was on a disability pension and didn't stray far from his home base. They had no idea whether Ron might be armed and/or dangerous. Buck Dauthier also had no way of knowing whether or not Ron kept in contact with Leila Mulla.

He decided to plan the duo's arrest simultaneously to avoid any chance of one alerting the other. There was also one more person Buck Dauthier thought might have knowledge of the murder: Rick Stockmeier, Leila's ex-husband. He still lived in the same Cincinnati suburb.

So Dauthier selected six homicide detectives, splitting them into teams of two. One team was sent to the Ohio home of Rick Stockmeier to question him for any information he could provide. The hope was that Rick and Leila's divorced had been acrimonious, giving Rick added motivation to talk.

Joe Rawls and Mary Ann Godawa were assigned to arrest and question Leila in Astoria, Queens. Mary Ann worked in Internal Affairs and was given the assignment after FBI profilers suggested a policewoman should be part of the team. They further suggested that when the officers questioned Leila, they should be in street clothes, not uniforms.

They began making preparations with detectives in New York City. Finally, Ross Williams and another Baton Rouge detective traveled to Bossier City and joined deputies from the Bossier City Sheriff's Office and Louisiana State Police officers to apprehend Ron Dunnagan, the schizophrenic clown, casino barker, and once again, accused murderer. He offered no resistance to his capture or the cuffs. Did Ron suspect this day of reckoning would eventually come, even after almost thirty years? By this time, the unkempt and overweight Dunnagan, with his unruly white hair and oversized white beard, had the look of a dingy, demented Santa Claus. He shuffled along, favoring his one strong leg and protecting his ailing back. Although he had turned sixty-four a few days before his arrest, Ron Dunnagan looked a generation older.

He remained quiet while he was read his Miranda rights,

until he was asked about the incident with Gary Kergan. He responded only with, "I'm innocent."

Ross Williams continued to question him, until Ron opened up enough to describe events of the early hours of November 29, 1984, from his point of view. Yes, he agreed, Gary Kergan was at their apartment on Byron Street, but there was no sex involved. All three of them were there. Ron added that they talked for a few minutes and Gary Kergan left the apartment around 3:15 a.m. Ron suggested he may not have been the last person to see Gary Kergan alive. Finally, he claimed he had never been in contact with Leila Mulla during the ensuing twenty-eight years.

"You don't have a body, do you?" Ron asked Detective Williams. It was hard to discern whether the question emanated from a mocking killer who had definitively disposed of the body, or from a simpleton who was asking an earnest question about the possibility of additional damning evidence.

CHAPTER 14

TED AND GARY

Early in their lives, both boys found that their humble beginnings left them with an appreciation of the value of money. They were awakened most of all to the idea of living every day without financial worry, free to live in dignity and respect. Gary figured, and Ted agreed, they already knew too much about how to be poor. The Kergan boys hungered to move in the opposite direction.

As for the means of getting that done, their mother's hard work and honorable way of life wasn't lost on them, so it didn't occur to them to do anything except work for it, shoveling snow, mowing lawns, or doing cleanups for people around the neighborhood.

The secret behind the brothers getting enough work to make real money lay in Gary's natural sales ability. He was already hard to miss, with his large size and gregarious nature, and his easy-going personality could get him included almost anywhere. By contrast, Ted was painfully shy at that period of his life, and he was astonished by how easily Gary seemed to converse with people and get along with them. For Ted, it was like hearing someone speak an unknown foreign language. It was hard not to envy Gary's outgoing nature.

Once they had a little pocket money between them, they were able to help themselves out in small ways. Since they knew they weren't going to get new bicycles under their mother's strained finances, they put their job money into used bikes, then restored them to gleaming life. Ted admired

Gary's ability to look at something and visualize how it might look after some work. Gary saw both of the old bikes as the shining restorations they became.

Neither of the brothers ever had time to get into trouble, since they were too fired up on seeking opportunities and working to make them pay off. When Gary was still in his high school years at their parochial school, he ran afoul of one of the Catholic brothers who taught there. This classroom instructor was a Catholic "brother" in name only. He had a reputation for verbally tormenting students, and walking up and down the aisles ready to smack errant students in the back of the head with his heavy class ring.

One day this bully found cause to give Gary the same treatment. Just as he closed in for the blow, Gary's reflexes protected him and he was able to whip his arm up to deflect the blow.

This treason got him dragged to the front of the class, where he was mocked and derided, "So you think you're a tough guy?" When the instructor raised his arm to strike Gary again, Gary blocked the blow once more. The infuriated instructor retaliated by kicking Gary - hard - and resumed his mockery. Then he readied his leg to place another kick, which proved to be a big mistake. Gary exploded and jumped him, beating him to the floor. The Catholic brother's attack ended there.

Of course that wasn't the end of it, and Ted knew their mom had to make the difficult trip to the principal's office the next day, where it was assumed she would be informed that her son was being suspended or even expelled from school. That wasn't the result, however. It turned out that the school already had numerous complaints about this man and knew there was a problem. With this episode, all support for him was lost.

This impressed both boys with a solid lesson in never letting another person or group push you around unfairly. It turned out to be a great lesson when applied to sales.

Not long afterward, when Ted was fifteen, their mom's arthritis progressed to the point that she couldn't do her seamstress job anymore. She decided to sell their house and buy a franchise of some kind. There was no way for her to foresee how the franchise business model would come to provide for her sons in abundance.

So, at fifteen, Ted began going along with his mother to pitch meetings for various franchise operations, and then to look for suitable commercial properties. The activity required him to be aware of all the aspects of business real estate, from square footage prices to insurance costs and employee needs. Even at that young age, Ted could tell he was getting an education that felt far more relevant to him than his parochial school classes.

He explained his drive to his mom by saying he had no interest in growing up to be a lawyer; he wanted to *hire* a lawyer whenever he needed one to close another business deal. His eyes were open now to the opportunities to be had when in the right business and proper location. School became an obligatory distraction from his real interest.

Gary was eighteen now, and earned such high grades in his pre-med courses that he had already been awarded a scholarship to medical school. A fine career in medicine awaited him, and he had all the right stuff to get that medical degree.

In the meantime, Ted's desire to earn brought him into a job in direct marketing. He hadn't done it for long before he saw this work as a golden opportunity for a man like his brother who was a natural born salesman. He contacted Gary and explained the work to him, along with the potential market for a skilled persuader like him. Ted insisted this was a viable way for them to earn good money together, and to protect their mother from financial need.

After spending most of his life watching his mother make every possible sacrifice for her sons, Gary's desire to do right by her was as strong as Ted's. He quit his pre-med courses at school and came home to work with Ted.

Ted worked at learning, as much as possible, to emulate Gary's way with people, and came to regard the business world as a giant chessboard. As a natural introvert, he liked the challenge of planning successful moves, and his older brother's gregarious nature made it easier to put them into action.

They began to talk about going into business together.

CHAPTER 15

A CONFESSION

Baton Rouge police officers Joe Rawls and Mary Ann Godawa were well prepared for their trip to Astoria, New York. The mission was to apprehend Leila Mulla.

Beforehand, FBI profilers had sorted through Leila's past and come up with a plan on how to approach her and elicit her confession. Leila had a substantial internet presence, particularly blogs about a number of subjects: happiness, well-being, psychology, even wedding planning. The blogs were general in nature and extremely vague. There was absolutely no contact information for her on any of them. It appeared the blog spots were pre-programmed, scheduled in advance to appear on her websites with regularity. Since her subject matter was so varied and her photo accompanied each blog, profilers determined she must be confident, even narcissistic. They knew she was a nurse and the divorced mother of two children. So they combed through as much data as they could find and outlined the best approach.

There needed to be a female police officer in the mix. Mary Ann Godawa was selected, a long-time Baton Rouge police officer with experience in various departments. Profilers repeated that they wanted officers to wear street clothes when they apprehended her, and for them to use gentle tactics. Because of Leila's psychological profile, officers should suggest that perhaps she had been victimized by Ronald Dunnagan and the murder might not be her fault. They were also instructed to try to obtain the confession while still at her apartment.

If Leila ever thought about a future day of reckoning, the suspicion does not appear to have created more than a passing shiver. Mostly, Leila focused on one day, one situation, one person at a time. Such compartmentalization formed the crux of her life. Making her way to her apartment building on 11th Street after a nursing shift at Montefiore Hospital in The Bronx, Leila had no idea her life was about to flip upside down. In the morning hours of December 3, 2012, her cell phone rang while she rode the train home from work. Leila remembered looking out the window at the New York winter the moment the train rose above ground.

A Baton Rouge detective identified himself to her and asked where she was. Leila explained she was on the train, on her way home. The detective told her they were at her home and would be waiting for her. Leila could do nothing but stand on the speeding train and endure a frenzied barrage of thoughts.

Minutes passed, and just as the train went below ground, her cell phone rang again. The same detective asked the same question. Where was she? Leila told them she would be home shortly. She clicked off the call, then dialed Wadia. Her sister advised her to be careful, for whatever that was worth. Her next call was to her ex-husband, Rick Stockmeier. She explained what was happening and then asked him to take care of their kids. Leila exited the train in a trance. She was walking down Broadway in Astoria, Queens, toward her apartment, when her phone rang for the third time. She told the detective she was almost home.

When three professionally dressed men and women approached her near the door of her bland, four-story red brick block building, Leila knew her time was up. It was December 3, 2012. The mental boxes, into which she had so neatly shelved the past, now began to rattle around and fall over.

Joe Rawls and Mary Ann Godawa introduced themselves

as Baton Rouge detectives and asked if she knew why they were standing on the sidewalk outside the door to her third floor walk-up. Before she responded, Joe Rawls also asked if she knew Gary Kergan.

"Yes, I knew this day would come," she finally replied, turning pale and becoming flustered. Detective David Gilbert, one of two New York City detectives on hand, asked if they could go inside her apartment to discuss the case.

Meanwhile, unknown to the arresting group, Ted Kergan, Larry Tucker, and his daughter, Memry Tucker, were taking in the entire scene from a car parked along the street.

Ted planned to leave no stone unturned this time. To him, that meant that he had to be present every step of the way. No detail of this investigation was going to escape him. Leila Mulla was guilty. She murdered his brother, his business partner, his best friend. For all of the twenty-eight years since then, Leila had been free. She'd been able to marry, have children, and become a nurse.

Gary Kergan didn't even get to celebrate his son's tenth birthday. Ted remembered the last few days of his brother's life, and the unspoken burden Ted felt emanating from Gary during their incessant daily conversations. That bond was still intact after all these years. Ted had waited for this day for such a long time. On this chilly December morning, he realized he was one giant step closer to seeing Leila Mulla behind bars.

Still, Ted wanted to actually witness Leila Mulla walk into prison. As soon as he discovered the arrests were planned, he made arrangements for a flight to New York and a driver in New York City.

Even though they were only observing, Memry didn't tell any of her police compadres she planned to be in New York for the arrest. The trio coordinated disguises to "blend" in with the city's diverse, crowded population. Larry was a businessman in his dark suit, while Memry dressed down to play a college student. Ted Kergan, who donned so many different disguises during his information-seeking forays, chose to look as much as he could like a homeless man.

Before the detective entourage arrived, Ted roamed the corridors of Leila's apartment building, wanting to see for himself where his brother's murderer lived. At one point, Ted inched close enough to Leila's apartment, Number 3-D, to hear the fussy barking of her dog, Pumpkin. When he heard police detectives climbing up to the third floor, he took another stairway down and scampered back into the waiting car with Larry and Memry.

The official police party joined Leila inside her apartment, where she became visibly shaken and began crying. Between sobs, she asked Joe Rawls whether she was facing the death penalty. Joe Rawls advised her of her Miranda rights and told her she was not under arrest but rather a subject of the investigation into the disappearance of Gary Kergan. He had no idea what the consequences might be. Then, Detective Rawls asked Leila if she knew Gary Kergan. She responded positively and referred to him as "Sonic Gary." The story she related for the four detectives followed the same salient points as her previous confessions right after the 1984 murder, the one after her arrest in Las Vegas and another one once she was returned to Baton Rouge. Rawls interrupted her sweeping narrative, asking point blank what happened to Gary Kergan. She replied just as quickly and directly. Ron Dunnagan killed Gary Kergan in their duplex.

The Baton Rouge detectives were following direction given to them by FBI profilers, on the idea that it was imperative to get her to talk and hopefully confess to Gary Kergan's murder. By questioning her first at her own apartment, detectives nailed it. Now, they needed to get her to repeat it all on the record. Leila agreed to accompany detectives to the Queen's District Attorney's Office to give a videotaped statement.

Watching detectives get back into their car with Leila Mulla in tow, Ted instructed his driver to follow them.

They traveled the ten miles to the district attorney's office in Kew Gardens, with Ted in the front seat videotaping the entire procession. Memry couldn't believe the Baton Rouge detectives didn't recognize them. She received continuous text updates from Joe Rawls, who assumed she was back in Baton Rouge and wanted to keep her informed. Little did he know Memry was in spitting distance.

Assistant District Attorney Dana Cummings also traveled to Queens, hoping to question Leila. Dana had practiced law for more than thirty years. As a prosecutor, she had tried high-profile murder cases against the rapper "Lil Boosie" and serial killer Derrick Todd Lee. She had just been assigned the Kergan case by her boss, District Attorney Hillar Moore.

Even though she had a lot on her professional plate, Dana had been enticed by the working trip to New York City, since her sons live there. Her only hesitancy in taking the case was whether Ted Kergan still trusted the district attorney' office, since it had initially dropped the case. Once she met with Ted, Dana found she really liked him. There was no lingering animosity on his part, just a dogged drive to have the duo convicted for killing his brother. Even though Ted believed both Leila and Ron were both involved in the murder, he held Leila Mulla most responsible. Dana didn't know if she agreed with his take and wanted to meet and talk to Leila herself.

Dana and Marilyn Filingeri of the Queens County District Attorney's Office made their way to the first floor interview room, where they joined Joe Rawls and Mary Ann Godawa. Leila Mulla was in the restroom. Shortly after noon, the two-and-a-half-hour interview commenced with Joe Rawls showing Leila a photo of Gary Kergan, whom she identified once again as "Sonic Gary."

Leila had little outward reaction to the photo. She wrung her hands and leaned forward. Her demeanor was timid. As Sergeant Rawls continued his questions, Leila said little more than "sure" or "I know."

"Can I just have a minute to think?" Leila asked in a tiny, meek voice.

"Take all the time you need," replied Joe Rawls.

"Okay. We'll just do it and see what happens."

"So you want to talk to us without an attorney, correct? You want to tell your story?

"After I do this, will I be able to get an attorney?"

"Absolutely."

"I mean, then the damage will be done. I understand."

"You've had to carry this dark, deep secret for all these years. You know you felt better thinking that one day this is gonna come and it will all go away. The only way it's going to go away is with you talking about it. Otherwise, it will be there and I can promise you, it will be a lot harder. It will be dragged through the system for years."

"Am I ever going to have to see him (Ron Dunnagan) in court though?"

"I don't know that. I wish I could tell you. But I can tell you one thing: he will never be around you."

"Okay."

"So are you ready? Ready to talk? Tell your side of the story? You don't need a lawyer, right?

"I guess not."

"Okay, Okay. Well, I need you to initial this for me. Right here."

Leila had changed clothes out of her nursing scrubs. She now wore a gray two-piece jogging suit and a knit t-shirt in a tiny floral print. At forty-seven, she was still a fairly good-looking woman with a nice shape and shoulder-length dark, wavy hair. Leila looked defeated, however, when she once again related the story of running away from an Ohio halfway house and ending up in New Orleans.

"Someone said 'Oh, I'll help you' and they ended up taking all my belongings. Someone else said 'Oh, I'll help you' and they raped me. I had nothing. So I was living on the street."

"That had to be tough."

"So, basically, I met Ronald Dunnagan. He told me he had a place to stay and I could stay there. So I went and I stayed and before I know it, I'm caught up in prostitution."

Leila continued, saying Ron found her jobs dancing in clubs and johns with whom to have sex. Then he took all of the money.

"How did you feel about him? Weren't you scared of him?"

"Well, yeah. He had threatened me. Threatened my family."

"What did he threaten to do?"

"He said he was going to kill them. He said he had connections. He was part of a mafia and they would come and get me and my family if I left. And at one point, I did go home for a couple of days and he was calling and said if I didn't get back he was going to send someone up there. So I left and went back."

Leila described their move to an apartment in Baton Rouge and how Ron found her a dancing gig at The Night Spot, a place where she developed a small prostitution clientele, including Gary Kergan.

Mary Ann Godawa pulled out a bound notebook. Leila Mulla couldn't hide her surprise when she saw the copies of her journals from 1984. She went silent.

"Your journal and any of the writings -- Dunnagan, you know it sounds like to me, had total control over you," continued Mary Ann Godawa. "He even told you, you know, how to think, where to be 24/7, right?"

"He did."

"He told you what to do. He even told you what to write."

"Yeah."

"What did he tell you to write?"

"That started way back in New Orleans. He told me to start to write things down. And then, he started with the ghost in the closet."

"He told you there was a ghost in the closet at y'all's place and he just built on it."

"And I believed everything he said, once again, like an idiot. I believed in the ghost in the closet. I believed, you know, it was watching me. He was watching me."

"You get to Baton Rouge, you get an apartment. He said a ghost was there?"

"It was the same ghost."

"Did the ghost have a name?"

"Squeekee."

"Squeekee is still with you. Now, Ron went back to the apartment when you serviced your client during the prostitution?"

"Sometimes he would be there, yes."

"And why?"

"He'd say 'if anything happens to you.' Now I know, once again, it was just a control thing so I couldn't get away."

"Did he ever talk about stealing from one of your johns, from one of your clients, taking their money?"

"Mm-hm. I believed everything he said. I've heard, you know, stories about Patty Hearst being brainwashed and people laughing at it. But you know what? It's very real."

Leila continued talking about how Ron Dunnagan scouted for wealthy men she could lure back to their apartment for sex and then rob them.

"So, you think he was looking for someone," Mary Ann Godawa addressed her.

"Oh, he was looking. I heard it in New Orleans. I heard it in Baton Rouge. And, you know, whatever he told me to write, like an idiot, I'd write it, and I did whatever he told me to do. Just give me a minute please."

With that, Leila slumped a bit in her chair, staring at the tissue clutched in one hand.

"You need some water?" Mary Ann asked.

"No, I just need to..."

"Just breathe. Take your time. We're not here to judge you."

"No, I mean, I judge myself enough. And I'm sorry. Very sorry for everything."

Leila broke down a little harder this time, sniffling into the Kleenex.

"Oh Lord, I just need to...," she started. "How could this have happened? How could things have escalated? How could I have ever been in this situation? It's just hard to relive."

She continued to lament how the thirty-six-year-old Dunnagan dominated her then, as a nineteen-year-old naive teenager.

"He's the one that really caused this all to happen," Leila told Godawa.

"He did. So you know it and we know it." Godawa replied, cajoling her to continue.

"Let me go back to the writings," picked up Leila.

"The journals you're talking about?"

"The journals, yes. He bought some type of poison and was poisoning animals.

"Animals? Like what kind of animals?"

"I believe it was mice."

"So, he bought, it was like rat poison?"

"I don't remember where he put it. But I remember him telling me about dead mice. ...And, um, and I remember this. This particular night he was there. I brought him in."

"You brought Mr. Kergan? Gary?"

"Yes. I know I gave him a glass of wine because he liked to drink wine. He started drinking the wine, and he fell to the ground and it looked like he was choking. And I didn't know what to do. And then Dunnagan popped up. I'm sure he was in the apartment. And he grabbed him 'cause he was down choking and took him out of the room. And then, somehow, the door was closed. I don't know if I closed it; I don't know if he closed it. I don't know what he did with him."

"So, he dragged him out while he was still choking and you stayed in the bedroom?"

"After he left the room, I didn't see him."

During the interview, just outside the Queen's District Attorney's Office, Memry Tucker continued to receive text updates and relayed their contents to Larry and Ted. Suddenly, Memry became visible shaken and tears began to roll down her cheeks.

"They poisoned him," Memry told Ted and Larry.

"That's bullshit," was Ted Kergan's immediate response. Yards away, back inside the interview room, Mary Ann Godawa continued her line of questioning.

"Gary was a big man. I don't know how big Dunnagan was. Did somebody help him get Gary out of the apartment?"

"I didn't know he was going to do that. I knew at some point that Dunnagan was planning on (getting) somebody at some point."

"You didn't know it was going to be Gary?"

"No."

"Did you know when you served him wine you had..."

"Tainted wine? No, I didn't."

"Did Dunnagan say anything to you when he came into the room and he saw Gary down there?"

"I don't know if we did or not. I mean, I've pushed this out of my mind for so long. Honest to God, I don't know. I know he drug him out. I know he had trash bags."

"Dunnagan had trash bags? In the apartment?"

Leila's new revelations about poison pissed off Ted Kergan. This was total bullshit, he thought. Whatever she said, it's okay, Ted further reasoned. She was confessing to her role in the murder of his brother. Her confession was the most important goal. He couldn't help but recall so many years earlier, when the confidential informant attempted to extort him in New Orleans. The CI said Leila told him she poisoned Gary Kergan and that they took Gary's body and the evidence out of their apartment in six trash bags. They supposedly put each one in a separate dumpster in suburban New Orleans, near the Landmark Hotel.

Back in the interview room in Kew Gardens, Mary Ann Godawa produced the hand-drawn map. Leila denied knowing about it or even that the handwriting was hers. Mary Ann then gave Leila copies of the journals, which Leila admitted were in her handwriting.

"Why don't you take some time and read through them?" the detective suggested.

The change in Leila's demeanor was pronounced. Her back became a straighter. She soon appeared out of breath, so detectives offered her a drink of water or a bathroom break.

"You know, after I got out of jail before, I went to a mental institution for like a year. Now I know why."

"Have you talked to anyone over the years about this?"

"Not my psychiatrist. Not my ex-husband. Nobody, but nobody."

"Have you had any contact with Dunnagan?"

"Oh no. I don't ever want to see him. He's a scary man and he's one to be feared."

Sergeant Joe Rawls wasn't sure he believed everything Leila was saying. "You know Dunnagan dragged the body out (of the apartment). Then, you're saying you remember being in the passenger seat of Gary's car. And, then y'all driving somewhere. And you remember that it was very quiet. It's very hard for a man to take a grown man out of a trunk by himself."

Assistant District Attorney Dana Cummings saw Joe Rawls becoming frustrated. She used that as her cue to get some answers from Leila. "But wherever you drove Gary's car, you had to get transportation back. Correct?"

"I remember sitting in the passenger side of the car and I remember going somewhere. I don't know where we went. It was dark out and I remember having a crochet knit cap on."

From there, the interrogation stagnated. Finally, at 1:55 p.m., Leila asked for a bathroom break. Ten minutes later, when everyone reassembled in the white-walled room, Joe Rawls had enough of Leila playing the victim. Having read Leila's diaries, written in her own hand with a "take charge" attitude, Rawls believed Leila was more culpable than she was admitting. Things just weren't adding up.

"You know what I think?" Rawls asked. "I think you're lying."

"I'm going to tell you what happened," she responded meekly.

"All right, then start telling me. Let's quit the dance."

Leila reiterated the story about the poisoning and Gary Kergan falling to the ground. Then, Ron Dunnagan came out of a closet outside the bedroom, took Gary into the bathroom, wrapped him up in plastic and put Gary in the trunk of his own car. She said Ron told her to get in the car and they drove, stopping at a dumpster. They continued to drive, parked the car, and took a cab back to the apartment where they packed up their belongings and Ron cleaned the bathroom floor.

"Those dumpsters are, I mean even if the lid's open, they're pretty high," ventured Mary Ann Godawa. "So that means he had to lift that body over his head or pretty high up to get it into the dumpster."

"He did," replied Leila.

"Hard to believe he did it by himself. Tell us what happened, please? In the bathroom..."

"I can't."

"You have to tell us, Leila."

"I know. I know I do. I know. I know. I know."

"We need to know why he went into the bathroom."

"He cut him in half, OK?"

"With what?"

"It was... I know it was a saw."

Outside the office, on a Queens sidewalk, Memry Tucker was almost too upset to relay the text she has just gotten from someone inside the interview room. They cut him up, she said succinctly, in between deep breaths. Ted had the same reaction as he'd had when he'd learned of the poison, complete bullshit. Or, was it? He remembered once again that the CI talked about disposing of six trash bags in six different dumpsters. It just didn't make any sense to Ted. How could this then-teenager and her grifter companion accomplish such a difficult and disgusting task in such a short time and in such a small place? There was just no way. This was the supreme gut punch, a watershed moment. What was the truth? How in the world could they separate fact from fiction?

"Look, I'm okay with whatever she tells," he said to Memry and Larry. "I'm just fired up she's confessing."

Inside the interview room, Mary Ann Godawa kept asking questions. "Do you remember the blood?"

"Yes, there was blood. Well, I didn't see the blood. I asked him what he was going to do about the blood. He said, 'I'm going to clean it.' I didn't clean anything. He cleaned everything. I was just there and I did not see him cut. This is what he said and he said he was taking care of everything. And that's how he lifted him into the dumpster."

"And he had him in... and when you say plastic, was it garbage bags?"

"Yes."

"Let me tell you something," pointed out Joe Rawls. "When a body gets cut in half, the guts come out. And blood goes everywhere."

"But I did not see any blood."

"You know I don't think you're telling the truth, don't you?

"But that is the truth."

"You're gonna tell me Dunnagan chops this guy in half; this guy gets cut in half. He bags him up, right? We're gonna bag, we're gonna stuff him, get in the car, we're going, OK? That sounds believable?"

At this point, Joe Rawls started rapid firing questions,

even ones unrelated to Gary Kergan's demise.

"How many times had you ripped off people before? Doing the johns, the tricks?"

"I had never ripped someone off before."

"I'm a patient man, but I gotta tell you, when I see a lie, it kind of bothers me because I wouldn't lie to you. I have not lied to you."

"I know. I know."

"I came all this way to talk to you."

"I know. I'll be truthful."

"So you knew he was going to hit him (Gary)?"

"I knew he was going to do that, yes."

"So, when you served the wine, you knew?"

"I knew he was going to do that. He told me not to drink any wine. The poison was in the wine."

"Now, let me say this, his family deserves to know," began Mary Ann Godawa.

"Yes, they do," Leila responded.

"So, we need to know. He was married. He had a child. They need to bring him home. They need some kind of closure as to where he is."

"I mean, as far as where he is, it was a green dumpster."

Questions about the size and location of the dumpster went nowhere. Leila couldn't seem to remember anything except a long cab ride back to the apartment under still-dark skies. Everyone was tired and they decided to end the interview, thinking they had everything they needed, including a confession from Leila Mulla. After the interview, detectives secured an arrest warrant for Leila Mulla from Detective Buck Gauthier, who was monitoring things from Baton Rouge. Leila was charged with second-degree murder, criminal conspiracy, and simple robbery.

She was taken into custody and driven to the women's prison facility at Riker's Island, where Ted Kergan was waiting outside at a safe distance. Watching Leila Mulla walk into prison was something Ted was determined to witness after waiting twenty-eight years. She stayed in prison there, awaiting extradition back to Baton Rouge, until December 20. Detective Rawls returned to New York, took custody of Leila Mulla, and returned with her on a United Airlines flight out of LaGuardia Airport, located between Riker's Island and Leila's apartment in Long Island City.

Even though it was Christmas week, Ted Kergan traveled back to New York too, shadowing Rawls. Ted knew was he was missing holiday preparations with his wife and young son, Jean Luc, but, for him personally, Leila Mulla's arrest and extradition to Baton Rouge were his best Christmas present. Ted, once again disguised, took his seat on the United Airlines jet headed to Baton Rouge, the same one Leila Mulla later boarded in the custody of Joe Rawls. After making and remaking airline reservations a number of times tallying up an exorbitant price tag, Ted had managed to procure a seat on the same flight as the woman he knew killed his brother. Twenty-eight years later, Leila Mulla was facing second-degree murder charges back in Louisiana. Ted had waited a very long time for this day. She had slipped through his hands, through all of their hands, once before. He was careful not to let Rawls notice him as he passed down the aisle with Leila in custody, but it was hard to avert his eyes. He didn't want to let Leila Mulla out of his sight for a moment.

CHAPTER 16

THE REAL LEILA

Ted wanted to learn everything he could about Leila Mulla. Although he had already kept tabs on her for decades, when the case resurfaced in late 2012, he was even more determined to find out every minute detail about the killer's life.

He knew she was a nurse. Obviously, she was smart. When Ted discussed her profession with his friends at the Acadiana Parish Sheriff's Office, the deputies correctly guessed she worked in a hospital emergency room, a place where moments separate life and death, where medical professionals are in control of how patients are handled. The deputies pointed out that, among the ranks of female serial killers, nurse was a popular profession because of the access to potential victims, drugs, and other medical supplies.

They convinced Ted that Leila was the brains behind Gary's murder based on the profile they were building. Some of these same deputies were at the hotel with Ted in the summer of 1985, when the CI talked about Leila Mulla. They reminded Ted of the CI's description of nineteen-year-old Leila Mulla, someone the informant saw daily; a portrait which included narcissism, fantasies about prostitution, instability, and erratic behavior. Deputies saw a snapshot of her that fit a classic criminal profile.

After his conversation with the deputies, Ted's belief that Leila took the lead in his brother's murder was cemented. Even at such a young age, Leila had the moxie and cunning to charm and enlist the help of a man seventeen years older. Although Ron Dunnagan had street smarts, mentally, he was no match for Leila. Because of her youthful beauty, he would have done anything she requested.

The realization that Leila Mulla was likely the chief engineer in the plot to kill Gary was a defining moment for Ted. By going after Ron Dunnagan, he could have made a serious mistake, since it now appeared that Leila was chiefly responsible for Gary's death and Ron Dunnagan was merely her pawn and her brawn.

Ted knew Leila had two children and an ex-husband, whom she divorced when she turned forty. He wanted to know what type of lifestyle Leila Mulla chose in her mid-life single years, when she took jobs with hospitals in New York City and as a traveling nurse.

He linked her with the Leila Mulla he Googled periodically on the Internet, who authored numerous blogs on everything from planning weddings to discovering happiness. At first, the personalities of the serial blogger and murderess-turned-nurse didn't seem to jive. Ted couldn't believe the two could be the same person. After talking it over with detectives, he realized the more numerous the blogs about positivity, happiness, and even wedding planning that Leila Mulla amassed, the further down Internet search engine hits those troublesome articles about Gary Kergan's murder and on thecharleyproject.com were pushed. This latter website, designed to keep alive cold cases nationwide with its articles about unsolved murders, was just one of the places on the World Wide Web where Leila Mulla's name was mentioned in connection with Gary Kergan's murder. Ted figured it made sense that Leila intended to bury her connection to the long-ago crime with her multiple, multi-topic blogs. He still wanted to know much more about her. Ted never believed she was Ron Dunnagan's sex slave. Did she return to prostitution at any point in her life? Even more sinister, had she murdered again? It required extraordinary resources to paint a complete picture of this woman.

Larry Tucker was once again on board to help Ted with research. This time around, he engaged a friend to both of them who played armchair detective with him time and time again in the ensuing years regarding Gary Kergan's case. The re-arrest of Leila and Ron was a serious call to action.

Ann Edelman had heard Larry talk about the case for decades. These two first met when Larry hired Ann to help market his Sonic Drive-Ins. Ted was part owner of some of the same stores, so he began to interact with Ann as well. Years later, when word came down from Sonic headquarters that all franchisees had to disengage their local ad agencies, Larry and Ann continued to remain close friends. Ann also saw Ted periodically, for business as well as socially. Ann knew that when news was released about the re-arrest of Leila Mulla in Astoria, New York, and of Ronald Dunnagan in Bossier City, there would not only be interview requests from Baton Rouge media, but also from media in the regions where those two lived and worked, as well as nationally. She volunteered to handle the press. By then, Ann was already intrigued by the case.

"There were so many things that we needed to learn," Ann related. "There was no way two people could do it all."

There was also an urgency to their parallel investigation because they knew they evidence was light, only Leila Mulla's confession and the blood DNA match. They also feared that if Leila recanted her confession, there would be no reason to hold either Leila or Ron. But how could they help build the case? There were additional things Ted Kergan wanted to know, things not necessarily germane to the case, but which represented knowledge that could serve to weave together the entire story surrounding the crime.

The TV shows Dateline NBC and 48 Hours sent representatives to Baton Rouge to pitch Ted Kergan about possible future programs on his brother's murder. Media representatives from ABC News, the Huffington Post, New York City, and newspapers in Las Vegas and Leila's hometown of Kent, Ohio, called for information and interview requests. Ann had her hands full, scheduling interviews and crafting statements in conjunction with Ted. Brand management and crisis communication were Ann's forte, so she put those skills to work coordinating the bevy of media requests.

Ann knew plenty about Gary Kergan. His light still shone brightly almost thirty years later, inspiring so many friends, even strangers, to pledge support to Ted in helping solve the mystery of Gary's death. But it was Ted's ability to keep his brother's memory alive that kept his brother's murder case active for all these years.

Through Ted and Larry, Ann gained an arsenal of facts and suppositions about the case. Still, all three were just babes in the woods when it came to discovering the facts in the case and maneuvering through the legal system. They all believed Leila Mulla was the brains of the operation from the beginning. Ted's cohorts at the Acadia Parish Sheriff's Office produced enough of an argument to convince him. After Leila confessed at the New York District Attorney's Office in Queens, Ted, Larry, and Ann Edelman had more questions than answers. Leila's story had multiple versions, so they had to doubt everything she confessed. In fact, a veteran law enforcement official who was not involved in the case told them not to believe anything she confessed.

They sought to find the truth themselves and concentrated their search on Leila Mulla, but they quickly found themselves in a quandary. If the truth about what happened to Gary contradicted Leila Mulla's confessions, she would lose all credibility as a potential witness in the upcoming legal battle. What if she was needed as a witness in legal proceedings against Ron Dunnagan? What version of the night-of-the-murder story would she tell on the stand? Would it follow the same tenants as her confessions so far, even though there were variations in those stories? Or would she stray off course and into a path where opposing counsel could tear her story to shreds?

Before they leaped, Ted hired an attorney so they could discuss the legal parameters of how to proceed. The attorney was fairly straightforward. They could do whatever they wanted as private citizens, including hiring private investigators to solicit information about Leila's life. Whatever discoveries were made needed to be vetted through the attorney. He knew what information should be shared with the district attorney's office.

Meanwhile, the trio began to construct a timeline of events from the beginning of the suspects' lives to the present time. At first, there were many blank time periods. The price tag for Ted's private searches was mounting, and there was no way to budget for the future since no one knew what the future held. He told his long-time colleague and friend, Doris Reiners, that he did not want to be informed of what he was spending to help solve his brother's murder. Doris completely understood Ted's request. She had been employed with Kergan Brothers' Sonic-related businesses for a long time, and she, too, worked with and knew Gary Kergan.

"I've been saving for this for thirty years," Ted told Doris. "Let's do it all."

Ted brought Ann Edelman many boxes of information on Gary's murder case which he had amassed over three decades. They made a pledge to make no assumptions as they revisited all old leads in the case. They rethought the murder timeline, beginning by taking their own road trip to New Orleans, starting at the Byron Street duplex.

The duplex was condemned and demolished in 1994, and now a concrete slab was all that remained at 2956 Byron Street. They made trips to the Port Hudson area, north of Baton Rouge, and to the Alligator Bayou area, south of Baton Rouge, trying to rethink some of the telephone hotline tips from decades before. They proceeded on I-10 to New Orleans, getting off at any exits they thought might have been easy stops to dump a body. Once in New Orleans' French Quarter, they made their way to the Old Mexico apartment building on Decatur Street where Leila had moved in with Ron in late 1983. Jumping in and out of Ted's giant four-wheel drive truck, they walked the same paths that Leila and Ron would have walked back in their days together. They tried to survey their scene in New Orleans with new eyes. On the way out of the city, they made their way to the Severn Avenue parking lot where Gary's car was discovered. It was less than a quarter mile off I-10. When they reached the lot, they were in the shadow of the iconic building right across the street. It was the round tower of The Landmark Hotel, the same hotel the CI had led Ted and detectives to, so many years before.

Ted, Larry, and Ann all looked with fresh eyes upon the hotel directly across the street from the Severn Avenue lot where Gary's car was first spotted back on November 29, 1984. It was an emotional and disturbing moment, to realize Gary's car was found here and that an informant had told them his remains were put in dumpsters at the hotel across the street. Many puzzle pieces from the night of the murder emanated from this very spot.

Ted, Larry, and Ann mounted their own campaign to discover the truth about Leila Mulla. They engaged private investigators in ten states to question people who had known her at different periods of her life. That was just the tip of the information iceberg. Ted and company developed a library containing more than nine hundred digitized documents with cross-reference tools. There were so many private investigator interviews that as many as four transcribers were employed at one time. Hard copies of interview transcriptions, timeline information, and legal proceedings were stored in binders. This system formed the lifeblood of their investigation, allowing Ted, Larry, and Ann access to any document from their mobile devices. It was a painful process, but it proved well worth the effort.

As Ted became anxious about the slow pace of the complicated legal system, he thought of a way to literally shine a spotlight on the search for his brother's body. After all, Ted was the one who found the hand-drawn map in Leila's and Ron's Las Vegas apartment back in 1984. Ann Edelman had already determined from a lengthy session with Google Maps that there were only a limited number of places where railroad tracks were located perpendicular to levees as depicted on that map. Ted, Larry, and Ann began another driving campaign, veering off main highways and onto lonely levee-lined roadways north of Baton Rouge near Port Hudson and then east of the Capital City near New Orleans.

Meanwhile, Detective Jim Steele joined Memry Tucker in a helicopter to determine sites that mimicked the map from the sky. There was one place, on Shell property near the little town of Geismar, Louisiana, which was a close match with the hand-drawn map. There was even a dive bar on the property that fit the description of the building on the map.

Now, what? If Ted pursued a search for his brother's remains, that finding might discount Leila Mulla's confession. He decided the search was worth that risk.

Ted remembered reading about a non-profit organization called Texas Equusearch. Its mission is to assist victims' family members in physical searches to locate their missing and murdered loved ones. Founder Tim Miller was a wiry, outspoken man whose heavily lined face was emblematic of the tragedy and tough work he faced every day. His own daughter, sixteen-year-old Laura Miller, was murdered just a couple of months before Gary Kergan, in September of 1984. Her body was found in a League City, Texas, field more than a year later. Although Tim Miller has always believed he knows the killer's identity, no one has ever been convicted for her murder. Thus, the former construction contractor began Texas Equusearch to help family members search for and recover lost and missing loved ones to their families. Ted contacted Tim Miller and asked him in March 2013 to conduct a body search and dig for Gary Kergan's remains on the Geismar property.

Once permissions were attained from both the property owner and law enforcement, Tim Miller and company arrived with canines, which scoured the area and signaled the most likely dig sites. Next, they set up a camp on Shell property near the Mississippi River levee. Accompanying Tim was his girlfriend, Misty Lee Jumper, and a small army of volunteers, including a gentleman from Atlanta with sonar equipment. There were several tents, one of which acted as the operations center, with aerial maps of the site as it appeared both in 1984 and in 2013. Other tents held refreshments from Sonic Drive-Ins. Once key areas were identified, bulldozers and other pieces of heavy equipment helped cleared out areas of trees. Volunteers combed the dirt, using hand held rakes in the cleaned-out areas. Levee police assisted, along with canine units from two different law enforcement agencies.

Ann Edelman described feeling inspired as she drove up to the scene on Good Friday, March 29, 2013. The "dig city" remained out of view until she reached the top of the levee.

The scene was akin to an archeological dig from Raiders of the Lost Ark. Participants rode around in golf carts. Teams in khaki attire accompanied the Equusearch canines along with two other groups, including the levee police and District Attorney Hillar Moore III, Assistant District Attorney Dana Cummings, and detectives Chuck Smith, Buck Dauthier, Jim Steele, and Memry Tucker. Also on scene was renowned forensic anthropologist Dr. Mary Manhein.

In the thick of things, of course, was Ted Kergan. His $50,000 donation to Texas Equusearch gave them ample resources to conduct a thorough search operation. Even though they were unsuccessful in locating Gary Kergan's body, the search was a success on many other levels. For one, it instigated a friendship between Ted and Tim Miller, which would immensely benefit both. Secondly, Texas Equusearch gave real legitimacy to the search by taking an old murder case and moving it to the attention of law enforcement as well as to the public. Now with momentum building, the body search was underway just days before the grand jury was to meet and determine whether or not to indict Leila Mulla.

Miller felt a close kinship with Ted Kergan. He fought hard to find answers and justice for murder victims' families, having assisted with almost 1,500 cases in forty-two states and a few foreign countries. Members of Texas Equusearch have often actually located victims' bodies. For the rest of the cases, Tim and company hoped they brought some semblance of peace to the victim's loved ones. Ted and Tim both always kept the cases of their loved ones front and center, with files on their desks and even on the seats of their trucks at all times. After getting to know Ted, Tim thought he was one of the most functional human beings in this mostly dysfunctional world.

The Texas Equusearch dig wrapped up on the first of April. Private investigators continued to crisis-cross the country, conducting interviews with friends, relatives, and co-workers of Leila Mulla and Ron Dunnagan, with expenses paid by Ted Kergan. Everyone on the team awaited the grand jury's decision, which was handed down Wednesday, April 3, 2013. Although it was only a wait of a couple of days, the intervening time frame was a painful stretch.

On April 3, Ann Kergan joined her husband in state District Judge Don Johnson's courtroom. District Attorney Hillar Moore III and Assistant District Attorney Dana Cummings were also there when the judge read the grand jury's verdict. Leila Mulla was indeed indicted on first-degree murder charges, although she was not present for the announcement. She continued to be held without bail in the East Baton Rouge Parish Prison, where her attorney delivered her the news.

Ted told media members assembled outside the 19th Judicial District Courthouse, "Twenty-eight years ago, the District Attorney's office pledged to never give up on Gary's case, and it never has. Our family can finally move forward in seeking justice for Gary, who was an unwitting victim in a calculated act of murder. There's still a process to go through. We're going to be part of that process."

Later that day, an indictment celebration and appreciation party for members of Texas Equusearch was held at Larry Tucker's home. Dana Cummings and her team from the district attorney's office attended, along with detectives and private investigators involved in the case. The prevailing mood at the occasion was near jubilant. Finally, so many years later, Leila Mulla had been indicted in Gary Kergan's murder.

However, uncertainty remained. How would Leila Mulla plead? A not-guilty plea meant she would go to trial. The district attorney's office had her confessions and her diaries to use as evidence in any upcoming legal action. Behind the scenes, legal wrangling ensued. Leila's attorney sought a plea deal for his client, meaning she would plead guilty and testify against Ron Dunnagan at his trial in exchange for an agreed-upon prison sentence.

Attorney C. Frank Holthaus pushed for a lenient prison sentence in a plea deal for his client, claiming that Ron Dunnagan forced Leila into prostitution, acting as her pimp. In exchange for a light sentence, Holthaus offered Leila's testimony citing Ron Dunnagan as the murderer of several people, including Gary Kergan. Leila's attorney correctly pointed out that without her testimony, there was little chance of convicting Ron Dunnagan.

Dana Cummings met with Ted Kergan, who maintained what he thought was fair: a thirty-year sentence for Leila in exchange for her testimony against Ron Dunnagan. Ted's insistence upon a thirty-year prison stint for Leila corresponded to the thirty years she remained free after

Gary's death. Dana Cummings was convinced Leila would never accept such a long term in prison, but Ted refused to relent.

Holthaus also refused to budge, asserting that without Leila's testimony, Ron Dunnagan would never be convicted. If the impasse continued, Leila would plead not guilty and go to trial for Gary Kergan's murder. Tension mounted. Ted Kergan and Dana Cummings decided, if the events came down to it, she would try Leila Mulla. The prosecution volleyed this serious message to Holthaus, which Dana Cummings and company felt they had evidence to convict Leila Mulla and would proceed readying for an upcoming trial. In an even more extraordinary move, Ted Kergan thought about cutting Ron Dunnagan loose and putting all the pressure squarely upon Leila Mulla, who faced a no-win decision: take the thirty-year plea deal and testify against Ron Dunnagan at his trial, or plead not guilty and go to trial for the murder of Gary Kergan.

On Friday, April 12, 2013, a little more than a week later, Leila took center stage at a media-filled arraignment. She stood directly in front of Ted Kergan, who once again took his seat on the front bench in the spectator portion of the courtroom, and pleaded not guilty in a tiny, meek voice. After all the back-and-forth drama, Leila picked going to trial over the thirty-year plea deal. She was dressed in drab green prison garb and tan rubber sandals, with her hands cuffed and legs shackled. Her curly, wiry hair was pulled back into a bun. She showed very few ill effects of four months spent in parish prison.

CHAPTER 17

PRETERMIT

In the end, Ted Kergan made the bold move to cut Ron Dunnagan loose. He knew Assistant DA Dana Cummings needed a witness to prosecute Leila's murder case. There were only two people in that Byron Street duplex the night of the murder, and one of them, Ron Dunnagan, wasn't talking. That left only Leila Mulla to divulge the events of November 29, 1984. After all, she had already admitted her involvement.

Back in 1985, Ron's and Leila's liberation had caught Ted Kergan totally by surprise. He had truly believed the State of Louisiana would indict both of them, and subsequently gain convictions against the murderers responsible for putting an abrupt end to his brother's life. Instead, both of the accused were granted their freedom and, for twenty-eight years, lived separate lives in separate states.

The tables were turned, however, this time around. Ted Kergan had earned respect and a seat at the table when District Attorney Hillar Moore, Assistant District Attorney Dana Cummings, and their staff discussed the case's strategy prior to the grand jury meeting. He had seen Leila Mulla's diaries and knew she had confessed several times to killing Gary. Not only was Ted convinced she was the mastermind in the plot to kill his brother, she had just been indicted by an East Baton Rouge Parish grand jury on first-degree murder charges. Although Leila implicated Ron Dunnagan during her confessions, Ron had revealed absolutely nothing up to this point. Ted asked if Ron could be charged later if he was released now. The lawyers in the district attorney's office explained to him that the grand jury could decide to "pretermit," legally defined as "to let pass without mention or notice." Under pretermit, the grand jury took no action against Ron Dunnagan. Thus, he was released but indeed could be charged with murder at a later date. Dana Cummings was skeptical about the choice for pretermit, waving her hands descriptively, telling Ted that Ron would be gone, "Poof! In the wind!"

But the man who had kept tabs on Ron Dunnagan for twenty-eight-plus years only smiled. Ted Kergan thought that pretermit was exactly what he wanted. Sure, it was a bold move, but after all, there were checks and balances. Next, they could concentrate on Leila Mulla's upcoming trial and talk about keeping a plea deal on the table for her, in the event she decided to change her plea to guilty and testify against Ron Dunnagan.

So, Ron Dunnagan was a free man. His release from prison was so immediate, it caught Ted and company off guard; they were used to the legal process being painfully slow, and there had been no time to come up with a plan. Leila's attorney, C. Frank Holthaus, was surprised to find out Ron was being released from prison. That meant the district attorney was indeed focusing the case solely on his client. He would have to prepare to go to trial.

When Ron was given his pretermit pass in April, 2013, Ted found satisfaction in knowing Ron would never really be comfortable, always looking over his shoulder, wondering when the authorities would come for him once more.

Although private investigators began following Ron after his release from East Baton Rouge Parish Prison, they lost track of him within the first hour. Ron was used to living on the streets, which meant he could be almost anywhere. Although he was out of jail, he was hardly what anyone could call free. He had chalked up nearly a dozen prior suicide attempts, so there was also a real possibility that he might kill himself.

It was almost twenty-eight years to the day from when he was originally released from East Baton Rouge Parish Prison for lack of evidence in the murder of Gary Kergan. This time, when Ron was unceremoniously dumped out of jail and onto the streets of Baton Rouge, he was pointed toward a bus stop and given directions to the Salvation Army Homeless Shelter on Airline Highway some ten miles away. Ron was still somewhat confused over his newly found freedom, but he realized he needed his schizophrenia meds, and returned to the East Baton Rouge Parish Prison to obtain the pills. This time he nixed the bus, walked to a gas station and begged a ride to the Salvation Army shelter.

The Salvation Army complex housed a store where used furniture, clothes, and other donated goods were sold. The shelter was around back, on Maribel Drive. Because of the erratic nature of Ron's course across town, Ted Kergan's private investigators lost track of him. Still reeling over the surprise of Dunnagan's sudden release, Larry, Ann, Ted, and one hired investigator fanned out across north Baton Rouge, worrying that Ron Dunnagan, used to living homeless on the streets, could stop under any overpass or bridge and they'd miss him. One of the investigators headed to the Salvation Army Shelter, one of the only places for homeless men on that side of town. He parked in the lot and waited, and eventually saw Ron Dunnagan arrive on foot and go through the front door. Shortly after, the investigator went inside. At 9:00 p.m. on April 4, he confirmed that Ron Dunnagan had checked into the shelter and settled in for the night.

Inside that shelter and inside Ron's head, he was not very clear on why he was a free man, but he knew Gary Kergan's body had not been recovered. The voices in his head continuously echoed in unison, telling Ron his freedom was likely to be short lived.

Tim Miller and Misty Lee Jumper were still in town after

wrapping up the Texas Equusearch dig in Geismar, while Ted and company were scrambling to come up with a plan to contain Ron Dunnagan. Ted approached Tim Miller about appealing to Ron face-to-face, with the goal of hopefully obtaining his murder confession and even the location of Gary's body. Ted and Tim both had a determined attitude in their pursuit of justice, but while Ted's investigative methods were meted out in more of a smooth, covert manner, Tim Miller's way was forceful and direct. Tim told Ted not to worry; he and Misty would be at the Salvation Army Shelter bright and early on April 5. They all knew Ron Dunnagan was headed back home to Bossier City soon and Tim wanted to get that confession first.

When Tim and Misty arrived at the shelter, they found Ron Dunnagan in the parking lot, amid a group of men huddled under the hood of a car, checking out an engine in distress. As a one-time auto mechanic, Ron's help in diagnosing the car's dead battery was legitimate. Tim barged into the group and got their instant attention by offering to help pay for a new battery. Then he offered to give Ron a ride. Ron accepted.

They all got into the dusty pickup truck with Texas license plates and Texas Equusearch stickers, its tires still muddy from the body search dig the previous week. Their first stop was the closest Walmart, to pick up sundries and other basic items, where Tim Miller made a brilliant move, purchasing a pre-paid phone for Ron under the guise of being able to talk to him at any time. Tim's expenses were being picked up by Ted Kergan but he knew Ted would agree to such generosity under these circumstances.

Meanwhile, Ron became infatuated with the perky, fast-talking Misty, who fancied tight t-shirts and jeans and was much younger than Tim. She was sugar-sweet Southern charm meets tell-it-like-it is, and Ron seemed awestruck by her. Both Tim and Misty chatted with Ron as if they had been friends for years. Even with his penchant for paranoia, Ron relaxed. They stopped at Church's Fried Chicken on busy, commercially-choked Government Street, where Ron, much to his chagrin, found himself the center of attention after a diner approached him, recognizing him from a photograph on that morning newspaper's front page. His doughy frame, disheveled mass of white hair, and long white beard made him easily recognizable.

The newspaper story had documented Leila's indictment and Ron's release from prison, so Ron started to walk away from the nosy newspaper reader. He quickly changed his mind and decided to engage, specifically to find out what happened to Leila. When he found out she was still in jail for Gary's murder, Ron was clearly confused. Why was she still in jail while he was free? It didn't make sense. Voices, voices ... all talking to him at once. Ron blinked hard a couple of times and gawked around the room, taking in everything in the small Church's Fried Chicken dining area. He realized that the loudest of the voices was coming from the diminutive Tim Miller.

In his not-so-subtle way, Tim related the story of his own daughter's death and the fact that her murderer had never been charged or prosecuted. He told Ron about his mission of founding Texas Equusearch to search for and find missing persons and murder victims to give peace to their families. Tim even revealed that he and Misty were in the Baton Rouge area to help Ted Kergan find the body of his brother, Gary. He then pressed Ron for the body's location and urged him to put an end to Gary's family's suffering. Without any attempt at a smooth segue, Tim continued by explaining that he and Misty wanted to help Ron return home to his own family. In fact, they wanted to help him in any way they could. If Ron was ruffled by any of Tim's rapid-fire revelations, he never showed it. If Ron thought he was being set up, it appeared he made a decision to go along with it for his own benefit. After all, who else could he turn to for help? He determined he would play along and outsmart both of them.

Misty keyed her phone number and Tim's number into Ron's new prepaid phone while they worked their way down busy Florida Boulevard, one of Baton Rouge main arteries. Ron didn't take his eyes off of her. Meanwhile, Tim glanced in the rearview mirror and confirmed that Ted's investigator was following them in his car.

He saw I-10 cross over Florida Boulevard in the distance, just as they reached the asphalt parking lot of the Greyhound Bus Station. They had missed the first bus to Bossier City, but arrived in plenty of time for the last bus out, at 6:50 p.m. Tim pleaded again for Ron to give up the location of Gary Kergan's body. He tried a number of tactics; he was demanding, then empathetic, and continued alternating the techniques. None of it got any reaction from Ron. He was too busy paying attention to Misty, with her cute manner and enticing brand of chatter. Tim could not help but notice, realizing that Misty could be the key to getting something out of Ron. After saying their goodbyes, Tim and Misty headed to their rendezvous point with Ted Kergan.

It took most of the night to travel the 250 miles to Bossier City, where Ron would bunk with his daughter, Tammy, at her home. For the past few years before his arrest, Ron lived with Tammy; her fifth husband, Larry; and her children, ranging in age from five to seventeen. It was a loud and busy household and Ron longed for peace and quiet.

More than once, Tammy tried to obtain reward money in exchange for turning Ron over to authorities for the murder of Gary Kergan, but she really didn't have any damning information. Larry drove a truck on long, cross-country routes and Tammy didn't see him for weeks at a time. Once, while Larry was home, Ron told him he had beaten a man to death with a baseball bat, but Larry just dismissed the tale. After all, the household was sustained in part, bizarrely enough, by Ron's monthly disability check.

While he was in Bossier City, Ron's new cell phone rang regularly with calls from Tim and Misty. After a week or so, the couple insisted on picking up Ron in Bossier City and bringing him back to Baton Rouge. Tim continually urged Ron to confess the location of Gary Kergan's body. For some reason, Ron agreed to come south with them. Perhaps he was tired of living with Tammy and family in such a noisy household. Maybe he wanted to see Misty again. Tim hoped he was ready to help them retrieve the body.

Ted Kergan went over all of the details of the murder with Tim, including the fact that one of Leila's diary entries, dated November 11, 1984, just a couple of weeks before the murder, talked about the couple shooting guns. Then, Ted and company made a tremendous leap of faith using the hand-drawn map. The mysterious map depicted levees, which are popular rural sites to shoot guns since they are shielded from the road. Ted encouraged Tim to get Ron talking and pinpoint the exact location of their "shooting range." Once Tim succeeded in getting Ron to reveal they indeed shoot guns at the levee in Iberville Parish, on the opposite side of the Mississippi River from Baton Rouge, Tim was determined to have Ron take them to the site. Ron, Misty, and Tim arrived at the West Motel in Port Allen in mid-April, where they checked into two rooms. The next morning, the trio headed down Highway 1 through Plaquemine, then on the River Road to White Castle. Without Ron's knowledge, Tim was being followed by a black SUV driven by Ted Kergan and a silver SUV with Larry Tucker at the wheel. When they stopped to eat at a truck stop casino, the two SUVs parked inconspicuously in the lot.

Ted decided to go inside for a closer look, and Ann Edelman joined him. Would Ron recognize Ted? Ted doubted Ron read any of the front-page newspaper stories bearing Ted's photographs, and they had never been face to face. While an incredulous Larry Tucker watched from his own car, Ted and Ann went into the truck stop. On their way to the restrooms, they passed the booth where Ron, Tim, and Misty lunched. "It was really hard not to come across that table and strangle him," Ted remembered. To be so close to his brother's murderer and not react required supreme self-restraint. Larry was nervous that Ted might try to take matters into his own hands, but soon Ted and Ann were back in their vehicle and that point of danger was over.

Once lunch was over, Tim and Misty got into the F-150 truck, still accompanied by Ron, and the convoy continued off road, into fields and, finally, atop the levee to the location noted in that 1984 diary entry. After almost thirty years, Ron Dunnagan led Tim directly to the place where he and Leila had shot guns on the riverside of the levee so many years before. Tim kept pounding Ron for answers about the murder, about the location of the body. Ron, tired of denying, just clammed up.

After that long and frustrating day, Ron confessed to nothing. Tim and Misty were tired. They returned to their respective rooms at the West Motel and retired for the evening.

Ted and Larry met early the next morning, April 18, at the Waffle House, adjacent to the West Hotel, where they had scheduled a time to powwow with Tim about another strategy to get Ron to talk. It was mid-morning already and Tim had not arrived. What took him so long to walk next door to the Waffle House? Tim finally dashed through the doors of the breakfast joint, flustered, and rambling about how, after numerous attempts, he was unable to get Ron to open his motel room door. The group quickly exited Waffle House and re-convened in the parking lot of the West Motel. Ted put on a baseball cap and sunglasses and positioned himself on a concrete bench, where he had a direct view of Ron's door. He pretended to be reading a newspaper. Meanwhile, Tim retrieved someone from the motel's office to force open the door to Ron's room.

Tim and Misty found Ron Dunnagan lying crosswise on the bed unconscious. On the nightstand sat an empty bottle of his prescription medication. There was vomit everywhere.

Tim immediately called 911. Minutes later, as Ted Kergan looked on from fifty yards away, EMS responders carried a lifeless-looking Ron Dunnagan from his room on a stretcher, his eyes closed and mouth gaping open. No one seemed to be in a hurry. A couple of cleaning ladies who saw the goings-on in Ron's room passed the victim's parade and brushed by Larry Tucker, who was stationed another fifty yards in the opposite direction, leaning against a post.

"What happened to him?" Larry ventured to the cleaning team.

"Took too many meds," one of them answered blankly, as if that was a regular occurrence at the West Motel.

Everyone under Ted Kergan's umbrella knew this was not Ron Dunnagan's first suicide attempt. There were at least ten others, but would this one be successful? Ron Dunnagan was one of two people who knew exactly what had happened to Gary Kergan in the wee hours of November 29, 1984. One of them, Leila Mulla, was lawyered up and in East Baton Rouge Parish prison. Now the other one might have just taken his own life.

Ted was aghast at the prospect of never learning the truth or getting justice for his brother's death. He couldn't even think about that now. He threw down the newspaper and headed to Ron Dunnagan's empty room at the West Motel. Once inside, Ted retrieved Ron's cell phone, hoping to later exchange it for a model with GPS to make it easier to track him. Ted looked for clues and even bagged some of Ron's vomit for the eventual possibility of later testing. Tim and Misty followed the ambulance as it raced east across the Mississippi River bridge to Baton Rouge General Hospital. They looked at each other with the same thought: *Is he dead or alive?*

CHAPTER 18

RON'S NEW FRIEND

Before Ron Dunnagan summoned the hospital chaplain to his bedside in the intensive care unit on the second floor of the Baton Rouge General Medical Center, he endured a day of pestering from well-meaning people. His suicide attempt was as unsuccessful as all the others. He had been unconscious for a long time, and now that he was awake there was a constant stream of visitors. Tim and Misty were ever present, and Tammy and her husband Larry made their way from Bossier City to the Baton Rouge General Hospital.

Each time they entered his curtained-off room in the large communal ward, Tim and Misty tried desperately to get Ron Dunnagan to confess to murder and give up the location of Gary Kergan's body. Misty used Ron's "crush" on her to try to obtain information. Tim pulled out all the stops, including the retribution from God card. Ron said nothing. A private investigator took his turn asking Ron questions but he got no answers. Tammy went into the room and played tough girl at one point, then tried to cajole Ron by tickling his side and feet. Even though Tammy told her father she would not allow him to return to her home upon his hospital release, Ron still gave up nothing.

A day after his suicide attempt, when Ron asked to see the chaplain, they all hoped the old bird had had a change of heart. He had told them he was ready to confess and requested the visit from the man of the cloth. Once the chaplain arrived,

Ron asked the nurse and Tammy to leave the room. He had something to say and he wanted to be alone with the chaplain. What was said between the two remained a mystery. Tammy implored the chaplain to tell her what her father had told him, but he replied that he wouldn't talk without being forced by a subpoena. Tim and Misty posited that nothing was revealed, but nobody really knew for certain. All the while, the ranks of those waiting at the hospital were swelling. While Ted remained in disguise down in the lobby area, Larry Tucker and his wife sat incognito on one side of the second floor waiting, facing Tim, Misty, Tammy, and Larry.

Later that day, on Friday, April 19, Ron was transferred to the hospital's psychiatric ward, where his visitors would be even more restricted. Tammy was fed up by this point and made plans to return home to North Louisiana the next day. Tim, as the head of busy Texas Equusearch, received a call regarding a drowning victim in Lake Charles, so he and Misty exited to make their way to that scene. Meanwhile, Ron agreed to see private investigators two more times, but those conversations went nowhere.

Tim kept in touch by telephone with Ron's social worker at Baton Rouge General and learned that he was still physically very weak. On Wednesday, May 1, Tim and Misty traveled back to Baton Rouge to meet with a private investigator, Ted Kergan, and Ann Edelman. As the group tried to sort out ways to elicit a confession from Ron, Ann Edelman concocted a totally bizarre idea. She had become used to extreme creative thinking while working on the Kergan murder case. Then there was Ted's mantra: *No stone unturned.* Ann asked herself why not do it; it was certainly worth a try. She mustered her courage, then turned to Ted and volunteered to become Ron's newest hospital visitor.

"I know it's a crazy idea but what do you think about me going in to talk to him?" she asked Ted. "I have no expectation of getting his confession but if I could get information about Ron's and Leila's lives together, then I could try to piece together all of these disparate parts we've gathered."

"Why not?" Ted responded, after a long pause. "You will be in a safe environment."

Ann Edelman consulted a psychiatrist who had dealt with schizophrenic patients, to learn more about the affliction and best ways to approach a sufferer. Denial, the psychiatrist said, was a schizophrenic's mainstay. So, Ann began thinking of how to obtain answers from Ron in a friendly, non-threatening way to ease his paranoia and tone down the voices in his head. The premise for her first visit was to deliver a new cell phone, one equipped with GPS, ostensibly from Tim Miller, for Ron to use once he was discharged from the hospital. Ron wasn't aware that the last phone he had, which had been left behind in the motel room during his suicide attempt, had already been retrieved by Ted.

On May 2, Ann got her name on the visitor's list to see Ronald Dunnagan. She went for an evening visit on the following day. Ann thought her best chance to connect with Ron would be through his love of being a clown. So she concocted a story about remembering Ron dressed as a French Quarter clown from trips to New Orleans during her college days. Ann told Ron he was her favorite clown. Then she continued with a personal story about how she promoted a circus show as part of a public relations job early in her career. She produced the show's brochure, trying to deduce whether Ron could read. It was obvious to her he was illiterate, which would explain why Leila was able to write freely about other men and even about him in her diary entries.

Ann introduced empathetic chatter about enjoying the circus and clowns. He responded with enthusiasm and told her how he began his own self-taught career as a clown. He described spending hours in front of the mirror developing clown tricks and making sure the secret steps behind his sleight of hand weren't detectable. Her one-hour session bore fruit; Ron responded to her non-threatening, casual demeanor with conversation about his life, filling in gaps in her knowledge.

He told Ann his two biggest regrets in life were getting married and quitting his job at Exxon. He also relayed the details about the death of his daughter, Angelique. She was struck and killed by a police car as she ran across a multi-lane North Louisiana highway in pursuit of her soon-to-be-ex-husband, who was trying to drive away with her car, a car Ron had given her.

Ann was determined to establish a relationship with Ron and she knew she had to consistently act sweet. She slowly engaged Ron until he ended up substantiating much of what Ted Kergan had already discovered through his own research. Ron told Ann that when he and Leila left Louisiana in November 1984, they indeed went first to San Diego, but found it too expensive and quickly retreated to Las Vegas, where they were arrested mere days later for murder. That revelation meant the duo did follow through on plans to head to San Diego where they forwarded their mail from New Orleans and ate up a few more days while on the lam.

Ann's subtle approach was a welcome relief to the heavy pressure Ron had received from the private investigators and Tim Miller. Ann had taken the first steps brilliantly, especially given that Ron Dunnagan was not a person who had much use for human contact.

Until their first meeting, everything Ted Kergan and his associates knew about Ron Dunnagan was filtered through the eyes of the authorities and members of Ron's unorthodox family. Until that meeting and subsequent ones between Ron and Ann, Ted Kergan had no idea what Ron Dunnagan was really like. Ted had gone from knowing almost nothing about Ron Dunnagan to having his envoy in the hospital room conversing with the man who killed his brother. This scenario was beyond anything he could have imagined.

"If ever the hand of God was touching a situation, this was it," Ann related. "We were pawns. This case had a life of its own. Gary (Kergan) and God were touching this thing and I knew that we were going to win."

Details about that first visit flooded her senses: the feel of the sticky vinyl of the hospital room chair against her skin, the jarring vision of partially dressed Ron laying on his side talking to her. Ann pushed those memories aside and went back to the hospital for another visit three days later, where she found Ron as completely coherent and engaged as before. Ron instructed Ann to leave the door to the hospital room open this time. He added he couldn't do "hanky panky" now because he was through with women.

To Ann's amazement, Ron discussed his failure to achieve an erection in his two sexual forays in the twenty-eight years post Leila. Ron told Ann that after his sexual relationship with Leila, he unsuccessfully tried to have sex a couple of times within a few years and then never tried to have sex again. Besides, he added, it would be unfair to begin any kind of relationship with a woman since he knew he was going to eventually be arrested again. He admitted to Ann that he wanted to die, and told her he would even confess to Gary Kergan's murder if he was guaranteed a swift death. He did not want to become a long-term prisoner on death row.

Ann Edelman waited until her third trip to see Ron before she brought up the story of Gary Kergan's murder. Ron suggested Gary faked his own death by planting blood evidence in the trunk of his own car, but he could see Ann wasn't buying any of that story. As conversation about Gary Kergan ensued between them, Ron began discussing Gary's disappearance as a murder. On the topic of Gary's Cadillac, Ron said it was stupid to leave the car in a parking lot with blood in its trunk. Ron declared he should have torched the car or perhaps dumped it into a bayou. Ron even pondered aloud why, although he was balding then, not one of his hair fibers was found in the car.

Ron recalled that Leila and Gary did go back into the bedroom of the Byron Street duplex on the morning of

November 29, but just to talk; there was no sex involved. He vehemently denied Leila was ever a prostitute. Ron said he bid Gary goodbye at just after 3:00 a.m. Ann posed her next questions as bait, trying to get Ron talking about Gary Kergan. Why was everyone making such a fuss over Gary Kergan?

Ron Dunnagan straightened his back and rose up in bed. He turned his head to face Ann and looked directly into her eyes.

"Gary Kergan was a great guy," Ron said animatedly.

Ann was stunned. Ron's response was not at all what she expected. A great guy? His emphatic response reinforced their belief that Ron was not the mastermind behind Gary's murder. Ron told Ann he believed his next arrest would come within the next six months and talked about how he was being hounded by the police and the private investigators who were hired to find Gary Kergan's body.

Ann's head was spinning when she closed the door to Ron's room behind her. She immediately called Ted for a debriefing, then composed her thoughts on the drive home. Ron's twenty-one-day mandated stay for observation in the psychiatric ward of the Baton Rouge General was winding down. He was scheduled for release on Friday, May 10. Since Ron had no other relative or friend in Baton Rouge, Ann stepped into another pivotal role and became the hospital's contact person for Ron, as well as the person given instructions about his medications, his therapy, and the group home where he could further convalesce after his hospital release. It was Ann who was there to pick him up in her own car when he was released. There was one caveat: She was always followed by private investigators who had their eyes on her at all times.

They traveled back to familiar turf for Ron: The Salvation Army Shelter building on Airline Highway. This trip took them further into the neighborhood behind the facility, winding around until they reached the address of the group home. Officials there had been notified that Ron was on his way. Ann accompanied Ron on a tour of the home and was so horrified by its condition that she had pause about leaving the suspected murderer there. When they reached and peered into the bedroom where Ron would have bunked with another man, Ann and Ron exchanged glances. The frightened look each gave the other was identical. This was a very unpleasant place to live, even temporarily.

Ann had to think quickly on her feet. What should she do with Ron? If she left him there at the group home, would he ever really trust her again, especially after that shared expression of fear? But, where could she take him? Ann asked Ron to follow her outside. Once there, Ann asked Ron if he wanted to stay at the group home. No, he quickly replied. She motioned toward her waiting car. Much to Ron's relief, they got back into Ann's car and headed south on Airline Highway, putting the scary group home in the rear view mirror. They were followed, of course, by the perplexed private investigators. Close to a main intersection at Florida Boulevard, quick-thinking Ann pulled into a cheap motel parking lot and rented a room for Ron Dunnagan. They made a trip to the grocery store and filled a cart with provisions, including his favorite Miss Debbie snack cakes. There, on Airline Highway, tucked away in that motel room, Ron was very content to lie in bed, eat, and watch television. He was once again living the good life, this time sponsored by Ted Kergan. Ann still hoped to obtain a confession or the location of Gary's body from Ron, but it would have been unsafe to be alone with him in the motel room, as she had been at the hospital. Ann picked him up a few days later and they dined together at El Rancho Mexican Restaurant next door to the motel. It was a logistical nightmare lining up private investigators to follow them while they dashed around town or ran errands. Per instructions from the private investigators, Ann found a table in front of a large picture widow, where the couple could be easily observed. Ron's lack of teeth made it difficult to find suitable menu items. Ann's concern was not eating but getting Ron to talk.

After a few weeks, Ron said Ann wasn't spending enough time with him; he wanted to return home. Ann soon waved goodbye to him from her car in front of the Greyhound bus station. Ron took his new phone with him so he could stay in touch with her. When she wasn't talking to Ron on the phone, the device's GPS tracking let her know his exact location. Often, Ann discovered, Ron spent $800 of his $1,100 monthly disability check to reside for a month at a time at the Ramada Inn. There, he had free daily breakfast and maid service. With the leftover $300, he could ride the bus or buy a stash of his favorite junk food.

Ann wanted to visit Ron in Bossier City, to continue their conversation and hopefully gain more substantial clues. Ted Kergan knew she could not left be alone with Ron Dunnagan, so they hatched a plan. Thereafter, when Ann Edelman made trips to see Ron Dunnagan, she did so in a car, complete with a chauffeur dressed the part in a black suit, dark glasses, and a stiff brimmed cap. He wasn't a real chauffeur, but none other than Ted Kergan in yet another of his disguises.

CHAPTER 19

WHAT'S THE DEAL?

Assistant District Attorney Dana Cummings was frustrated while she railed in Mike Erwin's courtroom in response to numerous delays in moving forward with the State's case against Leila Mulla. Her speech became louder and more affected. "My witnesses aren't getting any younger. None of us is getting any younger!" The last court date was Leila's arraignment on April 12, 2013, during which she pleaded not guilty. Her attorney, C. Frank Holthaus, had asked for a continuance of the first date for motions, originally set for September 2013. Now, although they were finally in court, on February 5, 2014, Holthaus had still not filed any motions.

"This case needs to move," continued Dana. "The victim's family needs to have their day in court. If he needs something, he needs to let me know he needs it."

C. Frank Holthaus wore wire-rimmed spectacles and a red tie displaying an image of part of a Scrabble board to boldly complement his gray double-breasted suit. Flanking Dana while they faced Judge Mike Erwin, Holthaus stood erect, his six-foot frame towering over the petite assistant district attorney. He appeared emotionally removed from Dana's rant. In reply, he began one of his own.

"Your honor, I filed a motion and left service copies with the clerk. They are notoriously unreliable. And consequent to knowing that, I mailed copies, but it was snail mail. And apparently, those didn't arrive either. So, I'm warranting to you and to counsel that I will email and hand-deliver those copies to the DA's office when I file things.

"Secondly, this case arises consequent to a two- or three-decade (period), after a missing person's event arrest in New York. And I don't have the information I need about New York. And that is going to be the primary focus of the motion to suppress. It's a two-hour long video statement that was arranged in advance, and it had numerous authorities from Louisiana and New York in it; and she was arrested, even though she had counsel, me, and she was arrested and brought in to interview. I want to know those details because I'm moving to suppress that statement."

"Your honor," Dana fired back, "in the first place, the last time Mr. Holthaus had any connections with Ms. Mulla to my knowledge had been thirty years before. She certainly was not still represented by counsel at that point. The case had long been over. In the second place, he was provided with just about everything I have. If he needs anything else, it was his obligation to let me know."

"Your honor, the case that we're here before is the same case," Frank Holthaus insisted. "There is no law that says thirty years later, it's a different case. The case I represented Ms. Mulla on in this court is this case."

"Mr. Holthaus, if I were to ask you five years ago if you represented Leila Mulla, you would have a said, 'No, I don't even know where she is,'" replied Judge Erwin.

"That's not correct. I would have said, "Yes, I don't know where she is. But if you asked me, 'Do I represent her in an accusation of a homicide?' I would have said, 'Yes, I do.' And I'm asking your honor to allow me ....'"

"You know and I know what this case is all about," interrupted the judge. "You did not represent her for the last thirty years because nobody knew where she was."

"Your honor, I think the case law is clear," interjected Dana Cummings. "That somebody doesn't remain your client for thirty years."

"At the beginning of this statement, she asked to be

told my name," C. Frank Holthaus said, referring to the videotaped interview at the Queens, New York District Attorney's Office. "She couldn't think it up. It ain't an easy name."

"Well, you would think if you were representing her, she would know your name," said Dana.

"You would think..." Holthaus replied. "But, your honor..."

"I love America," answered the judge, dismissing the topic completely.

Next, Frank Holthaus inquired, on behalf of Leila Mulla, whether this would be a capital punishment case. Dana Cummings didn't commit one way or the other.

"See, there you go judge," said Holthaus. "Now, I have got to treat it as a death penalty case because the government is taking the position it can do it later. I'm going to be criticized for not having taken all of these motions that are necessary in a capital case, for not having done it now. So now I have to do it."

"I'd just be happy if he filed something," said Dana.

"All right," concluded the judge. "Pick a date."

Ted Kergan was tired of Holthaus' delay tactics even though he knew it was part of his overall strategy to draw this case out as long as possible, hoping something would happen to eliminate a trial for his client. After all, the defendants and the witnesses were getting old. Evidence was hard to come by. Ted felt like he was back at square one, starting over. For months, he had worked behind the scenes and with Dana Cummings' team, dotting i's and crossing t's. Now, they were facing another damned hiatus. Ted looked over at Leila, dressed in the drab prison uniform, relegated to a bench on the left side with other inmates. She looked older than her forty-eight years. Her curly, kinky hair showed streaks of gray and her face was devoid of emotion which allowed her skin's wrinkles to drag down her face. With all the delays in this case, at least seeing she had aged so harshly as time marched on let Ted feel there was a subtle form of justice at work. Both sides agreed to a new motions hearing on May 15, 2014.

A full moon rose amid Baton Rouge skies early on the ides of May and temperatures dipped to a record-low fifty degrees. It had been an extremely unusual two days. As promised, attorney C. Frank Holthaus filed timely motions on behalf of Leila Mulla, notably a motion to suppress any evidence gathered from Leila's and Ron's Las Vegas apartment address at 4050 Palos Verdes Drive, alleging a warrantless search and seizure.

If granted, this meant Leila's journals and diaries could not be entered into evidence. Without the diaries, the state wouldn't be able to prove that Gary Kergan's murder was premeditated.

Dana Cummings spun into high gear, trying to produce the executed search warrant for the Las Vegas apartment, but authorities in Clark County, Nevada, said the decades-old document no longer existed. Time was running short and Dana Cummings was a bit ruffled. Ted and company were panicking. Larry Tucker called a friend of a friend, powerful Las Vegas attorney Paul Padda. On Tuesday, May 13, Larry had arranged a conference call between Padda, two trusted private investigators, and the heart of the Kergan murder team: Ted, Ann Edelman, and himself. Ted explained that they needed the executed search warrant from December 1985, for the Las Vegas apartment as soon as possible. He added he didn't care what it took or how much it cost. Meanwhile, Ted continued preparing for the motion hearing and there was a volley of calls about the court date.

The next day, the day before the May 15 hearing, Padda sent an email with a succinct yet satisfying message: "Attached are the documents you requested. The original documents are on their way to you." Kergan and company rejoiced over another miraculous turn of events. Ted personally delivered the papers to Dana Cummings, who was once again amazed at Ted's wherewithal. The Kergan investigation team breathed a huge, collective sigh of relief. This was a major turning point for the prosecution. Going forward with the case without those diaries would be much more difficult. Now Leila's diaries and journals proving the murder was planned were entered into evidence. As a result, in lieu of a trial, attorneys for both sides attempted to work out a plea deal. After all, the state had multiple recorded murder confessions from Leila in addition to the diaries. Dana approached Ted for his thoughts. He affirmed that he wanted to again offer Leila Mulla a thirty-year prison sentence if she agreed to testify against Ron Dunnagan.

Dana thought there was no way Leila would agree to that long of a sentence, and suggested they offer her a twenty-year-sentence but Ted said no, no way, reasoning that she could be out of prison in fifteen years for good behavior. Ted strongly felt that thirty years seemed like the perfect number. After all, she had been free, living her own life, for almost exactly that period of time. Thirty years was his best offer, knowing, in all likelihood, she would only serve twenty-five years of that sentence anyway. He also wanted Leila to give him the location of Gary's body but realized that could cause a problem with her testimony. Although Leila confessed several times with the same basic story elements each time, revealing the body's location might nullify or conflict with pieces of her confession stories. That resulting Catch-22 situation meant Ted could not ask for the one thing he really wanted to know.

Holthaus told Dana Cummings he was certain that his client would not accept the lengthy term of the offered plea deal. Dana relayed his thoughts to Ted, who stood firm on his three-decade offer. After unsuccessfully trying to reduce the thirty-year prison term, Leila's lawyer traveled to prison to discuss the stringent plea agreement now on the table. Meanwhile, Marianne O'Donnell, the Dateline producer for NBC, was traveling from New York to Baton Rouge for the

Thursday morning hearing. She was gathering information for a television episode about Gary Kergan's murder. For TV purposes, Leila going to trial for the murder of Gary Kergan was Marianne's best possible dramatic outcome. She had begun working on details for this story shortly after the arrests of Leila and Ron in December 2012.

Ann Edelman had been talking with Ted via telephone off and on all afternoon. Besides discussing the details of a possible plea deal, they had to get ready for the next day's hearing in case they couldn't reach an agreement. Since Ted was playing hardball with thirty years on the table, the court hearing looked more and more likely. Ted called Ann to relay his fear that Leila would not agree to such a lengthy sentence. Ann had an entirely different perspective.

"Oh, they're going to take the deal," Ann said. "If not, we would have heard by now. Her lawyer is working this long and hard." Ann wondered if Leila's attorney was really prepared to go to trial, wondering aloud who would foot the expense of such a legal effort and whether Leila would want to start over with new legal representation, which this time would have to be a court-appointed attorney.

At 5:30 p.m., Wednesday, May 14, Ted called Ann Edelman, and jubilantly gave her the good news that Leila Mulla had indeed just accepted the tough terms of the plea agreement. They took time to relish this moment of triumph before their thoughts went to Wade. Ted cut the call short so he could deliver the good news to Wade, and told his nephew to pack a bag and head to the Detroit airport. He wanted Wade to be in the courtroom the next day to see his father's murderess sentenced to thirty years in prison. The best flight arrangement Ted could make at that late hour got Wade to Houston, where a waiting car drove him several hours to Ted's Lafayette home. Even though it was supposed to be a done deal and his nephew would be there to witness Leila Mulla take the plea, Ted tossed and turned all night.

He didn't feel at all rested when he entered Mike

Erwin's tenth floor courtroom the next day, May 15, 2014. Rumors of more delays were once again swirling. Ted feared Frank Holthaus was going to ask for another continuance. Once again, Leila Mulla, in her army green jumpsuit, was in attendance among the male prisoners in their orange jumpsuits. Ted noticed that on this day her hair was dyed, with no more traces of gray.

One by one, the male prisoner's cases were heard and they disappeared back through the door and into their cells. Another defendant was called from the audience. His attorney recited details from his case and their proposed [?] resolution. The judge ordered this particular defendant to write "I will not take drugs" a thousand times, an old-school-style punishment he often meted out.

The court stood in recess. Leila was alone in prisoner row on the left side of the courtroom. She stared straight ahead, undistracted by the courtroom's noise. Behind the gate, the case's ever-present gaggle of reporters chatted away on the front left row of the spectator side of the courtroom.

Ted tore his gaze away from Leila to greet District Attorney Hillar Moore III, who had just arrived. He introduced Moore to Wade, who was now in Louisiana for only the third time since he and his mother moved to Michigan three years after his father's murder. When Dana Cummings finally entered the courtroom, she was all smiles, shaking hands with Ted and Wade, before making her way back to the judge's chambers. C. Frank Holthaus quickly followed behind her, up the aisle and back into chambers. Within a few minutes, the judge and lawyers were all in their places and court was back in session.

"All right," said Judge Erwin. "Let's do Leila Mulla."

"There's been a change of plea," noted C. Frank Holthaus. He explained that Leila Mulla was pleading guilty to a lesser charge, manslaughter, and that she had accepted a thirty-year prison sentence. The judge asked Leila to raise her right hand, which she did with difficulty since they were attached with cuffs.

"First, you have a right to a lawyer," said the judge. "Has he explained the consequences of your decision and your constitutional rights? You are waiving your rights to a jury trial."

"Yes, sir," responded the meek version of Leila.

"Leila Mulla will be cooperating in the prosecution of Ronald Dunnagan," Dana Cummings explained.

"She will be thrilled to do that," responded C. Frank Holthaus.

In the hallway outside the courtroom, members of the media surrounded Ted, Ann, and Wade Kergan. Some quickly filed online news updates. By the time Ted joined Ann Edelman and placed a call to Larry Tucker, who had missed the big day because of an obligation to remain at his remote vacation home in North Carolina, Larry was already jubilant. He had already received a news alert and he knew Leila had pled guilty and was subsequently sentenced to thirty years in prison for manslaughter.

Doris Reiners and Janet Hebert were two of Ted's longtime colleagues who knew and worked with Gary Kergan. They traveled from Lafayette to be in the courtroom for the guilty plea. So did Gary Wilkerson, Ted's close friend and president of Kergan Brothers, the company Ted and Gary Kergan started in the late 1970s and which still embraced the word "Brothers" in their title so many years after Gary's passing. Many of the investigators were there, including District Attorney's office investigators Chuck Smith and Jim Steele, Memry Tucker and Buck Dauthier.

They discussed who would head to Louisiana State Penitentiary to tell the ailing Bob Howle the news. On the courthouse steps, District Attorney Hillar Moore and Assistant District Attorney Dana Cummings made celebratory statements to the media. Just inside the courthouse doors, C. Frank Holthaus waited, staring through a full-length wall of windows at the gathering, not particularly in a hurry to step into the media limelight. As soon as everyone in Ted Kergan's party moved on to continue their celebration, Holthaus finally made his way toward the cameras. Members of the media threw out a few questions as Holthaus collected his thoughts. One reporter asked Holthaus why his client didn't make a statement. Another asked why Leila didn't apologize.

"We don't recommend people say they're sorry," Holthaus answered. "Victims are not often available for the word 'sorry.' It's open for manipulation. So, I just don't recommend it."

"Do you know where Ron Dunnagan is?"

"Yes. He's in Shreveport, probably drinking frozen margaritas and eating ballpark nachos."

C. Frank Holthaus was right about a couple of things. Ron Dunnagan was indeed in North Louisiana, but he was in Bossier City, not Shreveport. And, yes, Ron Dunnagan was totally oblivious to the day's proceedings in Baton Rouge. He had no idea a storm was brewing.

CHAPTER 20

BACK IN TOWN

Ted Kergan had the whole summer to ponder Ron Dunnagan's probable grand jury indictment. Leila Mulla had taken her plea deal and was now incarcerated at Louisiana Correctional Institute for Women, for the better part of the next three decades. One down, one to go. Ted had been in New York City to witness Leila's arrest and he planned to be in Bossier City after Ron Dunnagan's indictment when authorities took him into custody. No stone unturned.

On September 4, 2014, Ted had his bags packed and a private jet waiting at Baton Rouge Metro Airport. It was the day the grand jury met to decide whether or not to indict Ron Dunnagan. Ted planned to fly to Bossier City as soon as the indictment was handed down, to be on hand when authorities got there to arrest Dunnagan for his brother's murder. This arrest was Ron Dunnagan's third. Ted felt confident, finally, that things would go as the State planned. He had no doubt the grand jury would vote to indict Ron Dunnagan. Leila Mulla had already taken the plea deal and agreed to testify against him at his trial.

Once again, as they had on so many court dates before, Ted met Ann Edelman downtown at the Capital Hilton for breakfast. They went over another of Ann's outlines for the day's agenda, particularly Ted's post-indictment talking points for the press. Ann also brought along a packed bag. She planned to be on that flight to Bossier City, as well.

They talked optimistically about the indictment and

Ron's future trial while they walked the few blocks to the courthouse. Making their way to the tenth floor courtroom, they saw Dana Cummings standing at the end of the long corridor, talking with two other attorneys from her office, Ted just assumed they were bantering back and forth, working out the case's legal options. He and Ann spanned the stretch of the hallway with determined, confident strides.

When they got close, Dana greeted them, asking how they felt.

"Great!" Ted and Ann said, almost in unison.

"No, you're not," responded Dana. The smiles evaporated from Ted's and Ann's faces.

Standing at the end of the hallway, Dana quickly went on to explain. Leila Mulla had filed post-conviction relief papers, citing "ineffective counsel." She had also decided not to testify against Ron Dunnagan.

Deflated again. Another delay.

Dana and her team poured over legal options and the ramifications of each one. Mere moments later, C. Frank Holthaus motored down the same hallway, his body angled forward like a speedboat lurching ahead. His client, Leila Mulla, waited for him in a private room at the end of the tenth floor corridor. Lawyer and client had spent time alone together before Holthaus called for Dana Cummings to join them. Ted Kergan and Ann Edelman were ushered into another private room on the same floor, where they waited, nervous as cats while time crawled and nothing happened. For Ted and Ann, the wait in the private room to hear the grand jury's outcome continued for hours, but felt like days. Detective Chuck Smith came by to visit them. So did Memry Tucker and Detective John "Buck" Dauthier.

Dana eventually returned to their room to report that both issues had been resolved. The assistant district attorney threatened to charge Leila Mulla with first-degree murder if she reneged on testifying against Ron Dunnagan. Dana had also reminded Leila that she confessed to Gary's murder multiple times on tape. Ted Kergan's stomach churned, his breakfast was now inching back up his throat. He had just taken yet another roller coast ride in the halls of justice, this one before ten that morning.

Finally, they received the call to come to the courtroom. Once all the players were in place, the judge called for the decision. As quickly as it began, it was over. The grand jury brought back an indictment against Ron Dunnagan. At last, there was the good news Ted Kergan and his supporters had hoped for.

Dana Cummings joined a scheduled conference call with FBI profilers to coach her team about how to approach Ron Dunnagan when they traveled to Bossier City to arrest him for second-degree murder. Ann Edelman, who had spent so much time with Ron, had already given the profilers background information during an earlier session with Chuck Smith, who was super diligent researching the case as an investigator for the District Attorney. Smith helped Ann fill out a comprehensive questionnaire about Ron Dunnagan shortly after she befriended Dunnagan in the spring of 2013. Profilers honed in on Ron as an institutional man, suffering from schizophrenia, who would be happy to serve time in prison.

"I think he'd be very comfortable there," ventured one of the profilers. "I mean he'd have his medicine. 'Three hots and a cot' for every inmate. It's all right there for him."

They touched on topics about how to structure interview questions and about how he is receptive to women interviewers. A question Ron asked during his last interview with detectives stuck with everyone there.

"You don't have a body, do you?"

Detectives originally took the approach that Ron Dunnagan was playing the part of a savvy killer who knew he disposed of Gary Kergan's body so well that no one would ever find it. Perhaps Ron was just trying to find out if additional evidence had surfaced. Naturally, detectives wanted to know how to handle the question when it came up in future interviews.

"The answer is, you don't need the body," responded a female FBI profiler on the other end of the call. "We just finished publishing something about 'no body' homicides and this is the most frequent thing with somebody dismembering and getting rid of a body. They get rid of it under the very naive and juvenile notion that if there's no body, they can't possibly be prosecuted for the homicide, which obviously, as we all know, that's not even close to being true. What that is, though, is that's very reflective of his mindset in where he's at and what the spot patterns are. The answer is pretty easy. The interviewer can tell him, 'You don't need to have a body to prosecute for homicide and it's been done successfully,' and lay a path for the legal precedence for that happening across the country."

"The interviewer could say, 'That was true thirty years ago, but it's not true anymore,'" chimed in a male profiler on the call. "And now, over the last probably ten years, there have been dozens of cases and there's dozens more each year of successful prosecutions on 'no body' cases."

After the call, the entire Baton Rouge contingency moved to District Attorney Hillar Moore's office to devise a plan to send detectives to arrest Ron and return him to Baton Rouge. Although it was getting late in the afternoon, no one seemed worried that Ron Dunnagan might read about his indictment online or in the media and decide to flee. In Dunnagan's world, current events as well as local and national news were nowhere on his radar. He remained in a totally insular existence.

"Where is Dunnagan?" Chuck Smith inquired.

"He's in Bossier City, at the Ramada Inn Bossier Convention Center," Ann Edelman replied confidently. After all, she remained in touch with Ron via the cell phone for which Ted continued to pay the bills. The telephone was equipped with GPS, and in addition Ron continually updated

Ann on his whereabouts.

Hillar Moore got off the telephone on the far side of his office.

"OK, I got the governor's helicopter for tomorrow morning," he said. From there, a plan developed to apprehend Dunnagan. Chuck Smith and Jim Steele were assigned to take the helicopter north to State Police Headquarters nearby and work out a plan with Bossier City police to arrest Ron Dunnagan at the Ramada Inn. After everything was settled, Dana Cummings looked at Ted Kergan and Ann Edelman.

"So, when are ya'll going to Bossier City?" Cummings asked with a knowing grin. Ted and Ann just laughed. Once out of the district attorney's office, the two headed straight to Baton Rouge Metro Airport, where the private plane waited to take them to Bossier City. After the hour's flight, a rental car was waiting for them at the charter plane terminal and they drove to their accommodations at the Margaritaville Hotel and Casino. After a sushi dinner, Ted splurged on a $4,000 pair of binoculars at Bass Pro Shop. He didn't want to miss any part of the next day's arrest and he figured they wouldn't be able to get very close to Ron Dunnagan. Then, they headed to a convenience store to buy props such as newspapers and magazines to hide behind the next day at the scene of the arrest. Even though the arrest wasn't scheduled until 8:00 a.m., Ted and Ann were dressed and ready to go at 6:15 the next morning. They couldn't wait to see Ron Dunnagan back in custody. He had been free for seventeen months following the grand jury's decision to pretermit. Their anticipation was great, knowing that Ron Dunnagan was going to be arrested and charged once again with Gary Kergan's murder and Leila Mulla was going to testify against him.

When they pulled into the Ramada Inn parking lot, Ted positioned the car so Ann would have a bird's eye view of the hotel's entrance from the driver's seat. As they talked, Ann spoke confidently because she knew all about the layout of the Ramada Inn, including the location of Ron's room close to the buffet area, having visited there before, when Ted Kergan posed as her chauffeur.

Ann suggested Ted go inside and wait in the breakfast area, pretending to be just another overnight guest reading the newspaper and eating from the buffet. After a short time, three Bossier City police cars passed Ann's position and parked on the other side of the lot. Ted texted Baton Rouge Investigator Chuck Smith to let him know they were there. In turn, Chuck also informed fellow deputies, adding that neither Ted nor Ann would be anywhere close nor in any way interfere with Ron's arrest.

Barely five minutes passed before Chuck and deputies removed an extremely disheveled and freshly awakened Ron Dunnagan from the hotel and into the back seat of one of the police cars. Ted emerged from the hotel, Ann got out of the car, and true to their word, they stood side by side to watch the police cars from afar as they drove off with Ron Dunnagan in tow.

An overwhelming sense of satisfaction washed over Ted and Ann. They hugged, and Ted expressed deep appreciation of everything Ann had done which led to his moment. Then they looked at each other, both thinking the same thing. *We've reached an entirely new level.* Once the two were back in Baton Rouge, they got into Ted's car and were quickly in route back to the Capital Hilton, where this crazy episode began early the day before.

"You know where we need to go now?" Ted asked Ann.

"Yes, to Byron Street," Ann said, nodding her head knowingly. The murder scene wasn't far from the airport, so they quickly arrived at that lot. There, Ted and Ann had a moment, a spiritual celebration with Gary.

Once back in the car, Ted called Wade.

"He's indicted," Ted said loudly into the phone. "He's behind bars where he belongs."

Emotions ran high for both of them.

Ten days later, on September 15, 2014, Ted Kergan once again took the elevator up to the tenth floor for Ron Dunnagan's arraignment. It took everything he had not to shout "Yes, you ARE guilty!" when Ron pled not guilty to the second-degree murder charge.

There had been many times in the past when Ted maneuvered himself into close proximity of Ron Dunnagan. He had actually been close enough for Ted to touch him at the West Baton Rouge lunchroom in the spring of 2013, when Ted and Ann had followed Ron and Tim Miller. Ted had also been chauffeur for visits between Ann Edelman and Ron in Bossier City. But, that day in court, after the arraignment ended, from his regular front row position, Ted quickly rose and stood up very tall, all six foot four of him. He took one large step toward the gate that separated spectators from the courtroom sanctuary, where Ron was surrounded by a couple of deputies.

Ron Dunnagan sensed Ted stirring as he got into position at the gate. Ted believed Ron could feel Ted Kergan's eyes burning through his right side and into his entire being. When Ron swiveled his head, his eyes met the fury in the eyes of Ted Kergan. Their gazes locked and held for the longest twenty seconds ever. A hush fell as the entire courtroom watched. Finally, Ted Kergan turned and stormed down the aisle and out into the corridor, where reporters were waiting.

"I wanted to make sure it registered with him who I was," explained Ted to Baton Rouge Advocate reporter Joe Gyan. "I think it clicked. I think I look enough like Gary. If he hadn't been looking at me, it would have been very disappointing. I was very pleased with the exchange. I'd love to tell him I've been tracking him for thirty years."

It was shortly after the thirty-first anniversary of Gary's death, on November 29, 2014, that Ron Dunnagan's trial date was scheduled. All eyes, those in the district attorney's office and those in Ted's entourage, focused on July 9, 2015, the day Ron's trial for second-degree murder was set to begin. Dana

Cummings began to form her game plan, lining up witnesses and untangling the complicated timeline. Meanwhile, Ted continued seeking answers just as he had for thirty-one years, this time turning to nationally recognized experts in criminology and toxicology. Ted turned over to these experts the same data he had given to his private investigators and other researchers through the years; copies of crime scene photos containing images of what appeared to be blood evidence, copies of the diaries in which Leila Mulla penned how she and Ron could have practiced poisoning on animals they purchased, a copy of the curious map, and, of course, copies of reports concerning the blood in the trunk.

***

After studying the crime scene photos, the criminologist analyzed the position of the blood, noting that only cast-off splattering was located, and that it was three feet or lower on the duplex's bedroom walls. She believed Gary Kergan was never poisoned, as this evidence suggested that he was not lying on the floor, but rather was seated upright as he fought for his life in the bedroom of that Byron Street duplex.

One toxicologist posited that arsenic poisoning was ordinarily done incrementally and thus, one dose of poison in a glass of wine would not have caused Gary Kergan to choke or fall to the floor.

Once the experts weighed in, it seemed highly unlikely that Gary was poisoned. Yet, Leila had already confessed that she poisoned him. How could she be telling the truth? Was she telling the truth about anything? Knowing she was the star witness for the prosecution, he was not about to question anything she confessed, particularly anything that could convict Ron Dunnagan.

With just a month to go until the trial, momentum-crushing news came down. The trial was postponed until September 8, 2015, because of a witness's scheduling conflict. Then, less than a week later, Ted Kergan had an accident during a fishing trip with his son and shattered his shoulder. The summer of 2015 was not turning out as Ted expected.

In August, Ted joined Dana Cummings and R.E. Thompson, one of the original detectives on the case, at the site of the former duplex on Byron Street. Dana was preparing Thompson as a witness for the upcoming trial. She had some shocking news for Ted. State Police uncovered more evidence from the scene of the 1984 murder. Blood splatters were discovered on a ceiling tile from Byron Street. However, once those tiles were tested, lab workers determined that not only was the blood on the tile not a match to Gary Kergan's DNA, but that the DNA on those ceiling tiles belonged not to a male, but to a female, and not to Leila Mulla. Ted was speechless. How could that be? He began to worry about how this finding might derail Ron Dunnagan's trial. Ted called Ann Edelman.

"Are you driving?" Ted asked her.

"Yes," she replied.

"Then pull over."

After Ted relayed the news to Ann, he began to theorize that the evidence on the ceiling tile could throw Ron's trial off track and dilute the case against him. Ted wondered if they should engage their own DNA experts.

After her initial shock, Ann Edelman had an entirely different reaction.

"Maybe they killed more than one person there," she told Ted. "Now it all makes sense. If they were serial killers, maybe that's why Leila took a thirty-year plea deal. She doesn't want any further investigation if there are more bodies out there."

It always seemed curious that Leila agreed to such a lengthy plea deal. Dana Cummings had certainly been surprised, thinking there was no way Leila would take it. Even though in their discussions Ted held fast to the thirty-year sentence, Dana acquiesced to his demand, knowing she could have rolled the dice and gone to trial herself. The case and the evidence were decades old, any outcome might have been possible, including a probable outcome that meant Leila would serve less than thirty years. Yes, it had surprised everyone that Leila took the plea deal, as if wanting to put the case behind her as quickly as possible. Was there additional evidence Leila was afraid might be uncovered?

Ted wasn't ready to open that or any other Pandora's Box. Leila Mulla was in prison and was once again committed to testify against Ron Dunnagan in less than ten days. Ted was counting on Leila telling the same story about the night of the murder. Her version implicated Ron, which would, hopefully, secure a conviction sending Ron to prison too. Whether they committed one murder or many murders, Ted Kergan's concern was keeping both of them behind bars for killing his brother for as much of their lifetimes as possible.

CHAPTER 21

AT LAST

The Honorable Michael R. Erwin entered the 19th Judicial Courtroom where he had presided over an assortment of proceedings for the last twenty-four years to the familiar "All rise." It was precisely 9:30 a.m., Tuesday, September 8, 2015. He glanced over his glasses and found Ted Kergan, his family, friends, and associates, who filled up the first several benches on the right side of the courtroom. Looking inside the courtroom from the doorway, a short dark-stained wooden fence with a gate in the middle dissected the room. Before the gate, in the two rear quadrants, benches on both sides of the room held those waiting for their names to be called. Beyond the gate, only authorized personnel came and went freely. Prisoners were escorted into that area via a side door, and all others only went through it when their names were called.

The courtroom was packed. Numerous members of the press waited for Ron Dunnagan's trial to begin from where they were seated on the left front row. The trial was front page news in Baton Rouge's daily paper, and its long-time crime reporter, Joe Gyan, had been following the story since the arrests of Ron and Leila in 2012.

Today he was joined by competing print journalists from Baton Rouge, Lafayette, and New Orleans, as well as by a trio of regional television reporters. Awaiting news from the trial were media outlets from Leila's hometown of Kent, Ohio, and those from Astoria, N.Y., where she lived when she was arrested. Dateline NBC was also present, following the case.

Within the gated section of the courtroom, Dana Cummings shook hands with Ted, Ann, and Wade Kergan, before taking her seat directly in front of them. Her no-nonsense taupe suit and short bob hairstyle were softened by a burgundy blouse. Dana greeted Ron's attorney, public defender Susan Hebert, shortly thereafter, when she entered, green garment bag slung casually over one shoulder. The two had been acquainted for two decades, but this was the first time they tried a case against each other. Susan, who wore a black structured jacket and black floral print skirt, walked over and began whispering in Dana's ear. Dana turned and introduced her to Gary Kergan's family, all the while Susan continued whispering in Dana's ear. When she finished, Susan disappeared out of the same door that allowed prisoners to be brought into the courtroom. The garment bag held Ron's clothing for the trial. It was time for him to get ready.

On the left side of the interior part of the courtroom were the usual inmates clad in bright orange prison jumpsuits, accompanied by uniformed police officers. Today there was also a woman dressed in an army green drab prison jumpsuit. The prisoners, wearing hand and leg shackles and awaiting their turn in the legal limelight, turned around when Susan Hebert re-entered the courtroom.

A clerk began calling names from the day's docket and individuals made their way with their attorneys to the podium to face various charges. Judge Erwin meted out the next steps in each prisoner's judicial journey in monotonous tones. One attorney argued that his client, who had been waiting a couple of years for his trial, should be able to be tried as part of that day's proceedings. This supposition brought Dana Cummings to her feet.

"I feel the need to speak for the State," she proclaimed. "The trial for our thirty-year-old case has been bumped several months. It was supposed to be first thing today."

The frustration from so many delays, particularly the last one resulting in the postponement of the trial date from early July until September, spilled out in Dana Cummings' abrupt interruption. The tension and anticipation leading up to this trial date were boiling over. Dana was determined to not let this other attorney push his client to the forefront of the court's docket. She had delivered bad news at so many twists and turns in this case, that she would do all she could to prevent Ted Kergan from being disappointed again. Sensing the counselor's mounting exasperation, Judge Erwin turned toward Susan Hebert and confirmed that she would be trying the case for the defendant. She nodded and the judge called for a recess and ushered both Dana Cummings and Susan Hebert behind the courtroom and into his chambers. Within five minutes, the two lawyers emerged from the back room. Dana briskly headed outside the courtroom to talk with Ted and Ann Edelman.

Judge Mike Erwin realized a lot of people had waited a long time for this day, however, he was suffering a personal dilemma. He felt uneasy about his role as presiding judge in the matter, and wanted to recuse himself because of contributions from Sonic to his political campaign for judge. He was aware that by continuing as presiding judge under such circumstances, he could be writing the defense's grounds for appeal should Ron Dunnagan be convicted, as his counsel would surely allege that it was a conflict of interest which served as a detriment to his ability to act impartially. Dana had received a telephone call first thing that morning from Judge Mike Erwin's clerk, informing her that the judge was considering recusal.

Judge Erwin had been re-elected to the bench in November 2014. The donation in question was from a Sonic Drive-Ins franchisee Larry Tucker, who had a longtime friendly relationship with the judge. During the time of the conference between Dana and Ted out in the hallway, Judge

Erwin continued through the day's docket filled with alleged thieves and drug dealers while everyone who had assembled for Ron Dunnagan's trial was left waiting.

At last the court emptied of other offenders. It had been two years and nine months since Ron Dunnagan had been re-arrested for the murder of Gary Kergan. The wheels of justice had moved ever so slowly, and now it seemed they might come to another halt. At 11:00 a.m., Judge Erwin summoned both lawyers to the bench for a hushed conversation.

"I spoke to Ted Kergan," said Dana. "The contribution did not come from him."

"I know. It came from his company," replied the judge.

"No, there was a Sonic that is owned by Larry Tucker," clarified Dana.

"Larry Tucker?" asked the judge.

"...who was a friend of the victim, and then there are Ted's Sonics. Ted thought it was a bad idea and he did not (contribute)," continued Dana. "Larry did it. I asked my appellate people to do a little research and they did. They said that you have more than fulfilled your duty by disclosing it, as long as you don't think that it would cause you to have issues."

"I thought Ted had given money too," said the judge. "I didn't realize he didn't."

"No, he felt like it was not appropriate," responded Dana.

"Okay, that's fine with me," allowed Susan Hebert.

"All right," said the judge, signaling the trial was to finally begin.

"And one other thing that maybe I just need to put on the record because we did try to talk negotiation," said Susan Hebert. "I know that the state did make us an offer to plead way back on the manslaughter and the robbery (charges). So I just want to put that on the record that (Ron) did turn that down. And then we did some talking about possibilities, you know, that would help him if he would disclose, if he knew where the body was. And we were never successful with that."

That plea offer to Ron Dunnagan had been a bold one. If Ron revealed the location of Gary Kergan's body, all charges would be dropped and he would go free. Ted and Dana made it as simple as possible. Still Ron refused the plea agreement, leaving Ted and everyone else with an obvious question: What would make him refuse the chance to become a free man and instead stand trial, in a case where the woman testifying against him had already confessed multiple times and had implicated him every single time? Was it just the opportunity to be in the same room with Leila Mulla once more? After all, Ron had not seen her since they were separated in Las Vegas in 1984. They had not seen or spoken to one another in the ensuing thirty-one years. Supposedly, she was the great love of his live.

But Ron Dunnagan was schizophrenic and denial was his mainstay. There was no way he would ever admit he was a murderer. Besides, given his paranoid nature, how could he trust the prosecution? Even with the generous offer on the table, he could not, would not, admit he killed Gary Kergan, much less reveal where his remains were located.

The judge and lawyers ended their sidebar conversation, and another short recess was called prior to beginning this second-degree murder trial for a crime committed more than thirty years before. The silence was broken by the cling-clanging of the prisoners' leg shackles as he was escorted out of the courtroom via a side door. Ron re-entered through the same door minutes later. His hair was shorter than it had been for his last court appearance but still somewhat disheveled and parted oddly on one side. He wore old school penny loafers and no socks. After he sat down, Ron put on a pair of preppy-looking tortoiseshell glasses.

Susan Hebert took her seat next to Theo Jones, who was assisting her in the case. The young man, who had recently finished law school and awaited results from the bar exam, sat between Susan Hebert and Ron Dunnagan. At 11:10

a.m. on September 8, 2015, Judge Michael Erwin re-entered the courtroom from his chambers, and five minutes later, prospective jury members entered and made their way to benches in the back half of the courtroom.

"Ladies and gentlemen, good morning," began Judge Erwin.

"My name is Mike Erwin. I'm the judge in this matter. Dana Cummings is from the district attorney's office. Susan Hebert is the criminal defense lawyer, and Mr. Dunnagan is the defendant.

"Now, I'm going to tell you this right now. I don't know how many of you read the newspaper this morning, but it was headlines in the newspaper, this case. The newspaper is not evidence. The only way you can make a decision in this case is based on evidence that comes from the witness stand. So, if you read anything about this case or heard anything about this case or know anything about this case, then you have to put that aside or not pay attention to what the paper says, and the news reporters or radio or television people say."

Next, he admonished anyone in the jury pool who attempted to shirk his or her jury duty and waxed on eloquently about how jury service was the most important civic duty that a person could perform with the exception of military service.

"So, as we sit here right now, the defendant is presumed to be innocent. And under the law you must presume him to be so, until and unless, the state, through the district attorney, proves that he is guilty of the main charge or any lesser charge. The burden of proof in all cases is upon the state. The defendant is not required to prove anything or present any evidence. The defendant has a constitutional right to not testify. And, if the defendant chooses not to put on any evidence, then you can't hold that against him. You're going to hear in this case that the burden of proof on the state is proof beyond a reasonable doubt."

Ah, reasonable doubt. That no man's land between reason, common sense, and one hundred percent certainty. The selected jurors had to be convinced beyond a reasonable doubt that Ron Dunnagan committed second-degree murder, which means the killing of a human being with the specific intent to kill or inflict great bodily harm. The three elements included in the state's burden of proof are always the confirmation of the murderer's identity, that a human being has actually been killed, and that there is specific intent to inflict great bodily harm.

A group from the jury pool was called to the jury box for questioning. Amid myriad questions, Dana Cummings posed this one to a perspective juror.

"The defendant is old. Are you going to be sympathetic to the defendant because he's older?"

No, replied that particular juror. However, minutes later, another prospective juror, a young female, admitted to feeling overwhelmed. "It's (the case) is thirty-one years old. I do see the defendant over there. I mean, I don't know."

"Are you feeling some sympathy the defendant?" Dana asked. The young woman nodded her head.

Dana continued her round of questioning. When Susan Hebert talked to the prospective jurors, she addressed the same young woman.

"Let's just talk a little bit about Mr. Dunnagan. You said he looks like a grandfather. Are you feeling actual sympathy because of his age? Or, you know it's not every day that we have a thirty-one-year-old case that comes up here. This is pretty much, I would say, one of a kind. So, is it just his appearance that surprises you, that he's elderly at this point, because it's been thirty years?"

The young woman answered in the affirmative.

"But you don't just feel sorry for him," asked Susan Hebert.

"No, I don't," said the prospective juror. "I don't know him. But I just look at him and try to imagine thirty-one years ago, is what I'm really trying to do."

Meanwhile, Ron Dunnagan removed his glasses and remained alert, occasionally shaking his hands and turning his upright head very slowly in hawk-like fashion. He swiveled side to side in his chair during jury questioning. At one point, he casually placed one arm over the back of the chair, looking very relaxed. Once the panel of twelve jurors and one alternate were agreed upon by the defense and the state, Judge Erwin re-addressed the concept of reasonable doubt.

"If you're putting together a puzzle, let's say of a dog. And you start fitting it together and fitting it together and fitting it together. And you can pretty much tell at some point, even though you don't have all the pieces of the puzzle in there, that it's going to turn into being a dog. And some of those pieces might be missing, but you can still tell it's a dog. Does that help anybody?"

A chorus of "yes, sirs" followed.

Dana Cummings had another point she wanted to make to be certain the jury understood.

"The person who has committed the crime is in control of that crime scene. They choose whether or not they put gloves on, they choose whether or not they put a mask on, they choose whether they committed it at a Circle K or a dark parking lot. They choose where they throw the gun in the river or they put the gun under the seat of their car, where they leave the gun at the crime scene. Do you get where I'm going with this?

"The defendant is very much in control of what's left behind. And I add, I like to make that distinction with juries so that, you know, because a lot of times it's like, well, you know, there was no whatever, no gun. There was no gun there. Well, he was apprehended a week later. There was no gun there? He had a week to dispose of a gun."

Some jurors nodded. Dana moved on to question individuals in the jury pool on how they felt about such an old cold case.

"I'm okay with it," replied one woman. "It seems like things you do, except that it's murder, things you do when you're young and stupid shouldn't always carry over thirty-one years, but murder, that's a different case."

"And that's such a good point," said Dana. "I mean, because we all do things when we're young, those foolish mistakes of youth, but murder is not in that category. And I think you made a really, really good point. And that's why there's no prescriptive period for murder. That's why you can prosecute it anytime because that is not a crime that society is willing to go, oh well, it's a silly mistake; or it was a mistake."

There was another subject Dana Cummings needed to broach to get a reading from these members of the jury pool. She had to find out what they thought about the state making a deal with Leila Mulla in order to get her to testify against Ron Dunnagan. How did they feel about her credibility as a witness? Initially, the answers were tepid; some prospective jurors admitted it would be difficult to keep an open mind. One went so far as to say he believed a witness might lie to get a plea deal. There were confusing looks all around.

"Let me put it to you like this," offered Judge Erwin. "Sometimes you have to make a deal with the devil's little brother to get the devil. Do you understand that? And that's what happens in a lot of criminal cases."

After Dana Cummings wrapped up her questioning, it was Susan Hebert's turn and she was ready to make her own points.

"One of the things the judge said a few minutes ago caused me a little concern, and it's something we all have to go through here. I've had to do it myself with clients. He made a comment that sometimes you have to make a deal with the devil's little brother to get to the devil. Sometimes that's correct. That is correct. And there's always a reason or a motive behind making a deal with someone, you know. It is done regularly up here.

"One of the things you're going to have to judge, if you're chosen, that happens is, you've got to determine the credibility of the person who's doing the telling. You can look at demeanor, the way they answer, tell a full story, tell a partial story. Now, you also have to look at their motivation, okay?"

After more questioning, some potential jurors continued to have trouble with the idea of a plea bargain.

"Basically what happens is sometimes the district attorney will make an offer. Sometimes the defense attorney, after speaking with his client, may make an offer," explained Susan Hebert. "And so it's a negotiation, kind of. You know, sometimes it's trying to get the best for your client."

Twelve jurors and one alternate were selected by 5:15 p.m. The jury's demographic was skewed older and female. Of the eleven females, nine were Caucasian, two were African American. The other juror was an African American male. Eight of the jurors were older than 50. Among their last instructions for the day from Judge Erwin was a final warning

"I can't stress to you enough: Don't read, watch, or listen to anything about this case. It's going to be all over the news. It's going to be all over the radio. It's going to be all over the television. Your neighbors are going to want to know; your dogs are going to want to know; your cats are going to want to know. Everybody's going to want to know what's going on. You can't tell anybody. Also, I have to remind you. Do not get on the Internet, iPhones, smart pads, or whatever that crap is."

And with that, the trial was ready to begin, at long last.

CHAPTER 22

TED AND GARY

Ted was twelve and Gary fifteen when they began their initial entrepreneurial training. It took the form of home delivery paper routes, since newspapers of the time delivered their products by having them tossed onto doorsteps by local kids. Such jobs represented the first opportunity to earn regular money for kids with ambition, provided they could endure sleep deprivation and were willing to bicycle the streets in any weather. Ted had to have a paper route because Gary had one.

Early each morning, the brothers were up before the sun and pedaled about six blocks to the main drop-off point. There the newspaper delivery truck driver tossed out bundles of the day's editions, which then had to be folded and thrown by each of the boys on their scheduled routes. They suffered through inclement weather, pumping along on their refurbished bicycles with canvas bags full of papers swinging from the handlebars. On wet days, each paper also had to be wrapped in plastic, which was paid for by the delivery boy, in addition to the rubber band holding the paper closed, also paid for by the delivery boy. A few cents at a time, drip, drip, drip. They learned how it feels when the weather itself is costing you time, energy, and money.

It didn't matter if they felt like rising early or not. The customers expected to greet the day with a fresh newspaper, regardless of whatever conditions the delivery boy endured. If a few subscribers complained about their service, the job was lost and the spending money gone.

However, the method of billing subscribers back then was to make each paperboy visit each subscriber to collect in person. The boys learned that while some people were honest and cheerfully paid their bills, others seemed to resent the three or four dollar cost for a month of service, and would refuse to answer the door. Or husbands couldn't pay because their wives took care of it. Or wives couldn't pay because their husbands took care of it. Or kids couldn't pay because their parents took care of it. A few would blatantly refuse to pay at all, citing some feeble excuse or complaint. Unscrupulous subscribers who planned to leave town sometimes allowed their bill to accumulate and then left the delivery boy to eventually come and knock on the door of an empty home.

Each paperboy had to pay the subscriber's bill himself until he collected the fee, if ever. The law offered no effective way to force payment for amounts that small, even when they were significant to the one being ripped off. Such things caused Ted and Gary to share the frustrating sensation of having an invisible hand reach into their pockets and steal money they worked hard to earn.

Of course the brothers heard other paperboys talking, and realized a delivery boy who combined entrepreneurial ambition with juvenile delinquency might choose to rise a little earlier one morning and use the cover of darkness to take out a deadbeat's front window with a rock. If the theoretical boy wanted to expend a little more effort, a doorbell could mysteriously ring in the wee hours, leaving the resident to rise and to discover a burning paper bag on their doorstep. Then, if the proposed evildoer had any luck at all, said deadbeat might try to stomp out the flames and encounter the gooey dog crap waiting to greet his foot like an enthusiastic welcome from a smelly pooch who loves you and refuses to go away.

Nevertheless, and regardless of the collection methods

others might employ, Gary's way of dealing with unscrupulous customers was to ignore they damage they did to him and press ahead with the work. Ted admired his restraint and took the same attitude. He could curse the crooks all he wanted, but the job remained in front of him and his reasons for doing it hadn't changed. It became Ted's first lesson by way of personal experience in the value of dealing with honest people. The difference between the behavior of honorable subscribers and that of cheapskates who took advantage of a kid's vulnerable position registered loud and clear. Good and decent people became the heroes of his working life, and the lesson never left him.

The reward for difficult work was the dignity and freedom of having his own pocket money. Even though the amounts he and Gary earned were never great, they each got their first taste of how much satisfaction a job can offer to those who are willing to put in the effort and stick to the task.

For the first few weeks on their delivery routes, Ted felt so grown up in working alongside his brother that he never mentioned the odd fact that Gary always struck off for the rallying point using a different route each morning. Since they always arrived on time, Ted just followed Gary's initiative and pedaled along after him.

One day curiosity overtook him. He asked Gary why they didn't just stick to the shortest route and use it every day. Gary replied as if explaining the obvious, *"If we always take the same streets, we'll always have to see the same things. We'll miss everything else on the other routes. Just because we do this every morning doesn't mean we have to live in ruts."*

Of course twelve-year-old Ted had no way of knowing how well he would recall his brother's response many years later, and how powerfully it would resonate with him.

CHAPTER 23

WADE

Wade Kergan sat down on the front-row courtroom bench next to his Uncle Ted and the rest of his family, who were all trying to keep their emotions in check.

Representatives from local TV stations and newspapers took their places on the left side of the courtroom. Assistant District Attorney Dana Cummings readied herself and chatted with investigator Chuck Smith. Detective John "Buck" Dauthier took a seat behind the Kergan family on the right side of the courtroom, interspersed among members of the Kergan's Sonic family, including long-time friends Gary Wilkerson, Doris Reiners, and Janet Hebert.

As the trial was finally ready to begin, Ted couldn't help but mentally travel back in time to 1984. He had constantly tried to shield Wade from the horror of his father's death, but today his nephew was taking the witness stand alone. Ted knew that in doing so, he would become that young boy again, the one who had just turned ten, and who, instead of experiencing the joy of his highly-anticipated birthday celebration that late November weekend, found out his father was dead.

Wade was now forty, and projected a dignified persona in his well-tailored gray suit with his neatly -trimmed hair and soulful eyes. He dressed much more casually in his vintage record store back in Detroit, where he and his mom, Susie, had settled decades earlier to be near her family. Once cancer took his mom, he felt his family circle narrowing. Ted had always been Wade's protector and champion in spite of the many miles that separated them. Each year, Ted planned a family reunion in Michigan so that he could maintain close ties with his family, particularly his nephew. Wade had only returned to Louisiana a few times since he left Crowley at age twelve. His first time back to the state which put such a bad taste in his mouth, he attended his Uncle Ted's wedding. His other trips were to witness criminal proceedings involving his father's murderers and to meet with Dana Cummings in preparation for the trial, both during the last year. Unlike his late father, Wade Kergan was not comfortable in the spotlight and he'd had little to say when news cameras rolled and reporters stuck microphones in his face. Ted knew Wade wasn't looking forward to taking the stand. In fact, Wade's apprehension kept him from paying full attention while Judge Erwin outlined the order of events of the trial for the jury: opening statements by the district attorney and the defense, evidence from the state, and possible but not required evidence from the defense, and then the closing arguments.

"On the fourth day of September, 2014, the grand jury of the Parish of East Baton Rouge, State of Louisiana, charged that Ronald Dunnagan at and in the parish, district, and state aforesaid, committed the offense of second-degree murder… on or about November 29, 1984. This matter came before the court for arraignment pursuant to previous assignment," called out the clerk. "The accused was present in court represented by counsel. Through counsel the accused waived formal arraignment and entered his own plea of not guilty as charged."

Dana Cummings was ready to give her opening statement. She knew they were all in the courtroom that day due to the sheer force of will exerted by Ted Kergan. Everyone who played a role in bringing this case to trial was amazed by his tenacity in tracking his brother's murderers, as well as the way he pledged his time, his money, and resources to this long, thirty-year saga. The love Ted Kergan shared with his brother, and Wade's father, Gary, was extraordinary, so extraordinary that it didn't wane with Gary's death nor the long, difficult decades that followed. Ted Kergan was doggedly determined to see both perpetrators in jail and locate his brother's remains.

"The problem at that point in time is there was no body," Dana said, relating events of November, 1984, to the court as she addressed the jury in clear tones. "Nobody could find Gary. What they had was blood in the trunk of a car, a substantial amount of blood, but they couldn't prove it was his. So that was a problem back then.

"Well, fast forward a lot of years and start in 2012 when John Dauthier becomes the cold case detective at Baton Rouge City Police. Although there was no DNA (testing) back in 1984, we certainly have a lot of DNA (testing capability) at this point. But still, you have no DNA from Gary. So what John Dauthier did was check with the lab to see if there could be some type of analysis done with Gary's son to determine whether this was, in fact, his DNA in his trunk. Oh, by the way, Mulla did acknowledge that Gary was taken away in the trunk of his car. So John Dauthier got the kinship analysis done. And the results were that this was Gary Kergan's blood in the trunk of that car, such a substantial amount of blood that we had enough of Gary Kergan's body in the trunk of that car to pursue this case."

Dana proceeded slowly through the history of the case, using simple and direct language, knowing that members of the jury were not allowed to take notes during the trial. Jurors were dependent on their memory to sort out activities from two time periods with three decades in between. Dana wanted to make sure jurors understood that there was proof of Gary's blood in the Cadillac's trunk, the key piece of evidence which led to Leila's and Ron's re-arrests. She pointed out that Leila took responsibility for her part in the murder during confessions, before a plea bargain was ever agreed upon. In doing so, Dana added, she gave up thirty years of her life for her involvement in Gary Kergan's murder.

Susan Hebert, dressed in a jewel-toned crimson colored blouse and long skirt, dutifully made some notes on yellow-lined paper as she glanced between the pad and watching Dana speak. Her client wore the same violet shirt from the day before, albeit a lot more wrinkled. This time, Ron paired the dress shirt with gray houndstooth checked slacks, accessorized with the same penny loafers sans socks. Ron looked a little more disheveled and a lot less at ease. When it was her turn to address the jurors with opening remarks, Susan Hebert quickly placed the blame squarely upon Leila Mulla.

"The state wants to paint a very wonderful picture of Leila Mulla, an innocent girl, who, at nineteen, had already been out prostituting herself, using drugs, and living on the streets before she met Mr. Dunnagan. And how she's done wonderful things with her life. She's become an R.N. She's a saint and has taken responsibility for her actions.

"She's been videotaped, questioned by police, and her story gets greater, and greater, and greater and (she) continues to blame him and minimizes her role. They videotaped and questioned her again May 28, 2014. And her details keep getting greater and greater and greater. I guess practice makes perfect.

"This whole case revolves around Leila Mulla's self-serving testimony. Other than that, there's no blood evidence in that apartment. There's no fingerprint evidence in that vehicle, that Cadillac. That plea agreement had been in the works between Leila, her attorney, and the district attorney's office. It wasn't an automatic thing that all of a sudden she pleaded, because remember her statement changed in preparation for the grand jury testimony. You will see that she may be serving a thirty-year sentence now, but once you see that plea agreement you will realize it is still open because everything revolves around her truthful testimony. And if the court determines that she is testifying truthfully, it's basically understood she could file for reconsideration of sentence and her sentence can be lessened. There is nothing, other than her testimony, that will place Ronald Dunnagan in this. There was a statement made yesterday about sometimes you have to make a deal with the devil's little brother. This time the DA made it with the devil himself."

John "Buck" Dauthier was the first witness called to testify. Since he was designated court agent by the district attorney, Buck was able to be present in the courtroom during all proceedings. Besides Wade, who was a family member, the rest of the witnesses weren't allowed inside until after they testified. He explained the evolution of the police department's cold case division and his position as the only cold case homicide detective in the department. In reviewing files for several hundred cold cases dating back to the 1970s, Buck picked the Kergan murder cold case to pursue because of the large amount of evidence. He first decided to take DNA from the blood sample in Gary Kergan's Cadillac trunk and compare it to Gary's son, Wade's DNA. The samples matched.

"The blood in the trunk, the donor of that blood was the biological father of Wade Kergan," Buck testified. "I felt we had the body of blood. I felt that we had satisfied what would ultimately be our burden in proving that Gary was, in fact, dead."

Buck went on to explain his coordination of the arrests of Leila Mulla in Astoria, NY, and Ron Dunnagan in Bossier City, LA, both on Dec 3, 2012. Since there was no way to know whether Leila and Ron maintained contact or whether Leila and her ex-husband, Rick Stockmeier, communicated with each other, three teams were dispatched to the three different locations. The ex-husband, who was living in Cincinnati, knew nothing. Ron was arrested, questioned in Bossier City, and brought back to the East Baton Rouge Parish jail that same day. Leila, apprehended at her apartment in Astoria, was taken to the district attorney's office in Queens, where she confessed, then spent twenty days in the women's jail at Riker's Island before being extradited to Baton Rouge on Christmas Eve. Buck explained how he contacted the two detectives, R.E. Thompson and Bob Howle, who originally handled the case in 1984. Since Dana already told the jury that Thompson would testify during the trial, Buck related news about Bob Howle.

"And where is he?" asked Dana.

"He is an inmate at Angola State Prison," replied Buck.

"And what was he convicted of?" continued Dana.

"He was convicted of murder."

"When you approached him, was he willing to talk to you?

"Oh, yes, very."

"And what is his physical health like?

"Extremely poor. He is unable to communicate for great periods of time without catching his breath.

"Basically bedridden?"

"Definitely."

"His conviction has nothing to do with this homicide; is that correct?

"Absolutely not."

As her questioning of Buck was wrapping up, Dana introduced another piece of evidence, the hand-drawn, double-sided map with its distinctive road, building, and levee markings. She asked Buck where he retrieved the map.

"This map was found by me inside of the case file from 1984," he explained.

With that, Dana turned over the witness to Susan Hebert for cross-examination. After establishing that Buck acted as coordinator of the arrests on December 3, 2012, but that he was not actually on site for any of the arrests that day, Susan Hebert's questioning became highly personal.

"I hate to do this, but I'm going to go ahead and... I think you probably know what's coming next. You, yourself, were arrested by the Baton Rouge police," Susan directed at Buck. Dana immediately asked Judge Erwin if opposing counsels could approach the bench. During their hushed, but on the record discussion, Dana made her case that this line of questioning was totally inappropriate. Susan Hebert fired back that the matter spoke to Buck's credibility.

"You can't ask him about arrests," responded Judge Erwin. "You can't ask anybody about arrests. You can ask only about convictions."

"And you know it was dismissed and he has sued over it," Dana said, eyes flashing at Susan Hebert. "So how can you bring that up in good conscience?"

"Because he walked around under a cloud of suspicion," fired back Susan Hebert.

"Oh, that is so off. I am so mad," retorted Dana. "But they're all asking about that; everyone asked about that."

"I have already ruled," interrupted Judge Erwin.

"Do you know what now, Judge," said Dana. "Now that she's brought it up, I have to explain, because otherwise, he's ... I withdraw that objection."

"Too late," said Susan Hebert.

"No, it's not," said Dana. "The judge gets to decide."

Judge Erwin dismissed counsels with "Go ahead" and motioned them back to court. Seconds later, Susan Hebert continued with Buck's cross-examination and the hotly contested line of questioning.

"Detective Dauthier, you, yourself, were arrested by the Baton Rouge Police Department back in November of 2010, correct?"

"I was illegally arrested for something that was not a crime; you are correct."

"Basically, you were arrested ... the allegation was purchasing the drug Tramadol over the Internet, correct?"

"That was the incorrect allegation; you are correct."

"I do know that subsequently you were not charged in the matter; is that correct? You were charged and brought with a bill of information, correct?"

"No, that's not quite correct. In fact, the attorney general's office flatly rejected the file with a letter that I have that says, 'We reject the file because you have not committed a crime.' So it's much more that that they just didn't decide to pursue charges."

"And, eventually, you did sue the police department, correct?"

"And I won."

"Okay, and you were still allowed to be on the force, correct? Because you're still here today, right?"

"You are correct. In fact, there was no discipline. I lost no seniority, no money, no anything. I am as whole today as I was the day before I was illegally arrested."

"But, basically, during that time, you did have to walk around with a cloud of suspicion over you, right?"

"Whether he walked around with a cloud of suspicion or not, nobody knows," retorted Judge Erwin, signaling he had had enough. Susan Hebert got the message, quickly replying "No further questions."

Dana quickly rose to her feet and approached Buck on the witness stand.

"Detective Dauthier, how much did you recover as a result of being illegally arrested?"

"Forty-five thousand dollars."

"Do you always have to answer this question when you take the stand now?"

"No. In fact, this is quite bizarre. This has been well established in previous trials. The incident she's referring to where I was illegally arrested occurred two and a half years before I was ever, basically, promoted to the position of cold case detective."

"Okay, and generally only convictions are admissible, correct?"

"Correct," Buck said emphatically. As Dana dismissed him from the witness stand, Buck was obviously incensed over Susan Hebert's malicious questions.

Wade Kergan was Dana's next witness. He stated his name for the record in a low, meek voice.

"Are you nervous to be up there?" Dana asked.

"I am," replied Wade, still very timid. Dana ticked through the timeline of Gary's death, asking Wade what he remembered about it.

"We spent a lot of time together. He took me on a lot of trips with him. And we did normal stuff. Hunting, fishing, you know, Louisiana stuff."

"Do you have any memory of the events that happened back then?"

Wade Kergan remembered the timing of his father's death well because it coincided with a planned celebration for his tenth birthday. He could never forget that he had no party because his father didn't return home.

Dana introduced into evidence a photo of father and son as well as a photo taken at Gary and Susie Kergan's wedding.

"Who else is in the photo?" Dana asked.

"My grandmother, my uncle, and my aunt."

"What are your uncle's and aunt's names?"

"Ted and Cheryl."

"And where is Ted?"

"He's here."

"Were Ted and Gary close?"

"Very, very. He was over at our house almost every day. They were very close."

"I know it's been a very long time ago. Do you recall Ted making efforts to find your Dad?"

"I do. As it happened, you know, at first you're not sure. And, then the longer they weren't able to locate him, the more information came up and the more determined the search became."

Wade never had that family birthday party. His ten-year-old birthday was draped in anxiety and sadness. He still remembered Larry Tucker, speaking gently to him in his bedroom, telling him his father was never coming home. More than thirty years later, Wade remembered the onset of that desolate, aching feeling, the void created by his father's death, a sadness that was constantly with him. He worked hard to keep it below the surface but sometimes that overwhelming familiar feeling got the best of him. Wade was fighting it now.

"I don't have any other questions at this time. Please answer any questions the defense has."

"Thank you, Mr. Kergan, but I don't have any questions," said Susan Hebert.

Wade Kergan was greatly relieved.

That evening, two hundred people on an email newsletter list, mainly Kergan family and friends, received the first of daily detailed trial updates from Ann Edelman. The goal was two-fold. Besides the obvious element of relaying news of the trial, the email update kept well-wishers from inundating the Kergan family during such a stressful time. Ann's expertise in crisis communication made her ever mindful of protecting the family.

CHAPTER 24

THE MAGEES

Dorothy Magee carried her purse to the witness stand. The purse was fairly new, but an aged memento inside had been a fixture in every one of Dorothy's handbags since 1984.

Back then, she and her husband, Gary Magee, owned The Night Spot Lounge. They were both at the club in the early hours of November 29, 1984, and saw Gary Kergan leave in the company of Leila Mulla, one of their dancers, whom they knew as "Erika." It was hard to picture this petite grandmother, dressed modestly in a polyester blouse and long, floral-printed skirt, as a former dancer in a titty bar. Dorothy wore matronly glasses and her shoulder-length blonde hair was now tinged with gray. Dorothy and Gary Magee had been married thirty-six years. Timidly, with her head bowed, she made her way to the stand.

"How did you meet Leila?" Dana asked.

"When she came in the bar with Ronald Dunnagan," Dorothy replied, in a meek voice.

"All right. Did you know Ronald Dunnagan prior to that time?"

"Yes, we did. We knew him because he did something before at the bar. I don't know if he worked there or if he was just there a lot. And he may have worked at the door for John Langlinais. But we also met him in New Orleans, making little balloons."

On a trip to the French Quarter sometime during the year before, Dorothy and Gary Magee were strolling around Jackson Square and ran into Ron, dressed in his clown regalia and entertaining children by making animal-shaped balloons. They remembered Ron from The Night Spot, where he had once worked, though at that time, the bar's owner was John Langlinais, from whom the Magees purchased it. Dorothy recalled Ron bringing Leila into The Night Spot, asking if they would hire her as a dancer. Why not? Dorothy had thought. Leila was young, beautiful and had no biker connection. Dorothy Magee remembered Gary Kergan fondly. Gary had become close to her and her husband during the year before his death. Dorothy stated she will never forget Gary Kergan coming into the Night Spot around 11:00 p.m. on November 28 and leaving with Leila Mulla around 2:00 a.m. on November 29. She told Dana she never saw Leila, Gary, or Ronald Dunnagan again.

Leila called her on November 30 and said she would not be at work until the next week. Dorothy testified that Ronald Dunnagan brought Leila to work and picked her up from work every day. When asked about Gary Kergan, she said he had been coming to The Night Spot once or twice a week for a year before his death. Dorothy had witnessed him leaving The Night Spot with Leila three times prior to the night he went missing.

"So you never saw him leave with somebody else?" Dana asked.

"No, he sat at the bar and bought drinks for several others, but he never talked to them."

"After this happened, when did you become aware that Gary was missing?"

"That Friday, his brother came into the bar, that Friday night. Ted came into the bar and I happened to be sitting outside the bar. I remember I was on the outside of the bar and I don't know if he walked straight up to me. But, anyway, he introduced himself as Ted. And he sat down and asked me if I wanted a drink. And I said yes, and he bought me a drink. And he asked me if I knew Gary Kergan and I told him yes.

And he asked me if I had seen him. And I told him I had seen him. I told him that he had come in the bar and he left with Leila."

"Is that pretty much all your conversation?"

"We probably talked about Gary some."

"Did he give you anything?"

"He gave me this half of a $100 bill," said Dorothy Magee, producing the one-half of a tattered $100 bill from her handbag.

"You still have it?"

"Yes, I've always kept it in my purse."

"For almost thirty-one years, you have been carrying around that half of a $100 bill?"

"I have."

"Why did he give you that?"

"When he handed it to me, he asked me if I had seen his brother. And I told him not since Wednesday night. And he asked me if I found out more information or if I heard from Gary or heard anything, to call him. If I called him, he would give me the other half (of the $100 bill)."

"And you held that for all this time."

"Yes."

"And you won't give it up?"

"No, I don't want to give it up. This is the only thing I have left of Gary."

"When you say that you knew him, I mean, more than just the club? Did you socialize with Gary a little bit?"

"Yes, we did. Sometimes he would come back without her. In fact, during the year we knew him, he would be there at closing time, and he followed us home and I cooked him breakfast."

"So he was friends with you and (your) Gary?"

"Yes, he was a friend."

The timidity briefly left Dorothy Magee when she spoke freely about teasing both men about "the Gary/Gary thing." Dorothy's stiffness quickly returned when it was Susan

Hebert's turn to question her.

"Did you ever know her given name of Leila?"

"I probably didn't pay any attention to it because we had like fifteen dancers. But my husband knew it. He knew most of the girls' names."

"And was it customary for them to take a different name and dance or tend bar?

"Most of the girls had nicknames."

"And so you only knew her as 'Erika,' correct?"

"Yes, I probably did not know her real name."

"Did Ron, did he come in to pick her up or did he wait outside or do you even remember?"

"He came in. He always came in and picked her up."

When Dorothy Magee was excused just before 2:00 p.m., she made her way to a bench in the back of the courtroom and passed her husband, Gary, on his way to the witness stand. Like his wife, Gary Magee was of slight build. He was casually but neatly dressed. Once he ascended into the box, Gary Magee testified that he had met Ron Dunnagan at The Night Spot a year prior to the Gary Kergan incident when Ron was there working for the previous owner, John Langlinais. After that, Gary recounted the story of how he and Dorothy ran into Ronald Dunnagan in the New Orleans French Quarter.

"(He was) taking balloons and putting them together," remembered Gary Magee. "Like for little kids, like making dogs out of them, stuff like that."

"So he was a clown and he was making balloons on the street," Dana recapped.

"Yes, ma'am."

"Did you know Ronald Dunnagan by both names at that point?"

"No ma'am. I only knew him as Ronald."

Gary Magee retold the unfolding of events at The Night Spot on the night of November 28 and early November 29. He, too, had seen Leila Mulla leave with Gary Kergan. His version of the story coincided with that of Wanda Magee, with one addition. Gary Magee testified that Ronald was not in The Night Spot lounge the evening of November 28 or in the early hours of November 29, either to drink or to pick up Leila. Both Magees had been questioned way back then, on Saturday, December 1, 1984, by one of the detectives assigned to the case, the man who was the state's next witness, retired Baton Rouge Police Captain R.E. Thompson.

R.E. looked like the quintessential old school police detective, with his close-cropped haircut, dress shirt, polyester slacks, and sports coat. Even though he was an older gentleman, R.E. kept his weight in check. He and his partner, Bob Howle, first met Ted Kergan two days after Ted filed a missing person's report back in 1984. Just like R.E. and Bob, Ted had shown up at the police station every day to work his brother's case. After a couple of weeks, Ted even had his own desk there.

R.E. and Ted were at the Louisiana State Police Crime Lab when the trunk of the Cadillac Eldorado was opened and the blood was discovered. It was Ted's quick thinking as well as Ted's American Express card that provided a Lear jet for immediate transportation to interrogate Leila and Ron in Las Vegas. R.E., Bob, and Ted had worked together to provide evidence for District Attorney Bryan Bush to prosecute the case. Instead, the district attorney decided to drop it. Now, here they were, R.E. and Ted, in the same room once again. It was evidence collected by the old school detective back in the day that solidified the cold case, and Ted's perseverance was the glue, the bridge between 1984 and the present.

R.E. retired from the Baton Rouge Police Department in 2003, then went on to work as an investigator for the District Attorney's office, as deputy director of investigations for the Department of Justice, and as a federal court security officer assigned to the U.S. Marshall's Office. Like others in local law enforcement, R.E. had crossed career paths with many of the same people time and time again. His former partner and fellow investigator, Leo Innerarity, worked with the ABC Board in 1984 and was the one who pulled the exotic dancer's license for Leila Mulla, aka Erika. Once they knew her real name, they were able to pull a duplicate license that listed her address, 2956 Byron Street, Apt. B, which fueled the investigation. Now it was the retired police captain's turn to take the witness stand for the state.

"Were you able to confirm that Leila Mulla and Dunnagan lived at that apartment?" Dana asked.

"Yes, actually through some driver's license information for Leila Mulla. And there was some forwarding mail and the address in the mailbox from New Orleans. I think 1021 or 1019 Decatur Street in New Orleans, in the name of the defendant, Ronald Dunnagan."

"Were you able to determine whether Leila Mulla and Ronald Dunnagan still lived in that apartment?"

"We were able to confirm it. They actually moved out around noontime. They contacted the apartment owner and he said that they halfway cleaned the apartment. They asked him if he wanted to buy some furniture, that they were leaving town. And, of course, he told them no, and he took a number from them, just in case he did, you know, hear of somebody, and that was it. They didn't request the deposit and he didn't offer it back, he said."

"Did anybody call that number?"

"He did, he said, but whoever answered said they never heard of him."

"Were you able to confirm that he was the one who rented the apartment?"

"Under an alias of Mike Karakas."

"Did the neighbors give you anything?"

"I picked up a mirror, one brown table lamp, a small lamp, two yellow plastic bottles. I think they're in my report. I think they're some type of feeder bottles. And two yellow plastic bowls."

R.E. Thompson testified he and Bob Howle were

notified days later, December 3, that the Cadillac Eldorado was located in Metairie. The two detectives traveled to the impound center and checked out the car. It was locked and they had the trunk forced open.

"There was assorted paperwork, a briefcase, several coin changers, several receipts. A large coagulation of blood was found in the trunk. We secured the trunk and physically followed the Eldorado back to Baton Rouge to the State Police Crime Lab."

R.E. noted there was no damage to the car at all, except for where they banged up the trunk prying it open. He also reported that Gary Kergan's wallet, with credit cards intact, was stuffed in the sun visor on the driver's side front seat. No money or jewelry was recovered from the car. As he talked, Dana showed photos of the car, taken at the crime lab, to those assembled in court.

"There's a significant amount of coagulated blood under or near the briefcase, as well as on that particular coin changer. There's a piece of paper to the left with bloodstains on it. "

"Is it a deposit slip?"

"Correct."

With the discovery of the car and new evidence, R.E. testified that he and Bob Howle returned to 2956 Byron Street to further process the apartment, this time with Hillar Moore, then a crime scene investigator with the district attorney's office. As he described the crime scene, Dana showed those in the courtroom photographs taken in 1984 of the tiny duplex on Byron Street.

"As you enter, there's like a small living room," said R.E. "It's like a little kitchen area to the left. There's a closet here in the center between the kitchen area and the bathroom. Right around the corner here, it's actually a bedroom with another closet and a dresser. It's a one-bedroom apartment. It's pretty small."

"How many closets in the apartment?"

"Two."

"Where were they located?"

"One between the kitchen and the bath in the little-bitty hallway here, and then one in the bedroom."

"What was the condition of the apartment?"

"It wasn't dirty. It appeared that an effort was made to clean the apartment before they moved out."

As Dana showed different close-up photographs taken in the apartment, R.E. described blood splatter on the bedroom ceiling and blood on panels from the closet doors. He also identified a photo of a piece of hard sugarcane with bloodstains on it that was left in the apartment. The two of them continued moving down the crime timeline, and noted the material witness warrant was obtained for Leila, since she was the last person seen with Gary Kergan.

"On December 7, about 3:00 p.m. in the afternoon, we were contacted by the Las Vegas Metropolitan Police Department. And at that particular time, not more than two days later, they ran a criminal history on Leila Mulla. She was applying for an escort license in the Las Vegas Metro Area. And in routine checking with escort licenses, they found that she was wanted by our agency for that particular warrant."

R.E. testified that within hours, he and Bob Howle were questioning Leila Mulla in the break room of the Clark County Detention Center. He noted the conversation was not recorded.

"She did, in fact, know Gary Kergan. She knew him through The Night Spot lounge. And she identified him as a trick. She said 'I know that he owns Sonic Drive-ins.' She said that she brought him home twice for sex and that Ronald, the defendant, was present both times. And, initially, she said they had sex at 3:15 and he left. He just left."

"That was her initial statement?" Dana asked.

"It evolved over the next several hours. It evolved to a different statement, so to speak. She said the same thing. They did come home; Ronald was present. They did go into the back bedroom. They had sex. During the act, I guess, he tried to force her, force things on her that she didn't particularly care for. She ran out of the room, laid on the couch. Ron basically intervened and, you know, escorted him out. That was one initial statement. Like I said, it evolved. Later, she did admit that the defendant did kill Gary.

"Did she mention the Cadillac?"

"She just said, you know, that Ronald Dunnagan panicked. After he went into the bedroom, she ran out onto the couch. He panicked. The next thing, Ronald basically threw Gary into the trunk of his own Cadillac and Ronald drove off with him. And that was it. She wouldn't indicate anything after that. Basically, she asked for an attorney and we stopped questioning her."

"Did she indicate during this final statement whether or not she heard anything going on after she ran out of the bedroom?"

"She did. She heard noises, some beating and banging, that type of thing. And that's when he, shortly thereafter, he came out. She stated that he panicked and, basically, threw him in the trunk and he drove off."

"And when she said he threw him in the trunk, did she indicate that he was dead at the time?"

"She did say that Ronald Dunnagan killed him, but it wasn't intentional at the time."

The state's line of questioning switched to the scene to Leila's and Ron's Las Vegas apartment. Dana showed those in the courtroom photos from that dwelling. A photograph showed one of Leila's diaries, located inside a kitchen drawer. Another photo pictured a lockbox, which contained another of Leila's diaries. A third photograph showed Leila's notebook, recovered from a bedroom chest of drawers. Also procured were weapons and zip ties.

R.E. continued the chronology. An arrest warrant was obtained for Ron and he waived extradition. Detectives waited to question him until he was back in Baton Rouge on December 11.

"We asked him about the night in question. We asked him if he knew Gary Kergan, to which he said, 'Yes, I do.' He identified him as the Sonic Man. He knew him. And, then, of course, the statement evolved that Gary was brought home by Leila Mulla for sex, and that there were issues back in the back bedroom. And he basically forced him out of the house and he drove off about 3:15 on his own. This is my report - 'Gary was last seen driving off in his Cadillac.'

"He said that 'How do you know he just didn't leave town or drive off? You know, how do you know? You don't have a body, do you?' And, for the most part, that was the end of the interview."

"So, he distinctively said, 'You don't have a body, do you?'" Dana asked.

"That's exactly what he said."

At that time, both suspects were charged with first-degree murder.

"Why was the case not pursued?" Dana asked.

"As far as I recall, District Attorney Bryan Bush, at the time, said that because there was no body, the *corpus delicti* had been established, and he preferred not to go to trial at the time."

With that, Dana released the witness to Susan Hebert, who lamented over and over the fact that the detectives did not record the interrogations of Leila and Ron in Las Vegas.

"So in that several hours, you continued to question her, correct? And her version of events continuously..."

"Evolved," R.E. Thompson interjected.

"From what you told us, would you say that she did not take any blame for what happened, that she tried to put the blame on Mr. Dunnagan?"

"Right. She didn't take any whatsoever. She just said that when she ran out of the bedroom, he ran in. That's when she heard the noises and the bumping and whatnot, like a struggle was happening. And that's when he came out, panicked. And the next thing she knew, or saw, was Ron throwing Gary's body in his own trunk and driving off."

"Actually carried him out to the trunk? She actually saw that. Is that what she told you?"

"Yes, that's what she said."

"And, basically, she did nothing?"

"She didn't implicate herself in any way, shape, or form of actually, the homicide or the disposing of Mr. Kergan."

Susan Hebert wanted to know how the conversation between Ron and the detectives began when they brought him back to Baton Rouge.

"Did you advise him he was being arrested? Did you tell him you were looking into a missing person's report or did you tell him you were investigating a murder?"

"Exactly that. The disappearance and a possible homicide."

"A disappearance?"

"A disappearance and possible homicide."

"As a missing person or a disappearance of someone, wouldn't it be unusual, but you didn't know it was a homicide at that point, correct?"

"Actually, according to Leila Mulla's statement in Las Vegas, yes, I did."

"Well, when you said missing person, it could be understood that you were looking for someone. You didn't have a body, correct?"

"Actually, no. We basically told the defendant there what Leila admitted to us; that it was a homicide."

During the redirect, Dana wanted R.E. to use his vast experience in criminal justice to familiarize the jury about a detective's techniques in getting to know and questioning a suspect, the typical evolution of a suspect's testimony.

"Is it your experience, is it unusual for a suspect or a witness that's being questioned, particularly a suspect, to start out denying involvement and gradually admit some things that happened?"

"Nine times out of ten, that's usually what happens."

"So nobody generally walks in and says 'Detective Thompson, I did it?'"

"It's a process. You kind of get to know them. And you know, sometimes people are very defensive, sometimes they are not. And it just depends on what they want to tell you... I've talked to people as long as eight, ten, twelve hours before, where everything changes from A to Z. In this case, this man right here, the interview was very short."

"How long is very short?"

"It was less than an hour."

"Would you have interviewed Leila Mulla again if she had not lawyered up?"

"Definitely."

"Do you see Ronald Dunnagan in the courtroom?"

"Yes, I do."

"And where is he?"

"That man sitting all the way to your left in the purple shirt."

"Did he look like that back then?"

"Uh-uh, no way!"

And with that exclamative punctuation, R.E. Thompson was dismissed from the stand just before 5:00 p.m., after almost three hours of weighty testimony. Although at times a bit red-faced, the former detective delivered details from a period of three decades ago with little hesitation. He drove deep into the facts of the case, remembering how he and his partner, Bob Howle, worked practically around the clock during those first few weeks following November 29, 1984. Meticulous investigations from The Night Spot and 2956 Byron Street folded into the urgent flight to Las Vegas. All of that was mulling about R.E.'s mind as Judge Erwin addressed the jury about next steps in the trial. He began by revealing how, when he was younger, he used to work late into the evening during criminal trials.

"But I found out it didn't do any good because you don't ever catch up. There's always another one coming so it doesn't matter."

He then instructed, "Don't read, watch, or listen to anything about it (the case). Don't go to the crime scene or the mentioned bars. I had that happen one time; first time I'd ever seen that in my life. Two jurors went out to the crime scene one night and were looking at it. I hadn't ever told anybody not to do it, but I never heard of anybody doing it. Because if I tell people not to do it, then unless it's court approved and we can all load up in a bus and go do it – but we ain't going to do that."

Ted Kergan watched Judge Erwin from his spot on the front, right side bench, but he was too exhausted to internalize the judge's statements. He had slept very little the night before, thinking about the trial and worrying about his nephew taking the witness stand. Even after thirty-plus years, there were mountains of information to internalize and process.

But the trial itself was something Ted had looked forward to for a very long time. He had no problem staring down Ron Dunnagan in court, he had done it before. The next day, Leila Mulla would testify, and Ted would come face to face with the woman who had lured his brother to his death, that evening so long ago.

CHAPTER 25

ALL EYES ON LEILA

Day three of the trial began with Baton Rouge Police Detective Ross Williams' testimony about his arrest of Ron Dunnagan on December 3, 2012. Williams had been part of the team who went to Bossier City and apprehended Dunnagan, then took him to the local police station for questioning. That videotaped interview was played for the courtroom. With his hands cuffed, Ron Dunnagan nervously shook one leg throughout the interview.

"I was there and I ain't murdered," Ron muttered on the tape. "As far as I knew, he's still around. I seen him alive. He got in his Cadillac and drove off." The interview was played for the jury as part of the detective's testimony, at the beginning of the trial's third day.

Ron dropped down one more rung on the hygiene ladder for Thursday's court appearance. Even though he finally sloughed off the vivid violet dress shirt and donned a fresh white one, he wore the same gray pants and penny loafers without socks. In person, he looked much better than in the videotape now playing for the court. The North Louisiana police station's small, stark interview room with its white paint, fluorescent lighting, and metal desk all served to magnify Ron's rough and ragged appearance.

He told the detective there had been nothing for the couple in Baton Rouge, and he wanted to head to California at the end of November, 1984, but they didn't have enough money, and instead went to Las Vegas. Ross Williams informed Ron he was charged with first-degree murder, conspiracy, and simple robbery. He asked if Ron knew how to contact Leila Mulla.

"I haven't heard from her since we separated in Las Vegas."

Ron Dunnagan claimed he had neither seen nor heard from Leila Mulla in almost thirty-one years. Today, Ron would see her at last, a woman he had once called the love of his life. Ted Kergan knew the background story better than anyone. He wondered if the old bird refused a plea agreement just so he could get another look at Leila, the once beautiful, naughty, and daring nineteen-year-old girl who had captivated him.

And who pushed him into murdering my brother, Ted silently added.

When Leila finally came into the courtroom, it was through the same door that all prisoners entered, which was also the door closest to the spot where Ron Dunnagan sat, at the far left side of the defense table. There was complete silence in the courtroom while she gradually made her way to the witness stand.

All eyes, especially Ron's, were upon Leila, dressed in dark, straight leg jeans and a striped prison shirt. Her hair was dyed back to its original brunette. She was much thinner than before, and was noticeably wearing makeup. At five-foot-two, Leila was small, almost tiny, and with her leg shackled, the trip to the witness stand lingered, almost like she was moving in slow motion. A police officer helped her up the steps and into the witness box. As she was sworn in, her speech was low and halting, her demeanor demure.

Leila was now a fifty-year-old woman who had spent the last two and a half years incarcerated, with the last year spent in a cell at Louisiana Correctional Institute for Women. She looked every day of it. Still, Ted felt no sympathy for the way prison life had taken its toll on her.

She responded to Dana Cummings' first few fact-establishing questions with a flat "Yes, ma'am" or "No, ma'am." Then Leila wove a dreary tale about running away to New Orleans, being robbed, raped, and homeless, living under a bridge with no place to go. She said Ron Dunnagan had offered her a place to live.

"He took me into his apartment and he would lock ... the apartment had a padlock on the outside of the door and he would lock me in. And then he'd show up. He'd bring me food and clothes and things. And then that's how it started."

Ron Dunnagan shook his head violently across the room.

"Did you start having sex with him at some point?" Dana questioned.

"Yes ma'am. He told me I had to have sex with him. First he was nice. He said he was concerned and he took my family's names and numbers and addresses and said if anything happened to me, that way he would be able to get in touch with them. And in time he told me I had to have sex with him. I didn't want to, but I went ahead and had sex with him.

"He took me to some strip clubs and had me start to work there. And he would walk me there and he would walk me back to the apartment. He told me I had to start to do prostitution as well. He was always right there."

The couple lived in New Orleans about a year, she said, until October, 1984.

"Did your relationship change over time, over that year period of time?" Dana asked.

"Yes, it did change. Where he used to threaten me and threaten my family, and I was very fearful of him for a long time where he followed me around, and it changed then. I thought, I actually thought I loved the man. Thought I loved him. So the relationship did change, and I became obedient to what he asked."

Leila said she begged to begin anew somewhere else and that Ron agreed to move to Baton Rouge.

"He said he knew people in Baton Rouge. He said he

could get me a job."

"Did you know it was going to be a strip club?"

"No, I didn't."

"Well, he took me to another strip club where he knew the owner. He talked to the owner and he introduced me, and that's where I started to work."

"Do you know the name of that club?"

"I believe it's named ... it was named The Night Spot."

"And what kind of club was it?"

"It was strip. It was dancing, exotic dancing."

"All right. So, you continued to work in a strip club. Did you also continue to work as a prostitute?"

"Yes, I did."

"What did Ronald Dunnagan do?"

"He drove me there. He drove me back. And that was it. Basically, he took my money and he didn't work."

"Is this the period of time where you're afraid of him or you're in love with him?"

"This is the period of time that I thought I loved him."

"Did you at some point meet Gary Kergan?"

Leila told the court about how she met Gary Kergan at The Night Spot. He bought her drinks and eventually became one of her customers. She said that although she noticed Gary Kergan wore nice jewelry and bought plenty of drinks for others at the club, Leila denied she knew Gary Kergan was wealthy.

"Well, Ronald Dunnagan told me that he was. He owned the Sonic restaurants. So then we started to call him Sonic Gary. And then Ron thought it would be a good idea for us to rob and kill him."

Ron continued to emphatically shake his head while Leila explained that a plan to kill Sonic Gary was hatched during mid-November, 1984.

"Ronald came up with the plan. The plan was that we were going to poison him. And Ron had done some research, and he was ... and we were going to rob him and he was going to dispose of the body."

"You said he did some research. What did he do research on?" Dana asked.

"Well, he called up different trash companies to find out about the dumpsters and the cost of what dumpsters he wanted to use," Leila said in a voice that suddenly became low and halting. "I guess the price of the... excuse me a minute."

She dabbed at her eyes with a tissue, a bit of drama she repeated several times during her testimony.

"Take your time," Dana said.

"The price of how much they charged because he wanted to dispose of the body in dumpsters."

"Why did the cost that they charged to dispose of the items in the dumpster make a difference?"

"He said that was important because the people who got paid ... What is it? BFI? Got paid less and they wouldn't look in any of the dumpsters."

"Why not just rob him?"

"That's a good question. You know, my fear of him (Ron) had turned more into love and obedience, and all I can say is, you know, he's a bad man. He's a very bad man."

"But you were at this point a willing participant, is that correct?"

"Yes, ma'am," Leila said for the thirteenth time.

"What did y'all do to prepare to execute your plan?"

"Well, first he went out and bought some poison. I don't know what type it was, but I know it was kept in a box and it was in the kitchen and we went and we bought some... well, he wanted to see if it works, so he went and bought some rats. At the same time, he bought me a couple of Guinea pigs as pets. And he poisoned ... well, I wasn't there, but he told me he poisoned and killed the rats. He said he wanted to run through the plan where he was hiding in the closet and how I was just to bring Gary in. I mean the practice took maybe a minute, maybe a couple of minutes."

"And, what did y'all do in the practice?"

"He just showed me where he would be hiding in the closet and that I was to give Gary this glass of wine."

Ron Dunnagan was now shaking his head and tapping his foot. It seemed he was about to burst as Dana prompted Leila to continue.

"I'm understanding that you planned to poison the wine, is that it?"

"The wine would be poisoned, yes."

"Why wine, why did y'all choose wine?"

"Because it was pretty much a routine that we drank wine."

"You drank wine with Gary?"

"Yes."

"How many times had Gary been back to the apartment with you?"

"I'm going to say like five or six."

"And did Gary pay for sex every time?"

"Yes, he did."

"Was Dunnagan in the apartment when Gary came over?"

"Yes. Sometimes even in New Orleans he hid in the closets."

"Why?"

"He said it would be for protection."

"Did he ever have to protect you from anyone?"

"No, ma'am."

"Certainly never had to protect you from Gary?"

"No, ma'am."

Here, Dana Cummings asked Leila to tell how events unfolded in the early morning of November 29, 1984, at the Byron Street duplex.

"We went into the apartment, went into the bedroom. I got glasses of wine. We both drank wine. I went out. There was a table, like in the bedroom, so I went out. I put the glasses on the kitchen table, went back in the bedroom, closed the door. We had sex and when we were done, I went to the refrigerator. I poured wine in both the glasses. In the one glass, I don't know if it was white powder or if it was wine residue, but I knew that was the glass I was supposed to give Gary, and I gave it to him."

"And what happened when he drank the wine?"

"Gary started to choke. He started to choke and I got scared. He said 'help me.' I jumped up and started to run out of the bedroom. Ronald came out of the closet. He pushed me back against the wall. He grabbed Gary, pulled him out, took a pillow from the bed, and held it over his face."

"Was Gary dressed at that time?"

"No, he wasn't dressed. He was getting dressed."

"Why did you freak out at this point?"

"I wasn't prepared. I didn't know. I've never seen anybody die before."

What happened after Dunnagan put the pillow over his face?"

"He quit moving and he quit breathing."

"And you saw that?"

"Yes, ma'am. He pulled him out then, out of the bedroom, and he pulled him into the bathroom. And he put him in the bathtub and he closed the door. Closed the bedroom door and then he closed the bathroom door."

"And what did you do at that point?"

"He pushed me against the wall and I sat there for a long time. I just sat against the wall. Eventually, I got curious as to what was going on. I got up. I walked out of the bedroom and I looked into the bathroom and I saw some blood on the wall."

"Which wall?"

"The bathroom's here and the wall right by the bathtub. And he yelled at me to get out. I got out and went back into the bedroom and I sat there."

Leila began sniffling and reached for another Kleenex. Dana kept up with the questions. Did you hear anything going on in the bathroom? Did you see anything else in the bathroom? What happened after you sat in the bedroom?

Finally, Leila spoke, asking for a reprieve.

"I just need a minute," she said, again dabbing at the eye makeup. It was less than 60 seconds but a heavy silence enveloped the court.

"After a couple of hours, he came out. He had some blood on him. He had a black plastic bag. He told me to get dressed. He put his clothes in the bag. He put the wine bottle, bottle from the refrigerator, the glasses of wine, the poison. He put Gary's clothing in the plastic bag. I don't remember how many plastic bags he had. I don't remember how many there were, but he was putting them in the trunk of the car. And I do vaguely remember helping him with one. And he put them in the trunk of the car and he said, 'We have to go.'"

"Whose car?"

"It was Gary's car."

"What did you do at that point?"

"I got in the passenger side of the car. He got in the driver's side and then he started driving. I don't know where he was driving to. I didn't know the area. I never drove in Baton Rouge. We hadn't been there very long. But he pulled up to a dumpster, one that was like behind an old building. I don't know where it was. Then, another one I know was like beside a road."

"Several different dumpsters?"

"Yes, a few dumpsters. And he opened the trunk of the car. At one point, I did get out of the car and watch, and then at another one, I just sat in the car and I saw through the mirror. He was putting the bags in a dumpster."

"Did he do that by himself?"

"Yes, ma'am."

"Where did y'all go after you left the last dumpster?"

"He drove; I don't know where. I know we went over a long bridge and he parked the car. It was like in a parking lot and there was a phone booth. He used the phone booth and a yellow cab came and picked us up. And I think he knew the man because he sat in the front seat with this man and they were chatting and I was in the backseat. And I remember it was early in the morning because the sun was starting to come up. And this cab took us back to the apartment."

"Did Dunnagan ever meet Gary at your apartment?"

"No, ma'am."

"Was he always present in the apartment somewhere when Gary came to the apartment?"

"Not always. Sometimes he was in the apartment; sometimes, he would be outside the apartment. If he was in the apartment, he would have been hiding in the closet. If he was outside, he would have been probably just outside somewhere close by."

"So he wouldn't just go out somewhere else?"

"No, ma'am."

"He was lurking around somewhere."

"He was always lurking."

Leila said when they returned to the duplex after killing and disposing of Gary Kergan, Ron began cleaning up with bleach. She said she was frightened, confused, and begged to leave Baton Rouge.

"We packed up his car and headed to Las Vegas."

"Did your financial condition improve after you robbed and killed Gary?"

"I don't know how much money Gary had on him, but it was enough to drive us to Las Vegas and stay in a hotel for a few days. And I know he rented an apartment, so it must have been enough for the apartment as well."

"Did you turn tricks on your way to Las Vegas?"

"No, the reason we went to Las Vegas is because he said he could legally get me registered; so that way I could turn tricks legally."

"Did he get a job in Las Vegas?"

"No, ma'am."

"But he took you to get your card?"

"He took me and dropped me off and told me to get registered so I could start to work.

"What happened when you went to get registered?

"I was arrested."

When Dana asked if she had seen Gary's jewelry, Leila related Ron approached her with a watch and two rings in his hand, saying "Look what I have."

"Did he tell you what he was going to do with the jewelry?"

"Sell it."

Dana ran Leila through the sequence of events after her arrest up to the point of her release from the East Baton Rouge Parish jail in March, 1985.

"Were you ultimately released from the charge?"

"Yes, ma'am."

"Was Mr. Dunnagan also released?"

"Yes, ma'am."

"Did you have any contact with him?"

"No, ma'am."

"Where did you go after you were released?"

"My parents picked me up and I went ... well, I was having a nervous breakdown and I was suicidal, so I went to a rehabilitation center for about a year."

Dana fast forwarded her line of questions to 2012. She established that Leila was working as a registered nurse in New York City when detectives came to her residence in Astoria, Queens.

"And what was your thought when they arrived there?"

"I knew what they were there for."

"Even though it was twenty-eight years later, you knew?"

"Yeah. I mean, I haven't done anything. You know; I've gone to school. I've raised my kids. I haven't done anything. I knew that it's got to be the only thing they were there for."

"Ms. Mulla, did you think about what you did to Gary Kergan over the years?"

"Every single day. I have thought about it and I've had a lot of pain and sorrow and I've had to try and move forward from it. And I've been very sorry and remorseful for my actions."

Dana Cummings relinquished her witness to the defense and, making her way back to her seat, she thought about how pleased she was with Leila Mulla's performance. After all, it had been many months since Dana last questioned Leila, so Dana had been nervous. She knew Leila's testimony was the key to the trial.

When Susan Hebert rose to question Leila Mulla, she began with "This is hard, isn't it?"

"Yes, ma'am," replied Leila, resuming her chorus of overtly polite responses, showing no less respect to the public defender than she did to the prosecutor.

"My name is Susan Hebert and I'm Ron's attorney. I'm going to start back with your testimony. And I'm going to take you back through things. And I want to talk to you about some inconsistencies."

"Yes, ma'am."

"You've talked to several people with the DA's office and the police department, haven't you?"

"Yes, ma'am."

"You never told them you were robbed or raped and living under a bridge, did you?"

"I don't know if I told them that or not, to be truthful."

"The first time you met him (Ron) were you hungry and did he give you some food?"

"Yes, I was hungry."

"And then did you see him some days later? Did you have a boyfriend at that time?"

"I was living in an apartment with this other man. I lost my job. He was a street musician and he was from Canada. And he was going back to Canada. And so then I didn't have any place to go or live."

"So, you weren't living under a bridge when you met

Dunnagan, were you?"

"After he left for Canada, I didn't have any place to live, so I went and lived outside, yes."

"Were you doing prostitution at that time?"

"No, ma'am."

"How were you supporting yourself?"

"I wasn't. He was pretty much supporting me."

"And how long did you stay with him?"

"Not very long."

"Did Ronald Dunnagan padlock you into the Baton Rouge apartment too?"

"No, ma'am."

"You basically stayed with him for about a year and a half, correct?

"Yes, ma'am."

"During that time that you say he basically kept you padlocked and made you do things - wasn't there a time, maybe twice, that you actually went all the way back home? Now, are you from Ohio?"

"I did go all the way home and I planned on staying at my mother's house."

"Uh-huh."

"And he called there and he was threatening to kill my family, so I came back. The second time, like I testified, my feelings had changed and I came back without any problem."

"So, you weren't afraid of him anymore?"

"The second time, no. The first time, I was very scared of him."

"And what family members did you give him, their names and addresses and telephone numbers?"

"My mother and father, and my brother, Omar, and my brother, Nejdat."

"If you were afraid of him, why didn't you give him some false numbers and addresses?"

"Because I was young. I was very naive. And he said he was going to help me."

"During a lot of your video statements and some of your audio statements, you blame a lot of this on your being young and naive. Isn't that correct? In fact, all along you keep blaming that you were young and naive."

"I don't know if I blame it all on being young and naive. I was young. I was naive. I was vulnerable, and I was also quite stupid."

"I think you blame a lot of things on stupidity, don't you?"

"No, ma'am."

Susan Hebert painted a picture of Ron Dunnagan moving to Baton Rouge to help Leila get a fresh start. She tried to catch Leila in inconsistencies but Leila suddenly couldn't remember certain things. Susan Hebert's tone was getting a bit rougher. When Dana Cummings tried to intervene, Judge Erwin decided Susan Hebert could "cross-examine her any way she wants."

"I'm trying to avoid playing all the videos," explained Susan Hebert. "They are very long, but if I get to that point that we have to play them; I may have to play them."

The videotape of Leila Mulla's interview in New York was at least two and a half hours long. Leila had also been questioned by detectives in Baton Rouge several times, and each of those interviews lasted about one hour. Susan Hebert's ploy of threatening to play more than five hours of Leila Mulla's taped interviews would draw the trial out at least one additional day.

"I'm great with that," Dana Cummings replied.

For more than an hour, Susan Hebert went through parts of all of Leila's confessions, trying to trip up the witness. Instead, Leila volleyed back with a chorus of "Yes, ma'am," "No, ma'am," and "I don't remember." Then Susan Hebert moved on to attack the plea bargain and the fact that Leila's sentence could be reduced.

"But the possibility for your testimony to have a sentence reduced exists, doesn't it?"

"It exists. But what I've been telling you is the truth."

"You've been trying to tell everybody the truth for almost thirty years now and there are little different versions every time you tell it," rebuffed counsel in a sing-song-y voice akin to an elementary school teacher.

"This has happened over thirty years ago. And these are things that I have truly tried to push out of my memory because they're so very painful. And I'm telling you the truth that I can remember them in bits and pieces. And I know sometimes it's not making a lot of sense, but that's what I remember and I'm doing the very best I can."

Susan Hebert maintained rapid fire questioning, sometimes without real questions. She folded her arms across her chest and raised her voice until it was just a few notches below a scream.

"Well, you changed your story again after you pleaded. You elaborated. Didn't you 'elaborate' more on your story?"

"No, ma'am."

Susan Hebert continued to dwell on the inconsistencies, stabbing in staccato tones at each one. Leila quietly fielded them all.

"Well, if you were so obedient to him, why didn't you try to reconnect with him?"

"Because in time I saw that he deceived me, he manipulated me, and he coerced me."

When it was time for her redirect examination, Dana Cummings zeroed in on the salient points of Leila's confessions, and the fact that she had been consistent in her story on all of them, beginning with her statement in Kew Gardens in December, 2012.

"At that time, who did you say committed the homicide?"

"I said Ronald Dunnagan did."

"At that time, did you take responsibility?"

"For my part, for my actions."

"Did you say it was planned or that it was spontaneous?"

"No, it was planned."

"How did you say the manner of death was?"

"That he was poisoned."

"How was he moved from the apartment?"

"In trash bags."

"How did you say the trash bags were transported?"

"In the trunk of his car, Gary's car."

"Where did you say the body ended up?"

"In dumpsters."

"Have you ever changed any of those big details or have they been absolutely consistent every step of the way?"

"The details have been consistent, the big things. The small, minor things, you know, I'm doing the best I can to remember those painful things, but I can't remember a lot of the small things and I'm doing the best I can. But the big things have been consistent throughout."

Next, for the first time during the trial, members of the jury received copies of a portion of one of Leila's diaries. Dana Cummings had Leila read selected passages regarding Gary and their plan to kill him. The jury was riveted.

"When we began plea negotiations, what was the one thing that you knew you could provide to the state and the victim's family that would make all the difference in the world?" Dana asked.

"My testimony."

"It was another thing, the thing that you kept being asked about. The location of Gary's body."

"I don't know the location. I've tried. I've done everything I could possibly think of to try and remember and I don't know. I mean, when I was offered to be driven around to look, but I was a little on the drunk side and all I know is it was dumpsters and it was BFI. And I tried to describe, to the best of my ability, the locations but it never came back to me."

With that, Dana Cummings rested for the state.

Quickly, Susan Hebert announced the defense rested too. That meant no testimony from any other witnesses, including

Ron Dunnagan.

But there was no surprise there, thought Ted Kergan. No one really expected Ron Dunnagan to publicly defend himself. It was difficult for Ted to listen to Leila's testimony objectively. He thought of her as a master manipulator and calculating murderer who, if she was remorseful about anything, regretted getting caught. Leila's portrayal in court as a pathetic figure, a diminutive concubine, tormented Ted, making it hard for him to appear respectfully calm. But anyone could see he didn't believe a word she said.

On the other hand, Ted was pleased because that same testimony would hopefully convict Ron Dunnagan. Ted observed jurors looking at Leila on the stand, then switching their gazes to Ron. He could tell from the jurors' expressions that they had begun to perceive Ron as dirty and evil. Ted allowed those expressions, that part of the trial, to soak into his entire being. He had waited a long time for this very moment, and he had to admit Leila's performance was downright spectacular. Academy Award winning material.

CHAPTER 26

VERDICT

"Closing arguments should be like a woman's skirt, long enough to cover the subject, but short enough to keep it interesting."

"And you just said that to a jury full of women," Dana Cummings replied, speaking loudly enough to cover laughter in the courtroom. Judge Erwin's cheeky closing argument rule was one he adopted long ago from a high school teacher.

"And with that admonition," he added, "we will begin." And with that admonition, tension sent a cold acid chill running through Ted.

There had been many tense moments along this journey, but Ted was extremely nervous today. All those years of pushing, so many years of searching, the continuous pain from not knowing, had converged in this moment. He thought Leila had been brilliant on the witness stand. But he knew she was a sociopath, with total disregard for the rights of others.

Leila Mulla maintained the same story line, once more. But this time her far-fetched saga was easier to swallow, by Ted's way of thinking. She was done, after all. She was toast, as they say, serving out her thirty-year sentence at Louisiana Correctional Institute for Women. Ron Dunnagan's fate would be determined soon. If Dana Cummings had her way, he was going down, and that thought made Ted smile on the inside. He thought Dana did a magnificent job interrogating witnesses. She had closed up any links in the chain of evidence and the events concerning Gary's death. Now all she had to do was succinctly pull it all together in one, big, finger-pointing delivery with her closing argument.

Though Ted had been physically close enough a time or two during the last couple of years to Ron Dunnagan to have touched him, or hurt him, or even killed him, none of those things could have given Ted the satisfaction he was looking for today.

The second-degree murder conviction of Ron Dunnagan meant he would spend the rest of his life in prison. Ron's incarceration would finally bring justice for Gary. It was that simple and that powerful.

He looked at the faces of the jury. All of them were fixed upon Dana Cummings, dressed in a funeral black suit with red patent shoes. Just like Dorothy from the Wizard of Oz, Dana Cummings was ready to bring this verdict home.

"For the last thirty-one years, everyone involved in this case has known that man is guilty of murder." She dramatically extended her arm and pointed at Ron Dunnagan. "For the last thirty-one years, the family has had to accept that justice may never be served. He skated for the last thirty-one years because he bought himself some time by doing a really thorough job of disposing of Gary Kergan's body. Time is up. Science has caught up with him. We know that the body of blood in the trunk of that car is Gary Kergan's."

"And unlike in '84 when Leila Mulla told just enough to implicate him and then shut up and quit cooperating, we have a witness now in addition to that DNA evidence."

The implicated one, Ron Dunnagan, decided to wear his white dress shirt a second time for closing arguments. For the duration of the trial up to this point, he had not uttered a sound, and he remained silent while Dana Cummings spoke to the jury, occasionally glaring, once even pointing directly at him while she tried to convince the jury that the state had proven all three elements necessary to satisfy its burden of proof.

"We're going to talk about what we have without Leila Mulla," Dana began. "...the blood in the trunk of that car is so much Gary could not have survived. There's strong circumstantial evidence that puts (Ron) with Gary Kergan at that Byron Street apartment in the early morning hours when this happened. The next day, they loaded the car and moved to Las Vegas unexpectedly, not giving a forwarding address and giving a fake phone number. Does all that show guilty knowledge? Absolutely. The timing... he even admits that Gary Kergan was at the apartment. He said Gary left at 3:15. The timeline is very clear.

"The third element is specific intent to kill or inflict great bodily harm. Gary was poisoned, put in the trunk of his own car, dismembered before he was put into the trunk and his body was disposed of in dumpsters. Now, on that one we kind of do have to rely on Leila for what is the actual sequence of events. She needed to fill in some of those gaps. And thank goodness, when she was arrested in 2012, the day she was picked up, she gave a videotaped statement, not only admitting her involvement, but again confirming that Ronald Dunnagan was the man who planned this with her, and the man who executed it with her."

Sometime during the course of the trial, even before Leila Mulla took the witness stand, any grandfatherly sympathy jurors felt looking at Ron Dunnagan evaporated. By the time Leila spoke in her hushed, halting voice, and pronounced him "a very bad man," there was little doubt jurors looked at him in the same way. Several of the women continually stared directly at him during closing arguments, but it seemed Ron was oblivious to them.

He listened intently while Dana Cummings continued, however. So did Ted Kergan. Ted knew the tide was turning but he was too nervous to claim victory yet. One thing he was confident about; Dana Cummings was a model of precision with her clear and concise closing remarks.

"Now, there's one piece of evidence that I didn't talk

about in the opening that I think is one of the most important pieces of evidence in this trial, and I couldn't talk about it in opening because it had to be admitted first. That's the journal that you read yesterday. And this is critical in talking about the intent, because it just lays it out. This journal was not written after Leila Mulla was arrested in 2012. When the search warrant was executed in Las Vegas, you saw where this journal came from. It came from a metal box in the closet of the apartment in Las Vegas. These are her words."

Dana then proceeded to re-read the chilling passages from the journal, the ones in which Leila talked about Sonic Gary the trick, how much money he paid her, and how she and Ron practiced and "hit Gary next time."

"I mean, it just lays it out," Dana continued almost incredulously, as if she had not already read those diaries countless times. She knew the jury was really familiar with the diary excerpts, handed out to them during the trial. In her mind's eye, she could still see the looks on their faces when they first read over them. Dana felt certain the excerpts only whetted their appetites and they would all like to read more.

"I mean, my gosh, they practiced. They ran through it. You can't get more deliberate. You can't show intent more than it's shown in the entries in this journal. Counsel can argue 'Leila's trying to please the state so she can get a deal' all she wants. This was written in 1984.

"The next entry is just interesting to me. 'We went to get field mice.' That certainly corroborates what she says. She uses field mice and rats interchangeably, but it definitely corroborates what she says about testing the poison on mice. I'm not going to read the rest of it to you. You read it. To me, those are the critical passages. And I think that definitely proves intent, absolutely beyond a reasonable doubt."

Here, Dana shifted to analyze the state's case with Leila's testimony. Leila had corroborated all three elements in the state's burden of proof. Although she was not physically back in the courtroom, she was present in spirit, a spirit that loomed much larger than her tiny five-foot-two frame.

"Let me make it really, really, really clear to you," continued Dana. "I don't think Leila Mulla is a saint. She was nineteen when it happened. Do I think that part of it was she fell under the allure of living this dangerous, evil lifestyle? Obviously. But she took responsibility. Whether she says, 'I was young,' that's just a fact. She was young.

"He was thirty-six years old," Dana said, as she raised and extended her left arm, index finger pointed squarely at Ron Dunnagan's nose. "A grown man, way past where you make errors in judgment to this degree. Let's talk about her statement, and she has been consistent since the day she was picked up on December 3, 2012, in all the major respects.

"We planned to rob and kill Gary. We decided to put poison in his wine. We put poison in his wine. I gave it to him. He choked. He fell. Ron Dunnagan came out of the closet, put a pillow over his head and then drug him out of the room. I totally admit to you that she gets a little foggy once he's dragged out of the room. But she has always, always maintained that he took Gary in the bathroom and that he loaded him into garbage bags.

"We wanted more details. But when she tried to come up with more details, she kept trying to remember. And I honestly believe that it was so horrendous, what happened in that bathroom, what she saw in that bathroom is so horrendous that she can't admit it to herself and never wants to admit it or she won't admit it to other people.

"Is she telling you the truth? Why in the world on December 3, 2012, would she give a full videotaped confession, that again (is) supported by a journal, and implicate Ronald Dunnagan, give up her life as she knew it, because she's been in jail ever since? And she has a sentence of thirty years. Why would she do that if Gary isn't dead, if they didn't plan to kill him, if Ronald Dunnagan isn't the one who was with her?

"Why would she do that? She walked away from her life.

Her life is in St. Gabriel now."

Dana wrapped up with a discussion of Leila's plea agreement and urged jurors not to be distracted by talk of a reduction in her sentence once she testified against Ronald Dunnagan.

"Her sentence is thirty years and the state will not file a motion to reconsider ...would never file a motion to reconsider without the full agreement of the victim's family. Never."

Got that right, mused Ted Kergan. He hoped thirty years would be tantamount to a life sentence for the now fifty-year-old Leila Mulla, and he would never agree to reducing her sentence. He still strongly desired to know where his brother's body had been placed and only two people could tell him: Ron Dunnagan and Leila Mulla. Ron would never give up the information. Ted had little or no leverage with a man like that. Leila, on the other hand, was a different animal indeed.

He watched jurors look at Leila, then glare at Ron, and that made him feel pretty damned comfortable. Dana Cummings' brilliant performance also put him at ease. When Susan Hebert rose to give her closing argument, Ted wondered how the defense could possibly combat the state's case.

"Sometimes in life, doing the best that you can is just not good enough," Hebert said. "You might get a participation award in a sporting event. But it should not get the state a conviction in a second-degree murder case, ever, doing the best that you can."

She went on to explain that Baton Rouge police, particularly R.E. Thompson, did the best they could with what they had in investigating the case back in 1984. "At the end of the day and everything that they had, the best that they could do was still not good enough. So, we fast-forward twenty-eight years to 2012. The cold case is reopened. What's changed? Well, DNA testing is available now, and also AFIS latent (finger) print analysis has been updated. So what happens? They are able to determine the blood in the trunk of the Cadillac is, in fact, that of Gary Kergan's. However, fingerprints haven't changed. There is no fingerprint evidence of Ronald Dunnagan ever being in that Cadillac. "There is no physical evidence that places Gary Kergan at that Byron Street address. There is no blood evidence, because what appeared to be blood samples may not have been. In fact, of the blood samples they got, there were two determined to be blood and it was that of a female who was not Leila Mulla. How do we even know where the crime occurred? How do we know that? We can put as much of that all into evidence and for me to even say it's flimsy at best would make it sound like I think it has some type of value. And, you know what, all of that is worthless."

Susan Hebert attacked Leila's testimony, calling it "verbal jujitsu."

"Just like in the martial arts, she can use it to deflect criticism of her inconsistencies. You can't pin her down on all of her previous statements or her lies because she can always fall back on that statement, 'I'm doing the best that I can.'"

Then, in an interesting move, Susan Hebert cast Leila Mulla as a possible victim of the state. "She relied on the DA's office, who made this deal with her, and now Ms. Cummings tells you 'Thirty years, I would never, never agree to something else, especially without consent of the family.' Well, you know what, it sounds to me like they tricked her. They tricked her into giving them what they wanted. Remember we talked about making a deal with the devil and the devil's brother? Don't forget that. They're not willing to honor their agreement now. Maybe they tricked her.

"The state asked you to look at Mr. Dunnagan during voir dire and said, 'You see this man right here. He's old. Are you going to feel sympathy for him just because he's old?' And every one of you said, 'No, I won't feel sympathy for him because he's old.' And I know you looked at him all throughout the trial. I saw you. I saw you when she was testifying. And you started to look at him and you started to think, 'Well, he's old. You know what, he might be a little strange looking. And, you know what, he might be even just a little bit scary when I looked at him. But you promised that you weren't going to use any sympathy."

Then, Susan Hebert reenacted Leila's testimony, almost mocking her.

"'I was very young. I was very naive. I was very stupid.'

"And I know that subconsciously, every one of you sat up there and began to feel sorry for her and feel some sort of sympathy as though she was under the power of this man. Well, if you felt sympathy for her, you were wrong. Because you cannot feel sympathy for him or her. It's not an element."

Susan Hebert droned on to the end of her closing argument, finishing by mandating the members of the jury look into her eyes as she urged them to find her client not guilty.

When Dana Cummings rose for her rebuttal, Ted looked around the courtroom and saw her boss, District Attorney Hillar Moore III, who had been the crime scene investigator at 2156 Byron Street back in 1984. He noticed R.E. Thompson, one of the original case detectives, who had testified two days earlier and was back for the trial's outcome. Gary and Dorothy Magee, Gary Kergan's friends from the Night Spot, were also back in the courtroom, as were a dozen family members, friends, and Sonic colleagues.

Yet there were many others Ted didn't know in the courtroom who showed interest in the outcome of this trial. It made him realize that during the last three decades, there were hundreds of people who helped him in this quest. Things had really come full circle. This was finally happening after such a ridiculously lengthy wait. Ted registered the scene in his memory.

This was the last chance for Dana Cummings to make

her case. She reminded jurors about the diary. She spoke of a plot to murder, jointly hatched by Ron and Leila.

"This was one of those dream cases where you actually have the people writing down what they are planning to do. That doesn't usually happen." She laid it out. "Remember when R.E. Thompson got on the stand and he said that man said, 'You don't have a body, do you?' That is what he has relied on for thirty-one years. You don't even have a body. Technology caught up with him. We got a body of blood and it took care of that."

Dana Cummings wrapped up the defense rebuttal with a few more small points. And with that, it was time for Judge Erwin to take over. He spoke in a low monotone voice while he issued the lengthy instructions, letting them know possible verdicts included: guilty of second-degree murder (as charged), guilty of manslaughter, guilty of negligent homicide, or not guilty.

Manslaughter, the judge explained, was murder committed in sudden passion. Negligent homicide is the killing of an individual with total disregard for the interest of others.

The judge wrapped up his instructions by reminding them that ten of the twelve jurors must agree on a verdict before it is valid. When the verdict is agreed upon by ten jurors, the foreperson was to write out the verdict on the back of the responsive verdict sheet, then sign and date the document before handing it back.

As soon as the jury was ushered out of the courtroom through back doors behind the judge's desk, Ted could hardly wait to leave the room himself. This had been such a long journey. Along the way, there had been a few times when he felt totally overwhelmed. This was one of those moments.

The moment would last as long as the jury deliberated. Ted and Ann Kergan traveled with Ann Edelman and Wade back to their downtown hotel in drizzling rain, not knowing if they would be there for minutes, hours, or even days.

Everyone with trial experience agrees that with a jury, things can go in any direction.

Ted labored to keep his emotions together while his mind raced at lightning speed. On one hand, he knew the jury would find Ron Dunnagan guilty. On the other, Ted thought about so many times during the past decades when things in this case did not transpire the way he expected them to. So many twists and turns, and now it all came down to twelve jurors determining the fate of the man who murdered his brother.

Ted tried to imagine what points the jury discussed, what hesitations they had, what they thought about Ron Dunnagan. To Ted, the group of jurors appeared to be reasonable people, but was he just hoping that to be true? His thoughts turned in a vicious cycle, making his head spin and his stomach churn. He took real solace that Dana had been so brilliant, taking the diaries and Leila Mulla's testimony and weaving them into a framework of premeditation. The jury seemed to ingest it, if he read their faces right. As if one can know any person's heart by studying their face.

Public Defender Susan Hebert had not delved as deeply into Leila Mulla's past as Ted had. After all, he had a thirty-year jump on her. Ted knew there were plenty of inconsistencies in Leila's testimony, many more than this attorney knew to point out. Even so, he desperately wanted the jury to believe her story, the version that would convict Ron Dunnagan. Ted continued to compulsively run the questions through his mind, feeling alone even though his family anxiously waited with him.

Less than an hour passed before Ted got the call letting him know the jury had made its decision. They hadn't been out long at all and Ted dared hope this was a good thing. He was joined again by his wife, Wade, and Ann Edelman, traversing the few blocks from the hotel to the courthouse. They rode in silence.

Meanwhile, Judge Mike Erwin's tenth floor courtroom

was at full capacity. Nine deputies of the East Baton Rouge Parish Sheriff's Office positioned themselves around the spectator area. Everyone who had been involved in the prosecution was there: Chuck Smith, Buck Gauthier, Jim Steele, Memry Tucker, Hillar Moore. Many of the witnesses had returned to hear the verdict, including Gary and Wanda Magee, the one-time club owners, and R.E. Thompson, whose original work on the case earned him the Detective of the Year Award in 1985.

Several of Ted's longtime associates, such as the group of deputies from Acadia Parish Sheriff's Office, a contingency from Kergan Brothers, including Doris Reiners and Janet Hebert, who had worked for the business long enough to have known Gary Kergan personally, were present. Filling in the few remaining spaces were courthouse workers who became enthralled with details of the case and heard the word that the verdict was being handed down.

A smiling Ron Dunnagan conversed with Theo Jones and Susan Hebert inside the railing during the short wait. Once news reached the courtroom that the jury was ready to announce its verdict, Dana Cummings hastened in to explain that the Kergan family was on their way and would arrive shortly. The buzz of conversation in the courtroom came to an abrupt halt a few minutes later when the doors flew open.

Ted and his family entered the courtroom, and right away he noticed the heaviness in the air. He could feel all eyes in the room fixed on them while he, Ann, and Wade Kergan took their regular seats on the front row bench of the spectator section.

Judge Erwin entered the courtroom from the left rear door, slid into the seat behind his desk, and spoke into his microphone.

"Before the jury comes in, I'm going to let everybody know that once the verdict is read, I don't want any commotion."

Minutes later, members of the jury entered from the right

rear door, filtered down the two rows of the jury box and took their seats.

"I have been informed y'all have a verdict," Judge Mike Erwin said, looking toward the jury.

"Yes, sir," replied the foreman. He tendered the verdict sheet to a uniformed deputy, who in turn made his way to the judge. Mike Erwin peered through his heavy black frame glasses onto the verdict sheet. He had perfected the poker face a long time ago. No one in the courtroom could guess the verdict by looking at the judge's face or body language.

"All right, the verdict appears to be in order," the judge said with no particular emphasis or inflection. "I'll hand it to the clerk to read."

Ted Kergan felt a lump well up in his throat.

"In the matter of State of Louisiana versus Ronald Dunnagan, Docket No. 9-14-1063, as to Count One, we, the jury, find the defendant, Ronald Dunnagan, guilty of second-degree murder."

Susan Hebert was first to respond, asking that the jury be polled. The deputy brought the polling sheet back to the jury,

"All right. Ladies and gentleman, I have a seating chart with your names on it. And, in the box where your name is, I want you to answer this question, yes or no: Was this your verdict?"

Tension mounted as jury members wrote their verdicts on the polling sheet. After they finished, the deputy handed the sheet back to the judge, who reviewed it briefly.

"All right," Judge Mike Erwin declared. "The verdict is unanimous."

As the courtroom's volume rose with people discussing the decision, Ron Dunnagan was escorted to the left exit, the one reserved for prisoners. Ted Kergan grabbed his backpack and escorted his wife and family through the courtroom's back double doors to a makeshift celebration in the corridor.

"Unanimous!" Ted said, breaking into a huge smile while raising his arm, pumping his fist and bringing that arm down quickly. "Kaboom!" He reached into the Orvis backpack and pulled out a large framed photograph of Gary, taken shortly before his death. Now the party was complete: Gary was brought back into the fold.

Ted embraced his wife, saying, "It's over; it's over." Ann Kergan began to softly cry with relief, and from the impact of the entire story. She had so deftly provided the safe place at home for her husband and son, but she had been insulated from talk of murder until this trial.

There were plenty of hugs and more tears. Doris Reiners and Janet Hebert, who knew Gary Kergan in the early days of Kergan Brothers, were crying. So was Ann Edelman, who had worked on case strategy so diligently alongside Ted Kergan for years. Emotions ran so high that even a couple of reporters were observed shedding tears.

One reporter asked Ted if the events of the day felt surreal.

"No, it's not surreal," he replied. "It's not. It feels very real."

Baton Rouge detectives and investigators, who played such integral roles in the case, patted each other on the backs. The party in the hall was in full swing. Sonic managers and employees, members of the Acadia Parish Sheriff's Department, and other friends and family members from Lafayette joined the happy gathering after the verdict. Acadia Parish Sheriff Ken Goss was one of the first to hug his old buddy. "You're the one who persisted and did it," he told Ted. "You did it for your family, for Wade and Ann."

Meanwhile, off to one side, Wade Kergan quietly reflected upon the proceedings. He received a hug from Dorothy Magee and a handshake from her husband, Gary. As Susan Hebert passed on her way to the elevator, she looked into his eyes and said, "Good luck to you."

A reporter approached Wade with the old how-do-you-feel question. He fought back tears. "It's a really good day," was all he managed to say. When asked if he wanted to address Ron Dunnagan, Wade was quick to reply. "I have nothing to say to him."

Dana Cummings said into another microphone, "I have gotten to know the family and I like them very much. I know how much they have put into this. You're invested in every case, but this was even more than that. Not being able to prosecute for so many years. The suffering this family has been through. Ted's efforts to keep this case alive. It was a unique case. Leila's confessions made it a strong case. And the diaries are what cinched it."

Ted grinned when he was asked about his relationship with his deceased brother, a bond which never wavered during thirty-plus years of Ted's battle to bring his brother's killers to justice.

"I'll always miss him every single day," Ted replied. "But we finally got Ronald Dunnagan. For thirty-one years, we worked on this. The Baton Rouge Police Department, the District Attorney's Office, Hillar, Dana, John, such a big team of people were involved, most of whom didn't even know Gary. I can't say thank you enough."

CHAPTER 27

ENTIRELY NEW LEVEL

Out on the steps of the courthouse, Ted's entourage continued celebrating Ron Dunnagan's guilty verdict. Ted jubilantly spoke to reporters. "I don't have to do this again tomorrow! I have seven large file boxes with everything that's ever gone on with this case on my conference table. Right now, I think I'm going to leave them there.

"To Ron Dunnagan: Enjoy the rest of your life in Angola. You're right where you need to be. Same thing for her. Leila Mulla is right where she needs to be. They need to be away from society."

The culmination of thirty-plus years of exploration, investigation, and dogged determination finally resulted in Gary's murderess spending the rest of her young years in prison, and now, her accomplice would spend a lifetime incarcerated. For most of that tiny sampling of people who find themselves savoring justice in the resolution of a cold case involving their loved ones, the sweetness of these victories would be more than enough. But not for Ted Kergan. The murderers were outed, but they would do their time without revealing the true location of Gary Kergan's body. His quest had always been two-fold: to bring his brother's murderers to justice and to find and bury Gary.

"One of my goals has always been to find my brother's body and to bring him home. It's like the story of Cain and Abel. Am I my brother's keeper? Yes, we are our brothers' keepers."

For Ted, it felt good to let out things that had long been pent up inside. With his wife, Ann, at his side, he watched reporters move the microphones toward his nephew.

Wade had tears rolling down his face. "I'm relieved," he said in a low voice. "This has been a long time coming. I am very grateful this happened and that I could be here for it."

Wade was a man of few words and today he was having trouble controlling his emotions. He was very grateful when reporters moved on to interview Dana Cummings.

"We had a great jury and justice was finally served. Ted has been a driving force throughout the prosecution. At last, he's got justice. It's a horrible thing to think someone can dispose of a body and never be brought to justice. The fact that he was found guilty is satisfying. This is the best we can do and I hope it helps Ted and his family."

The arduous process of obtaining long prison sentences for both murderers took three long decades. Most brothers wouldn't have been so persistent in the long haul. And in fairness, most couldn't have afforded the path Ted was able to take.

"I don't know anybody in my life who could have done what Ted has done, even if he or she had the resources," said Chuck Smith, who attended every court proceeding for the case, including the trial. "He listens, collects information, and then acts. It's as close to military precision as I've ever seen."

There were plenty of low moments, but all those negative markers on this long highway now seemed worthwhile. Ted Kergan won the war.

On the way back home to Lafayette later that evening, the energy of the super-charged day in court began to subside while Ted, Ann, Wade, and Jean Luc shared the highs and lows of the incredible trial week during an edited-for-family discussion. Indeed, the high of winning this case propelled Ted forward toward another victory, this one an amazing business recognition for his restaurants as well as for him personally. Ted was honored with the Troy Smith Hall of Fame Award, tantamount to a lifetime achievement award, at the Sonic National Convention, which just happened to get underway mere days after the trial's end.

In anticipation of both auspicious events, Ted packed two bags, one for the trial in Baton Rouge and one for the convention in Kansas City. He had no idea how long the trial might last, only the notion that the judge, an extremely loyal LSU fan, would work hard to end it before the football weekend began. And almost magically, the trial ended Friday afternoon and Ted traveled to Kansas City the next day, as originally scheduled.

Thousands of Sonic employees, dozens of managers, family members of Sonic employees and administrators crowded into the Kansas City Convention Center for the two-and-a-half-day gala event. At least a hundred of them were part of the Kergan Brothers Sonic organization based in Lafayette, Louisiana.

Clearly, Kergan Brothers owned this convention. The entire hall felt it. With the stars now aligned and a larger-than-life banner of Ted's likeness behind him, he walked onto the stage of the grand ballroom during the awards banquet, the culminating event.

A video presentation chronicled Ted's career while he and Ann looked out onto the massive audience. She felt a little intimidated, but the lights didn't bother Ted. As an experienced public speaker, he reveled in the moment. He had waited a long time for this. Some thought the Troy Smith Hall of Fame Award, which was presented to Ted by Sonic CEO Cliff Hudson, should have been awarded to him a decade earlier.

Ted knew the timing was perfect. What a month September turned out to be.

As he left the stage less than a week after the trial, he could feel Gary's presence. When he walked toward the backstage curtain, he saw members of the colorfully dressed band Earth, Wind and Fire, the evening's entertainment, waiting on the steps. They had been watching while Ted received his award. Band members all had their hands raised and palms extended, waiting to high-five Ted Kergan. *Now this,* thought Ted, *is surreal…*

***

Ted came face-to-face with Ron Dunnagan one more time, at his sentencing hearing on October 7, 2015. Everyone expected Ron to receive life in prison and serve his term at Louisiana State Penitentiary in Angola. Ted and Ann were joined at the hearing in their usual front bench by Ted's sister, Cheryl Maxwell, and her husband, Larry.

Ron Dunnagan was seated in a wheelchair when he was pushed through the left side door and positioned in front of his attorney's bench. His hair had been further sheared, revealing a large bald spot to those behind him in the audience. Ron definitely looked nervous.

At the call for "All rise," in anticipating the entrance of Judge Mike Erwin, Ron Dunnagan moved upward to a three-quarter standing position and quickly shot back down to the wheelchair. Judge Erwin proceeded through his day's docket, purposely leaving the Dunnagan sentencing for the last item of the day. Time dragged.

"Ronald Dunnagan?" Judge Erwin finally asked, looking once again over heavy black-rimmed glasses.

"Here," Ron replied loudly.

"Ms. Cummings?

"Yes, Your Honor."

"I understand Mr. Kergan wants to give an impact statement," said Judge Erwin.

Silence enveloped the courtroom when Ted walked to the witness box. He had thought about what he wanted to say to his brother's murderer. This was not the time to hold anything back.

VICTIM IMPACT STATEMENT

BY TED KERGAN

October 7, 2015

First of all, I would like to thank your honor and the court for allowing me this time to say a few words. And it's just going to be a few words, because there will never be ample time to express or convey the impact that this murderous, depraved act of that man right there, Ronald Dunnagan, had on my family, on Gary's wife, on Gary's son, on my sister who's here today, and myself, as well as the unbelievable waste of resources that the police and the district attorney's office and everyone has put into this.

My mother spent the last ten years of her life trying to find out what happened to her son. Every time I would go to her house, she would have maps of Louisiana spread out on the dining room table and all over her living room. And, she was praying to God, as good Irish Catholic women do, saying novenas, begging God to give her some kind of clue so that she would know what happened to her firstborn son. Then, you tossed my brother's remains away like a piece of trash. What's wrong with you? Do you not believe in retribution? Do you not believe that God is going to get you?

Your mother, on the other hand, is holding her head in

shame right now, reaching out to you from beyond the grave in shame and disgust that you killed a man who contributed so much, while you wasted your life, barely scraping by. The only thing you did, you were a clown; a clown and a murderer who interacted with children, for God knows what that was all about. And then you were a pimp, preying on young women. You seem to have a history of that. Leila was, what, seventeen years old? Your wife was what? Thirteen, when you married her? Thirteen years old! What kind of pervert does that? And then you used your good brother, Mike Karakas' name as an alias. And then you lived off disability. And now, the good citizens of Louisiana and the taxpayers are going to give you what you want: They're going to support you for the rest of your life.

How can you deny my mother the burial of her eldest child? Do you think your mother would forgive you, or that God will forgive you? And then you tried to very cleverly hide your murderous deeds. Oh, and you so liked to throw that up at the police when they'd ask you. You loved to come back and say, "Well, you don't have a body, do you?" Well, guess what, Ronald Dunnagan? We got enough of one, and you left it. This turned on you because of what you did. You're not only a murdering, depraved pervert, you're a stupid one.

I don't think there's a better example of my brother's legacy than all of the people here who have fought so long and hard for justice for him. And these were mostly people he didn't even know. But that's just the impact he had on people. The company he started will employ 4,000 people today, giving them a chance to provide well for their families.

And what do you have as your legacy? Where's your family? They're too embarrassed to be here. And even your daughter. Okay, she's not really your daughter; she's really Mike Karakas' daughter. That's not really your daughter, right? But anyway, even your daughter, your grandson, and every other member of your family called me repeatedly, and repeatedly, and repeatedly, to try to get me to pay them a reward so they could turn you in. And they did that time and time again. Your family has betrayed you in ways that you will never even know. It's got to be a little disconcerting for you because my brother and I look so much alike. So to you, this has got to be a lot like watching my brother sit up here, talking to you. And I think my brother has been here this whole time because there's been a lot of roadblocks over the years that we've been able to overcome that I can't really explain, so I know he had a lot to do with this. But if he was here right now, and it was him sitting here talking to you instead of me, what he would tell you, so you would hear it plainly, is, *I got you, you son of a bitch.*

***

When he had finished, Ted turned to the judge and added, "Thank you, Your Honor. I apologize for the language."

Judge Erwin merely replied, "No problem, sir. I would have probably said worse than that."

After that wrenching statement, Ron Dunnagan's formal sentencing was almost anticlimactic. In trial courts, it's known as LWOP, and the acronym means Life Without Parole. They don't kill you, they just lock you up and wait for you to die.

EPILOGUE

How did Gary Kergan really die? The question remained.

Ted certainly relaxed a bit, with Leila Mulla incarcerated for a long run at Louisiana Correctional Institute for Women, and with Ron Dunnagan doing life in Louisiana State Penitentiary. But he still hadn't located his brother's remains, and he wasn't ready to shut down his investigation. Even after all the years, he didn't know what really happened to his brother. The thing is, he would never get the answer if he gave up the search for it.

Just as he had done so many times, Ted carried out the continuing search by engaging experts. Criminologist Jennifer Juen had become quietly involved in Ted's private investigation months before Ron Dunnagan's trial began. She poured over crime scene photos, conducted her own tests, and came up with her own theories. And as it had happened so many times before, the act of obtaining more answers offered up more riddles.

Leila Mulla confessed she served Gary tainted wine the night of the murder. The immediate question became, what type of poison can be administered to a healthy adult without their knowledge, and produce instantaneous lethal results?

According to Dr. Mark Ryan of the Louisiana Poison Control Center, symptoms from cyanide poisoning can begin almost immediately. As Dr. Ryan stated in a telephone conversation with Detective Chuck Smith, cyanide poisoning would render the subject unconscious in less than thirty seconds, and death would likely occur in five minutes. He added that back in 1984, cyanide was contained in some of the rat poisons readily available in farm supply stores. Any determined shopper could get it.

However, if there was enough poison in that glass of wine to kill with devastating speed, wouldn't Gary have been able to taste it? Wouldn't he have spit it out as a reflex action? Forensic toxicologist Dwain Fuller stated he believes this is what he would have done but, scientists are not sure how strong the flavor can become, since the victims die finding out.

If Gary Kergan didn't fall to the ground after being given poison, or if he wasn't poisoned at all, what else is indicated by the gouges and the appearance of blood stains on the walls, the door facings, and the ceiling?

Gary was standing up and vigorously fighting for his life.

Leila also testified Ron smothered Gary with a pillow to put the struggle to an end. With Gary supposedly dropped to the floor and incapacitated by poison, was he smothered, or was he beaten to death? And afterward, if Gary's body was dismembered and hence most of the blood drained from it in the bathroom, as Leila Mulla testified, then how could so much of his blood be in the trunk of his car?

A cleaned up crime scene back in those days was not at all the same thing as a cleaned up crime scene today. Would blood evidence from the bathroom drain remain in the linoleum tiles glued to the concrete slab, or in underground pipes at that address?

Forensic science has given homicide investigators the ability to employ levels of detection at the molecular level. Meanwhile they share the results within a network of professionals, all of whom have the capability to physically locate and arrest a suspect.

There is no statute of limitations on murder.

"Leila Mulla's version of events is not supported by the evidence," said Jennifer Juen. "Most of the identified stains were higher up on the wall and ceiling. This means the victim was likely standing, not on the floor."

Juen also debunked Leila Mulla's dismemberment testimony. "It just doesn't add up. Dismemberment probably did not happen. If you dismember a body, you lose a lot of blood; there is bleed out. I have seen enough crime scenes. It's hard to clean up that much blood. Those photos of the bathroom just don't support that. There were no stains or evidence of that around the bathtub. And for there to be that volume of blood still in the trunk, it seems unlikely that he had been dismembered."

Gary's remains were placed in the trunk of his own car. But as to Leila Mulla's testimony that the dismembered body was put into garbage bags, Juen had more to say. "If there were multiple plastic garbage bags, there was no transfer pattern of the blood from those garbage bags. If there were those patterns, you would be able to see where the bags came into contact with the trunk or with each other. There might have been one bag, but there was no more than one garbage bag in the trunk."

Leila also said Ron Dunnagan drove Gary's Cadillac while she sat in the front passenger seat. She said she was wearing a hat. Were they both wearing hats and gloves? If so, maybe that explained why there were no matching fingerprints and/or hair samples when the car was checked back in 1984.

What happened to Gary's gold jewelry? Since Ron and Leila constantly struggled for money, it's safe to assume they sold the gold for cash. What about that curious map found in Leila's and Ron's Las Vegas apartment? Who drew it?

Juen ventured to suggest the map was not drawn to scale, but rather represented a visual list of landmarks along that specific route. If the exaggerated "X" on the map marked the location of a grave (and Ron and Leila show no capability of walking far enough away from any treasure to need a map), it leaves the question, were others buried there? Or else why use a map at all?

Then there was the extremely tight timeline of the murder. Leila brought Gary into the duplex shortly after 2:00 a.m. on November 29. He was killed and placed in the trunk of his own car, which was left in a suburban New Orleans parking lot before dawn. Leila said she and Ron took a cab some sixty miles back to the Byron Street duplex, arriving the next morning as the sun rose.

Next, they cleaned the duplex, doled out belongings, packed up, and hit the road, all by noon. It remains difficult to believe so much could be accomplished in so little time and that Ron and Leila would drive more than a few miles with a body in the trunk of their car.

Finally, that troubling little ceiling tile. The one from the duplex bedroom. Entered into evidence at Ron Dunnagan's trial, the tile was found to hold blood linked by DNA evidence to a female who was not Leila Mulla. So, whose blood was spattered onto that ceiling tile?

Of course, the room hosted many different occupants, over time. A few may have experienced some form of accident causing a cut and some bleeding, right there in the room.

But a ceiling tile?

How do people get blood on ceiling tiles? Did the female who was the source of the tile's blood also suffer blows rendered with wild swings of a blunt instrument?

And if so, by whose hands? Were Leila Mulla and Ron Dunnagan serial killers? Serial killers or not, neither was left in the position to repeat such evil. Instead they both were sentenced to exist in the constant inner torment and physical discomfort of life in prison. Leila, most of all, had to watch any chance for a better future melt away.

In August of 2016, almost a year after the trial and while Ted Kergan's private investigation continued, a freak natural disaster struck Southern Louisiana in the form of thirty inches of rainfall. That's thirty inches of rainfall in a single day. Experts termed it a thousand-year flood, inundating

140,000 homes in the Baton Rouge region.

The campus of Louisiana Correctional Institute for Women was hit with a floodtide of more than three feet of water from the neighboring Bayou Manchac. Even for the old Bayou dwellers with deep experience on the waterways, there was no fighting back the deluge. Still the rain pounded on. The region surrounding the prison came under immediate peril.

The prisoners, including Leila, were told to pack two bags, and were then shackled in pairs and marched onto buses. The escaping buses had to plow through water at the tops of their tires. For the first time in the history of Louisiana's penal system, a full prison population was evacuated. The entire complex was deserted just ahead of the rising tide.

The miserable toil of this process was yet another footnote of wretchedness for Leila, a woman with the ability to do positive work in the nursing field, a former violin prodigy, track star, and an honor student, and yet a woman who descended into street prostitution and drug addiction, and then cruelly plotted and carried out the murder of an innocent man. Talk of any rational motive is a waste of time here. It was supposedly done for money, but their pitifully poor planning and their bizarre reactions after the crime don't show money as their primary driver. Murder over pocket money is an act of momentary desperation, while these killers exercised plenty of mutual thought and planning.

No matter how different their personalities appear on the surface, a psychopathic link united them back then. They each held in their hearts a fundamental hunger to do evil.

The question of which particular weapon was used to commit this crime recedes in importance against the grim reality that the real weapon was another human being. This human weapon was fed and guided by its drone pilot, Leila Mulla. Although Ron Dunnagan has presented himself as a schizophrenic with paranoid hallucinations, as if incapable of plotting murder, and despite the claims of his abusively dominant control over Leila throughout their relationship, her weak appearance must not be mistaken for an inability to assert herself. Her diary makes it clear; she owns full partnership in their psychotic venture.

Ted Kergan walked away feeling grateful to have persisted in the long investigation. As far as the issue of culpability was concerned, he had followed the justice process on Gary's behalf all the way to a conclusion. He was no longer like Sisyphus from the Ancient Greek myths, forever doomed to roll the heavy stone uphill all day, slipping back again by night. There was a summit to that long trail, and he had reached it.

Word rapidly spread out to a private network of people, giving everyone who shared in the efforts of the long investigation their own moment of relief. It came with the rush of exhilaration accompanying long-awaited good news, as if a deep breath, held too long, is finally released.

Anyone would feel the same. That part of it was good.

That part felt just right.

ACKNOWLEDGEMENTS

I became intrigued by the winding tale of Gary Kergan's murder and his brother's lengthy journey to bring the killers to justice over lunch years ago with my dear friend, Ann Edelman. Like so many, I was captivated by her friend, Ted Kergan, and his drive and determination once his brother's murder case was resurrected in 2012. Memry Tucker, a former sheriff's deputy and district attorney's office investigator, was instrumental in organizing and placing those files in front of Baton Rouge Police cold case division leader, Detective John Dauthier, who made the decision to re-open the case. It was all very personal for Memry. Her father, Larry Tucker, was a close friend and colleague of Gary Kergan and worked side by side with Ted in efforts to locate and track the murderers.

But, that was just the beginning. I was allowed to tag along for quite the roller coaster ride as the aforementioned were so generous in sharing their time and findings with me. Chuck Smith, a friend as well as an investigator with the East Baton Rouge Parish District Attorney's office, was also instrumental in the resolution of the case. He, too, took the Kergan murder case personally and invested an abundance of his time and talent, as did his colleague, Jim Steele. The entire office, under the direction of District Attorney Hillar Moore and Assistant District Attorney Dana Cummings, did their jobs brilliantly and were very cooperative in helping me assemble information for this book. Thanks also to private investigators Scott Johnson and George Steimel of Bombet,

Cashio & Associates for laying groundwork through their insightful interviews.

At the trial, I met Gary's son, Wade Kergan, and Ted's wife, Ann Kergan. Their perspectives were invaluable. I also became acquainted with Doris Reiners and Janet Johnson, long-time executives with Kergan Brothers' Sonic operation. Their love and support for the Kergan family helped me paint authentic character portraits.

I learned a great deal about forensic anthropology from Tim Miller of Texas Equusearch; Mike Hadsell and Julie Starbuck of Peace River K9 Search and Rescue; and Jennifer Juen of Veritas Forensics and Veritas Investigations. Iberville Parish property owner Don Ristroph provided important historic data.

I owe a huge debt of gratitude to Leslie T. Sharpe. Her course on writing a non-fiction book proposal was the perfect template. Special thanks to my agent, Sharlene Martin; editor, Anthony Flacco; and publisher, WildBlue Press. Many, many thanks to the team at Zehnder Communications, especially Ann Edelman and Molly Feazell, who always greets me enthusiastically.

Finally, I want to thank my husband, Bill Blackwood, who was so very supportive during my long period of preoccupation with this project. Here's to many more orange-colored skies.

PHOTOS

Ronald Dunnagan's mugshot after his arrest in December, 2012

*The Astoria, Queens, NY apartment building where
Leila Mulla "got lost" for years before being arrested
there by Baton Rouge detectives in December, 2012*

*Ted Kergan (in khakis) at the Texas Equusearch dig
for Gary Kergan's remains in March, 2014*

Under one of the tents set up in the March, 2013,
Texas Equusearch dig for Gary Kergan's remains.
Tim Miller, at left; Ted Kergan, right

Heavy equipment on the scene of the Texas Equusearch
dig for Gary Kergan's remains in March, 2013

*Texas Equusearch founder Tim Miller, center, in doorway
of a West Baton Rouge motel room where Ronald
Dunnagan attempted suicide in March, 2013*

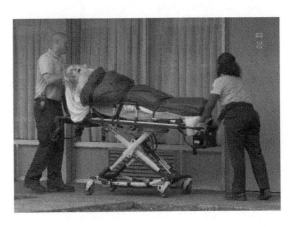

*Ronald Dunnagan taken from his West Baton Rouge
motel room after a suicide attempt in March, 2013*

Gary Kergan's son, Wade Kergan

Ted Kergan, center, responds to media questions after Leila Mulla's indictment in April, 2014. Also pictured are Assistant District Attorney Dana Cummings, left; Ann Kergan, second from right; and District Attorney Hillar Moore (Photo courtesy of Travis Spradling of The Advocate)

Ted Kergan with his nephew, Wade Kergan

Ted Kergan receives the Troy Smith Hall of Fame Award from Sonic CEO Cliff Hudson in September, 2015, as his wife, Ann Kergan, looks on.

Also Available From WildBlue Press

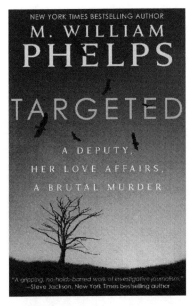

When her missing boyfriend is found murdered, his body encased in cement inside a watering trough and dumped in a cattle field, a local sheriff is arrested and charged with his murder. But as an investigative journalist digs in, the truth leads to questions about her guilt. In his first full-length, original true-crime book for WildBlue Press, M. William Phelps delivers a hard-hitting, unique reading experience, immersing readers in the life of the first female deputy in Oglethorpe County, Georgia, who claims a sexual harassment suit she filed against the sheriff led to a murder charge. Is Tracy Fortson guilty or innocent? Read TARGETED and decide.

Read More: **http://wbp.bz/targeted**

See even more at:
http://wbp.bz/tc

More True Crime You'll Love From WildBlue Press

RAW DEAL by Gil Valle

RAW DEAL: The Untold Story of the NYPD's "Cannibal Cop" is the memoir of Gil Valle, written with co-author Brian Whitney. It is part the controversial saga of a man who was imprisoned for "thought crimes," and a look into an online world of dark sexuality and violence that most people don't know exists, except maybe in their nightmares.

wbp.bz/rawdeal

BETRAYAL IN BLUE by Burl Barer & Frank C. Girardot Jr.

Adapted from Ken Eurell's shocking personal memoir, plus hundreds of hours of exclusive interviews with the major players, including former international drug lord, Adam Diaz, and Dori Eurell, revealing the truth behind what you won't see in the hit documentary THE SEVEN FIVE.

wbp.bz/bib

THE POLITICS OF MURDER by Margo Nash

"A chilling story about corruption, political power and a stacked judicial system in Massachusetts."–John Ferak, bestselling author of FAILURE OF JUSTICE.

wbp.bz/pom

FAILURE OF JUSTICE by John Ferak

If the dubious efforts of law enforcement that led to the case behind MAKING A MURDERER made you cringe, your skin will crawl at the injustice portrayed in FAILURE OF JUSTICE: A Brutal Murder, An Obsessed Cop, Six Wrongful Convictions. Award-winning journalist and bestselling author John Ferak pursued the story of the Beatrice 6 who were wrongfully accused of the brutal, ritualistic rape and murder of an elderly widow in Beatrice, Nebraska, and then railroaded by law enforcement into prison for a crime they did not commit.

wbp.bz/foj

Made in the USA
Columbia, SC
24 October 2017